D1246285

UNDER COLOR OF LAW

UNDER COLOR OF LAW

A. DWIGHT PETTIT

iUniverse LLC
Bloomington

Under Color of Law

iUniverse books may be ordered through booksellers or by contacting:

iUniverse
1663 Liberty Drive
Bloomington, IN 47403
www.iuniverse.com
1-800-Authors (1-800-288-4677)

Because of the dynamic nature of the Internet, any web addresses or links contained in this book may have changed since publication and may no longer be valid. The views expressed in this work are solely those of the author and do not necessarily reflect the views of the publisher, and the publisher hereby disclaims any responsibility for them.

Any people depicted in stock imagery provided by Thinkstock are models, and such images are being used for illustrative purposes only.

Certain stock imagery © Thinkstock

ISBN: 978-1-4620-5640-8 (sc)
ISBN: 978-1-4620-5641-5 (hc)
ISBN: 978-1-4620-5642-2 (e)

Library of Congress Control Number: 2013903921

Printed in the United States of America

iUniverse rev. date: 7/24/2013

Contents

From the Editor

I found *Under Color of Law* to be one of
the most emotional and fascinating books
I have read. I cried, I laughed, and I even
got angry, but most of all, I was proud.
From start to finish, this book will have
you question law as we know it and ask, in
terms of racism and prejudice in America,
"Has anything really changed?"

I am honored to have had the
opportunity to meet A. Dwight Pettit and
to play such an important role in the process
of completing this book. Compiling the information and the photos was
just as enthralling as transcribing and editing the text for this book. What
is so ironic is the comparison of innumerable phases of his father's life to
his life. For me, it was a journey that I took pleasure in taking.

For twelve years, the completion of this book had been anticipated.
I pray all who read it will feel as I do—excited. You, too, will laugh and
cry; it's a good read.

"Zinah" Mary Brown, CEO
Elocution Productions

Acknowledgments

To my mother, Mildred Miller Pettit, and my father, George David Pettit, who sacrificed so much to give me the opportunities of life, I give my thanks.

To my lovely and loving wife, Barbara Nell Moore Pettit, for your encouragement and support during forty-five years of marriage and four years of prior romance, I thank you.

To my wonderful children, Alvin Dwight Pettit Jr. and Nahisha Tamara Pettit, and to my beautiful grandchild, Georgia David Pettit, I thank you for your support and encouragement. My son, Alvin, helped me to put together the family history with pictures. My uncles John Pettit, Argel Pettit, and Joseph Pettit and my cousin Argel Pettit Jr. assisted with the family history. Many thanks also to my cousin Shirley Sumpter, my aunts Marion Conley and Ruby Pettit for their assistance with the family history.

I also extend my thanks to my office manager of the last twenty years, Felicia Jackson, for keeping the business moving during the times I was focusing on the task of writing and rewriting this book. Thank you to Marie Davis, my secretary, for your support. I would also like to extend appreciation to a family friend, Denise Lucas, for her hours spent listening to my stories. And I wish to express my sincere thanks to Ms. Carol Jones, who assisted in the editing of this book.

Last, but not least, Ms. Zinah Brown, my editor, who for the past twelve years transcribed, compiled, proofed, edited, and coordinated this book.

Thank you all for making the telling of this story possible.

Introduction

I am a civil rights/constitutional and criminal lawyer of some success. But I am also an actual progeny of *Brown v. Board of Education.* 347 US 483 (1954) I am a direct legal descendent and beneficiary of *Brown v. Board*—at a time when this nation is debating the necessity of continuing with the principals enunciated in *Brown* and determining the beneficial impact and contributions of *Brown* sixty years later.

This is not to say that my story affects the numerical or statistical result of *Brown*, nor is it just about *Brown*. But it is a story of an American family's battle to enforce *Brown* in order to give its child an education and that child's survival during those tumultuous times. I am probably the only American whose early life and family are traced in three early civil-rights decisions set forth in the *Federal Reporter: Alvin Dwight Pettit, a minor, by his parent George D. Pettit v. Board of Education of Harford County*, 184 F. Supp. 452 (1960); *George D. Pettit v. the United States*, 488 F.2d 1026 (1973) (my father's case in which I was counsel); and *Alvin Dwight Pettit et al. v. Gingerich* (Board of Law Examiners) 427 F. Supp. 282 (1977). This case chronology, which I refer to as the "legal trilogy" of my life, is of a historic nature in itself. However, I choose to develop my personal story around these cases—from the '40s through the present.

First, I deal with my mother's and father's families as a foundation as to why they would so vigorously attack the segregation policies of the day and sacrifice so much and struggle so long. This book continues into my life from early childhood in the black community to a sudden transition into a tensed all white world at Aberdeen High School where I was admitted by order of the U.S. District Court. I then transitioned from the white world in the '60s back into the black world of Howard University as an undergraduate and later in the School of Law. I entered the working world by being employed in Richard Nixon's Small Business Administration through affirmative action, taking racially controlled and discriminatory bar examinations and conducting subsequent litigation, and then entering into private practice in Baltimore City and venturing into the political arena. We will visit the Jimmy Carter campaign and my ascent to the top level of his presidential campaign, including the development of my close relationship with then-Governor Carter (eventually President Carter) and my involvement in the making of a president.

In the final part of the book, I address major litigation and representation in which I was involved, from alleged organized crime matters to US impeachment proceedings, civil-rights litigation, and high-profile criminal cases. Albeit most of the cases are of local interest. But for a criminal- or civil-law reader, I discuss landmark decisions in Maryland's Court of Appeals and the United States Supreme Court. I discuss civil actions involving heavyweight champion Mike Tyson, and the trial of Ray Lewis of the Baltimore Ravens. I also review and discuss a few high-profile cases selected from over one thousand civil and criminal cases that I have tried.

I conclude with my most recent involvements, including a $105 million verdict, the largest excessive-force and police-brutality verdict in the history of Maryland—possibly one of the largest in the United States. The *Clark v. O'Malley* case is now in the Maryland Court of Appeals, where we are awaiting a decision. Also, I have just completed the trial of Paul Shurick, the campaign manager for former Governor Robert Erhlich who was charged with campaign fraud. Last but not least, what I call the full educational circle, being appointed to the University System of Maryland Board of Regents by Republican Governor Robert Erhlich.

In the final chapter, I give a detailed summary of my greatest case, my father's case. That case involved the treatment and torment he experienced at his job, which was in retaliation for his bringing my school desegregation case to trial. This final chapter analyzes the case and concludes with my father's ultimate victory as set forth in *George D. Pettit v. the United States.* As I review the US Constitution and Amendments thereto with subsequent civil-rights decisions emphasizing equal protection and due process, it is and was the Civil Rights Act of 1871, as set forth in 42 USC (1983) (United States Code), that gave us the sword to challenge alleged legal and state-sanctioned "Jim Crow America" acting under color of law. The Civil Rights Act of 1871, 42 U.S.C. (1983), sets forth and provides the following:

> That every person who, under color of any statute, ordinance, regulation, custom, or usage, of any State or Territory, subjects, or causes to be subjected, any citizen of the United States or other person within the jurisdiction thereof to the deprivation of any rights, privileges, or immunities secured by the Constitution and laws, shall be liable to the party injured in an action at law, suit in equity, or other proper proceeding for redress.

As I reflect and look back over my life, this was the theme that was constant in my family's pursuit of justice in this nation, and it has been the constant theme in my pursuit of justice in my practice of law. Thus my desire to write this book springs from my observation of the reoccurrence of the abridgement of rights, although taking place in different forms. It is my desire that this book will warn the body politic of the dangers inherent therein. It is imperative that we as a nation and people, while celebrating our victories and successes, are aware of and not retreat from those dangerous pitfalls and dark caverns that still exist. It must be remembered that this is a young nation, where obstacles and entrenchment can easily be resurrected and refortified and put back into law while a nation sleeps in a fog of complacency created by past accomplishments. Before my father died, I promised him, George David Pettit, that I would tell our story. Although it has been twelve years in the writing due to trials, political campaigns, and illness, I have now completed this part of the story. Just as I am a continuing lawyer, this story will go on. Dad, with love, I dedicate this book to you.

Chapter 1: Role Models

My father's name is George David Pettit. My mother's name is Mildred Henry Louise Miller Pettit. My father's family came out of a place called Sylva, North Carolina, where they lived on top of a mountain. My paternal grandparents, Abraham and Nina Pettit had eleven children, ten boys and one girl. Although my father did not talk about my great-grandfather much to me, he was a man named Jim Crackcorn Pettit who was married to LouCindy Pettit, a full Cherokee Indian. The story was that Jim had fled North Carolina after shooting his white sharecropper. My great-grandfather obviously had a great influence on my father.

In the 1990s, I went to many funerals; all of those relatives seem to pass around the same time. My father passed in 1992. I am an only child, and my father and I were very, very close. By most standards, I would consider him a genius in mental aptitude. He was a brilliant man who taught engineering at North Carolina Central College. He and I had the unique experience of being in school together at A&T University (at that time A&T College, now North Carolina A&T State University). My dad's senior year at A&T was 1949, and I was among the first persons to graduate from A&T University's nursery school. I have a lovely picture sitting on my desk showing me holding his hand and wearing his graduation cap on my head. He was known as the man who carried his little boy with him wherever he went. Because my mother had many sisters and two brothers, and my father had mostly brothers and one sister, I had many role models of big, strong African American men. All of my father's brothers were athletes; most were big men. They were "the Pettit boys."

My father's baby brother, John, and I were very close. He went to A&T, as did his other siblings: Abraham, Argel, Joseph (known as JP), and Dorothy Mae. My grandfather was a Southern minister, and my grandmother raised the kids. Like many African Americans in the 1940s and 1950s, my grandparents never went to college. So I found it unique that out of their family's eleven kids, six of them went to college, helping each other and pulling each other through. This was the first generation of higher education for my family. I would be the first Pettit to break the A&T tradition by attending Howard University.

Anyway, the men—in terms of role models—existed mostly on my father's side; on my mother's side, I had all of these additional mothers. I recall the unusual fact that on both sides of my family, neither my father nor my mother was the eldest, but on both sides I was the firstborn. That fact gave me a unique status. If I went someplace on my mother's side of the family, the aunts, especially, Emma, Irene, and Florence, would always make over me. I was everybody's baby, everybody's young man. Being the oldest and firstborn on my father's side, I was the one they taunted, played with, athletically sparred with, and literally hung out and socialized with. This was especially true of my father's baby brother, John. When he passed, it was a very tragic loss. They all were tragic, but because I was an only child, John was the closest person I had to a brother. In so many ways, we were so much alike.

Even though he was not the eldest, my father, George David Pettit, was really the leader of the family. Whenever there were decisions that had to be made, the brothers came to my father's house. Now, it could be argued this was because my father had moved to Aberdeen in 1958, which meant we were located in the middle ground between Baltimore City and Philadelphia, the two cities where most of the brothers lived. One other brother had moved to Newport News, Virginia, and Joseph and Dorothy Mae stayed in North Carolina.

My uncles would later go on to become executives, entrepreneurs, teachers, a firefighter, a longshoreman, government employees, etc. Of the eleven children, none would go to jail or even be in any serious trouble except Argel. When Argel went into the Baltimore City Fire Department, he was set up in a sex-charge scandal while he was involved in a civil-rights action to secure promotional opportunities for blacks. He was always a step behind his big brother (my father) George, in his civil-rights activism. The establishment was always waiting for him. I think that matter was resolved when he resigned from the fire department. Nevertheless, all of these strong black men and women would live to be outstanding citizens, including my mother's sisters and at least one of two brothers, Lonnie Miller. He is the father of Larry Miller, who is the current president of NIKE's Jordan Brand and was the former president of the Portland Trailblazers.

Not only were these men outstanding citizens, but they were also distinguished in their military service. Ray was killed in Europe during World War II; my father survived the bombing in England. Argel and Willard were in the Navy; Donald was an Army paratrooper in Korea; Abraham was in the Army Air Corp as a mechanic; John, of course, was in the US Marine Corps with the shore patrol. What a lineup.

To some, my father would be what they called "a bad nigger." That was the term used in black novels, history, and folklore, and reserved for certain African American males who were somewhat rebellious. In reality, he was just a very proud, defiant, and ambitious black man who had no fear of anything that I ever perceived. His arrogance and his brilliance were almost to the point of belligerence. The belligerence probably built up because of the racist environment of this nation. It smoldered and carried over to other things because of the frustration of being a brilliant African American who the Southern white community, later the white community in general, would attempt to suppress. Because of his brilliance and the fact that they would not or could not accept a black person who was so far and above the accepted norm, he developed a degree of arrogance. This was something my father struggled with all of his life, starting in childhood.

My grandmother, my father's mother, was a very dark-complexioned woman, whereas my grandfather was a very light-skinned black man. Although he had African American features, my grandfather looked like an old white man, but you could still tell he was African American. They lived on the top of a mountain next to the Cherokee Indian reservation, and like many African Americans, we have Indian blood through my great-grandmother. My uncle Esses used to tell me, "Boy, you look just like a big old Cherokee. The older you get, the more you look like a big old Cherokee." Well, I never understood that because I thought all Indians looked a certain way. As seen on television, they were reddish-brown people, slender, with big noses. To me, I always thought I looked like my mother: sort of round-faced with light complexion and thick lips. However, a few years ago, I did see a historical special on the Cherokee and observed that the Cherokee are reddish people, light complexioned overall with big faces; they are big in their upper body, as I am. I watched how they left North Carolina and resettled and how they went to the eastern schools and tried to assimilate into white culture. These people did sort of fit my physical characteristics as described to me by my uncle. Maybe my appearance did not come entirely from my mother, as I thought, but more from my father's Cherokee heritage.

Most of the men on my father's side are big men. I am six foot two inches and approximately 250 pounds, and my father was about six foot one inch and 190 pounds. He was considered a large man in the 1940s and 1950s. Because of this, and his aforementioned personality, my father was considered a badass, a rebel. The family would always tell "George stories," as I call them. A typical George story told how, when he was a teen, an older man took his crutches and threw them and him in the river, and my father came back months or years later while that man was picking on some kids playing a marble game. My father allegedly put a knife in the man's stomach and almost cut him in half. The man never saw what hit him, and nobody ever told. There have always been these George stories about how treacherous George was and about his legendary temper. That had a pronounced effect on me, because I grew up with this man and witnessed this violence and his violent personality throughout my childhood.

My mother and father were together until he died in 1992. However, I must write that my childhood was very, very tumultuous. My father was a strong disciplinarian. He always demanded that I had chores and responsibilities. The chores, in my opinion, got more ridiculous as I got older, to a point in my late teens where they actually caused me to look forward to leaving home and going away to college. He was such a disciplinarian regarding responsibilities that I was not spoiled in my behavior in any way. I might have been spoiled materialistically though. I had everything I wanted as a kid. In our neighborhood, I always had the biggest and newest bike; I had the best of anything he could give or make.

Many of the things I had, though, were due to the values my father instilled in me. For example, I bought my first rifle when I was five years old, and I did that by selling Cloverine Salve. Cloverine Salve was a cure-all product in those days. You spread it on, and it cured all. At the time I was living in Dundalk, Maryland, before we moved to Turner Station, Maryland. I saw a magazine ad saying I could get different gifts by selling the salve. Cloverine Salve came twelve cans to a canister. The company also offered religious pictures, so when someone bought a five-cent can of Cloverine Salve, they would get a free religious picture: Jesus, the Last Supper, or what have you. As I accumulated enough sales, I could either keep a percentage of the money or transfer the money to the company and receive a gift. The gift that I chose was a .22-caliber rifle that, of course, my father allowed me to have. That was just the beginning of my business operations. I had different businesses. He instilled a sense of responsibility in me in terms of always having something to do, always having a cash flow, and always having some money. My father also encouraged and helped my mother to complete beauty school and set up her hair-care business.

I have my father's combative instinct, his defiance, and his arrogance—but not quite his temper. My tolerance to stay the course, my survivability, and my ability to reinvent myself in many aspects of my career are attributes received from my mother. Nevertheless, the volatility and the aggressiveness demonstrated by my actions as a person, an attorney, and a politician came from my father. This has had a negative effect as well as positive one: negative in terms of politics but positive in terms of my becoming a trial lawyer.

There are many examples of Dad's temper. Dad owned a restaurant and bar with my Uncle Argel. The bar was called the South Side Tavern, and it was located in Greensboro, North Carolina. John, the baby boy, was in and out of there too, although I remember that most of the time my father and Argel were running the operation by night while they were in college by day. I was allowed to wait tables and serve beer. I could identify different types of beers at the age of four. One night, I spilled some beer on a woman's white dress, and my father whipped my butt. That retired my bartender aspirations.

As a child, it seemed to me that every weekend my father would put somebody out of his bar—somebody who was fighting, somebody who was going to beat his woman or wife, somebody who was not going to pay his bill, or somebody who just got drunk. I don't remember him throwing anyone out of the door, although I am sure he did. However, the bar had a big plateglass window, and I remember him throwing somebody through that plateglass window every weekend. I would always say to myself, *Why doesn't he just open the door and save himself the expense of fixing this window every weekend?* I am not sure if it was actually every weekend, but it seemed as if somebody was going through that window on a weekly basis. And then there was whatever took place outside. Fighting or shooting or whatever other disturbance, my father would be in the middle of it. He just had that type of volatile temper.

My father's nickname on the streets was "TNT." I saw him do things that were very unreasonable for the time. Back in the early 1950s, over a traffic dispute, I saw him pull out a tire iron on a white man in Highlandtown. Now for people who do not know about Baltimore City, Highlandtown in the 1950s was totally redneck and generally still is today. What my father did in Highlandtown in those times was considered highly questionable. My father was a light-brown man with straight black hair, large lips, and a large Indian-type nose, but definite African American features. There was no mistaking that he was a black man. Of course, a white police officer arrived, and Dad argued with him. My cousin Shirley Sumpter was in the car with me, and we just looked at each other. I do not remember him backing down from anybody.

I clearly recall the times the police brought him home for being in a fight. One night, he came home, and all or most of the fingers on his right hand were broken. He had hit a man who had done something wrong or said something to him, and we had to wait for several days to determine whether the man, who was in a coma, would live. Until then, the police could not determine if my father was going to be charged with some type of homicide. I saw him on one occasion pull a man out of his house because he had hit my dog with his car and failed to stop. Now, we are talking about a man who was, at that time, a distinguished professional government employee, an electrical engineer. However, he had a tremendous temper, and alcohol did not help.

Years later, friends of mine like Marcellus Jackson, James (Biddy) Woods (who would later coin my commercial slogan, "If you need me, call me"), and others would tell me elaborate stories about my father. For example, how he would frequent the Sphinx Club and always do something that would eventually cause the owner to ask him to leave.

Marcellus Jackson used to tell this exaggerated story about my father. He said that my dad would walk into a nightclub or a bar and sit down, wearing his suit and tie. After his first drink, he would say to whomever was sitting beside him, "Yep, I'm George Pettit. I'm educated, I have a college degree, and I am smart." Then he would order a second drink. (He always drank his whisky straight.) By the third drink, he would say, "Yes, I'm brilliant. I write books, and I do [this], and I do [the other]." After he had his third or fourth Old Crow, he would take off his jacket and say, "And the rest of y'all in here are stupid." That's a word I distinctly remember as one of his favorite words. The story continued that after about the fourth or fifth drink (because he started to get high quickly), he would roll up his sleeves and say, "And I'm the baddest son of a bitch in here." For purposes of humor, my father's actions were always exaggerated in this story. This was an extreme example of my father's personality—the defining personality that my mother was strong enough to deal with. He had a volatile and quick-changing personality though. If he had been drinking, we never knew who he was going to be upon his arrival home.

My mother was tremendously strong, often indicating she was leaving my father, only to return, saying she was coming back or staying because of me. It never made much sense to me, because as much as I loved him, I never understood her ability to make the sacrifices she made. I could not understand how anybody could humanly allow himself or herself to exist in that type of atmosphere, even for the love of another human being, in this case a child.

Having said that, reflecting on the other side of the coin that was my father, I believe that he loved me more than life itself, and I loved him dearly. My father was always in the extremes in what he did. There was very little middle ground. Even with my children. He loved my children to pieces, and my children loved him to pieces. In fact, he would become the perfect grandfather. My kids made a pact that whichever one had a child first would name their first child after "Papa." My grandbaby, my daughter's child, is now fifteen and she was almost named George David, but instead her name is Georgia David Miguel Pettit (Miguel being the name of her father). We might end up with two George namesakes, considering my son still might do the same thing.

Even though I have criticized my father to some extent, no son could have had a more devoted father. It did not matter what I was involved in, he was involved in it too. I was exposed to things that other kids in the inner city could only think about. I am talking about before and after we got out of Turner Station and moved to Aberdeen. While still in Turner Station, my dad was scoutmaster, and he was advisor to the Day Village Boy's Club. He took all the kids camping, and he held neighborhood-cleanup crab feast. I could hunt and shoot at five years old. We hunted squirrels, deer, rabbit, quail, and possum. We lived in the woods. We would go out, catch fish, and cook them on the riverbank.

He did not like regular sports, except boxing. He did not care for football and baseball, although when I was about five years old, he did take me to see Jackie Robinson and the Brooklyn Dodgers. As he got older, he might watch a basketball game if Michael Jordan was playing, but as a young man, all of his favorite sports, aside from boxing, were in the woods. He knew the woods like the back of his hand, and that was how I grew up. I knew how to exist in the woods even before being exposed to the military.

That was the other side of my father when he was away from the stress of his occupation and competition with whites. He did not drink all the time like many drinkers, just in spurts. During my childhood, my dad and I did everything together. We had an old raggedy boat that we fixed up, and before that, we built and flew model airplanes, and we had ham radio sets. We had radios that looked like radio-station transformers, which had microphones and speakers. We could talk around the world. Dad could make and fix anything. When other kids made scooters out of old skates and two-by-fours, I had a scooter that looked like a limousine. My father was always trying to get me interested in high-tech things like radios, communications, Morse code, and so forth, but all I wanted to do when not hunting or fishing was go out and play marbles, football, and baseball. When I was sixteen years old, he got terribly upset with me because he wanted us to get our pilot's license together. You can get your pilot's license at sixteen. However, I wasn't really interested; I just wanted to get my driver's license. I will never forget my remark to him, "Dad, I don't want my pilot's license, because I can't fly an airplane to the drive-in." I was concerned only with girls, and for girls I needed my driver's license, not a pilot's license. He was a little upset with me but went on to get his pilot's license and fly extensively.

We now watch the movies about the Tuskegee Airmen, and I am convinced through the stories that I have heard and his memoirs that, at that time period, my father was one of the attempted predecessors. According to his memoir, he made application to the Army Air Corps before the creation of the Tuskegee Airmen, but he was denied even though he passed all of the tests. You have to realize, as my mother would say, in terms of African Americans or any minority racial or ethnic group, a lot of people who lead the way are not the people who enjoy the fruits. The people who lead the way in many cases are considered radicals, and they are swept over or destroyed in the revolutionary or progressive process. Other people come along and get the glory or fruits of the victory.

The above facts are the foundation of my personality, my beliefs, and my self-image. When I am engaged in public speaking, I tell the audience that I have never had to look to athletes or musicians for role models. In my father and uncles, I had the best role models—excepting, of course, my father's negative side with his temper.

George D. Pettit 1949 A&T Graduation

The Pettit Brothers
Top: Esses, Willard, Abraham, George, Donald, Hayes,
Lower: Argel, Joseph and John

My father's Family 1955

Argel in Training

The Pettit Brothers at Dad's House

Abe and Nina Pettit

Mom and Dad carrying Dwight in 1948 on Pennsylvania Avenue

Maternal Grandfather Garland Miller

Great Grandfather Jim Crackcorn (Pettit)

Maternal Grandmother Hattie Miller

Donald Pettit (middle) before Korea jump

Jump Team Over Korea

Dwight and Dad

George Pettit and Dwight

Chapter 2: Boxing

The Civilian Conservation Corp (CCC) was where young kids went to work in the woods and on farms during the 1930s. My father had boxed in the CCC camp while still in North Carolina before he went into college and the military. Uncle Argel boxed for North Carolina A&T College (Agriculture and Technology), Uncle John boxed in the Marine Corp, and Uncle Hayes, a longshoreman was always boxing down on the Baltimore docks and on the ships in the Harbor. In fact, Uncle Hayes had the reputation of being a very strong, athletic, and dominating fighter among the longshoremen. I grew up around this atmosphere of strong, smart, athletic men. When our family would get together on holidays, the first thing we did, along with grilling hot dogs or steaming crabs and drinking beer, was to start the boxing and athletic competition.

From the time I was a kid, I was slapped around by these two-hundred-pound uncles. To me, they were huge. This basic training would have ramifications as I became older, given my light complexion, freckles, and reddish hair. Sometimes when I describe my physicality during my early years, I think of the description of a young Malcolm X when he was growing up. One has to understand that, being light-skinned, I always had problems wherever I moved. Somebody was always going to whip my ass. I always had to go athletically on stage. What the other kids did not know was that I had grown up with a father and uncles who were very athletic men. I soon discovered that I could fight my ass off. At one point in time, I thought I was the first coming of a Muhammad Ali—until I saw him, still Cassius Clay, when I was fifteen years old. I saw him on television and thought I was looking at myself. I was a slight bit jealous. I remember thinking, *That's not me, but he looks just like me.* He was already doing everything I had thought about possibly doing if I were to choose to fight competitively. This fighting played a certain significant role in my formative years, both in terms of the integration and assimilation processes and in how other kids accepted and treated me.

I remember moving from Dundalk to Turner Station at seven or eight years old when I was going into the third grade. Although Turner Station had the reputation of being the badlands, people living down there all had good jobs because they worked for the Bethlehem Steel Mill at Sparrows Point. Badlands or not, moving meant there would be a physical throw-down or beat-down ritual. Using the boxing skills taught by my father and uncles, it was just a matter of time before I was accepted in school and around the neighborhood. The bigger boys (teens) always looked out for the younger boys they believed had heart. They were protectors against larger or older guys outside of my weight class. Reds was one of my protectors, he was also a badass and sort of respected by everyone. On a couple of occasions I was jumped by some older and bigger guys. Guess who tracked them down, went into their houses, and pulled them and their fathers outside—yep … my dad.

The kids loved the way I boxed. I was doing the Muhammad Ali before there was a Muhammad Ali. Eventually, however, I would become cruel with my skill. As I look back on it now, I became cocky and arrogant. I actually became a bully. Even though I might have been small, I would actually pick out people as part of a sideshow—a school sideshow—and all the kids would gather around. I would grab someone I knew I could beat. Once I grabbed a kid named Skippy Reid, but out of fear, he grabbed hold of me and almost whipped my ass. That's when I realized I had become a bully, and it was something I should never do again. It was a signal to me, a wake-up call. I had almost been embarrassed in front of the whole school by picking on a person just because I felt superior. That ended that!

Nevertheless, what my boxing ability did was to give me immediate respect wherever we moved or wherever I went to school. It didn't matter if it was Sollers Point or Turner Station, I could fight. When I went to Lemmel Junior High, I could fight. When I went to Havre de Grace Consolidated, the "colored" school, I was only there two days before a guy named Shug, the school's badass, came up to me.

"Boy, I'm gonna whip your ass," he said.

Then Frankie Sumpter said, "And after he whips your ass, I'm gonna whip your ass." Well, Frankie Sumpter went on to play for the New York Jets, and Frankie Sumpter and I really got tight. But first, we had to go to war. I didn't knock out Shug that day, but I didn't lose either. The next day Frankie Sumpter and I went toe-to-toe all over the school hallway with the same result as the day before. Frankie was a tremendous athlete, and as I said, he went on to be a defensive back for the New York Jets. I have not seen him for over fifteen years, but he used to call me for legal advice. Havre de Grace had three kids that went on to play for the New York Jets, which was quite an accomplishment considering they didn't have a football team. At any rate, after I went toe-to-toe with Frankie I was immediately accepted at Havre de Grace Consolidated. I never had any more fights. I had fought both Shug and Frankie, and even though I didn't beat either one of them, neither one of them beat me.

Everybody said, "That little red kid sure can fight. He can deal." This cycle would replay itself out again at Aberdeen High School and, in a way, at Howard University.

As I got older, around sixteen, my father and I could relate through boxing. It was just a family tradition. When I was about sixteen or seventeen years old, I finally knocked my father down. It was a major event. The whole family was in the backyard, eating and drinking. If I was not boxing with John, I was usually boxing with Hayes, but Hayes hit too hard. (I told this story at Uncle Hayes's funeral. He could not pull his punches.) Anyway, on this day, I was boxing with Dad. I hit him in the stomach, not the head, and knocked the wind out of him. He went down. The whole family went into a hush. They just had no idea what George's reaction was going to be. He was physically and mentally stunned. He got up, took the gloves off, and without saying a word went into the house. I guess he had to get himself together. I think the realization that your son might be your physical equal has quite a psychological impact. Anyway, he came back out, and we were all right. I do not remember us ever talking about this, and we never boxed again.

I had knocked my father down in a sporting set, which was different from other confrontations. I would never raise my hand and hit my father in anger, but we did have confrontations where we did engage physically. By the time I was seventeen years old, we were living in Aberdeen, and I was on the football and wrestling teams. On one occasion, we wrestled all over the place, and not in a sporting way, when I had interceded between him and my mother. When I came up on top, my father realized he could not get up and that I had him pinned to the floor. He looked up, and in a very calm manner said, "Son, I love you more than anything in life. But, when you get up off of me, and if you're still here when I get up, I'm going to blow your head off." I knew this was not an alcohol threat, that this was not idle conversation. I knew that if I did not get out of there, I would be a beloved dead son.

I never forgot that night. He let me get up, but he did not try to get up. I grabbed my mother, and we went running up Route 40. My mom and I went to a motel for the night. When we called home the next morning, my father had slept it off, and he wanted to know what happened, where we were, why we were not at home, and when would we be back. I lived with my volatile father for seventeen years.

Again, I do not mean to imply that I was an abused child, but he was very demanding and very physical as a parent. That was just the way he was. When my father asked me to do something, if I did not respond quickly enough or if I did not respond in the proper way, I would get the hell knocked out of me. I was not allowed to cry, but if I looked at him too hard he would say, "Who in the hell are you rolling your eyes at?" If I looked down, it was, "Damn it, look at me when I talk to you."

I never knew which hand was coming. I remember one occasion, at a very young age, when we were in the car coming up from Turner Station to visit Uncle Hayes in Baltimore City. I was leaning between the front seats, between my mother and father, while they were having a conversation. I was singing, "Eenie, meenie, minee, moe, catch a ni—" I never got the word out. The next thing I recall, I was knocked to the backseat. He never looked at me. He just caught me with the back of his hand and sent me from the front of the car to the back of the car. That was the type of quick reflexes my father had, and that was his type of tough, stern love. I knew then not to use the word "nigger" around my father. That might have been a street term, but it was not acceptable in his view of the world. I never heard him use the word, and obviously, I was not supposed to use that word. And that was the last time I ever rhymed, "eenie, meenie, minee, moe," around my father.

The Champ, Alvin, Jr. and Dwight

Muhammad Ali and daughter Nahisha Pettit

Dwight Boxing

Chapter 3: Responsibilities

Having responsibilities and being responsible were early lessons from my father. Thus, I was industrious. When I say industrious, I mean I really had a lot of imagination in the things that I did. As a youngster, I sold Cloverine Salve in Dundalk, Maryland. Later, while living in Turner Station, I would go around collecting bottles. I got a nickel for the big bottles and two cents for the small bottles. I would fill my wagon with bottles, and, between the ages of eight to eleven or so, I made two or three dollars every day in the summertime. That was my thing. I had kids working for me, and I would give them a certain percentage of the profit.

When we moved to Aberdeen, I developed a worm farm. I knew people liked to fish, so I got a big box, and I read books on breeding and caring for worms. I was an ardent reader of nature and wildlife books and novels. I spread the word that if people were going to go fishing, they did not have to dig their own worms, they could buy them from me and go straight out and start fishing. Dad designed an electric-shock machine that caused the worms to come out of the ground. That really got me into the world of entrepreneurship.

In the spring of 1959, I saw something in the newspaper involving the catching and selling of skunks. There was a place in Pennsylvania where baby skunks could be deodorized to keep as pets, or at least that was what the news article said. I think they paid ten dollars per skunk. My father and I agreed that if I took this on, and I figured out how to collect and store the skunks in captivity without exposing the neighborhood to the foul odor, then he would take me up to the Pennsylvania farm where I could sell the skunks.

Well, I had a very industrious summer. I read how to catch the skunks without being sprayed. I needed to shine a light into their eyes, which would temporarily blind them, and then I could pick them up by the tail. A person would not get sprayed handling them that way because they had to have their feet on the ground to secrete the spray. I could pick them up and just drop them into a bag. I built this compound, which was really a large ammunition box, and I started collecting skunks. In Aberdeen at that time, being on a military base, the skunks walked around like cats and dogs—mother skunks out strolling with five or six baby skunks. I would take the babies and then lock them up in my box. By Saturday, I might have fifteen or more skunks. My father would then take me to Pennsylvania. At $10 apiece, I would come back with $150 to $200. I did that for the whole summer. My little girlfriend and I were sprayed once, but the good part about that was we both smelled just alike, so at least we could keep each other company.

These projects showed the type of entrepreneurship that my father and mother instilled in me. My mother had finished beauty school near the campus at A&T, and she was a licensed beautician at a very young age. She did hair for almost all of the college girls at Bennett College, the sister school to A&T. Being a businessperson by day, as well as a mom and homemaker by night, she would leave cab fare for me in the morning, so at four years old I could take a cab to the beauty shop she shared. I would spend the day with the women, washing hair and sweeping up, or going down to Boss Webster's drugstore to read comic books all day. This was how I began to value having women as best friends. It was the beauty salon by day and the South Side Tavern by night.

Along with my jobs at age twelve, my chores included maintaining our family's gardens. We did not have much of a lawn in Turner Station, but in Aberdeen, after we moved off base, my father had two gardens, one at home, which was more like a field, and another up in Bel Air, Maryland. We grew enough vegetables to supply a whole town. Of course, I was the one who had to work the gardens. I played three sports during the school year: football, baseball, and wrestling. After coming home from practice sessions, I had to cut the grass or go out and plow the damn garden. We're talking about gardens that are half acres. Without brothers and sisters to help, I was doing that work by myself after two hours of sports practice unless it was a game day. My point is that I always had chores.

While in high school, I worked nights as a janitor on the military base. After my first year of college, I came home for the summer because I could not get a job in Washington, DC. I would interview at banks and so forth and would always score high or the highest on the application tests, but being a black male, I could never get the job. In my sophomore year, I saw my girlfriend (now my wife) get a job immediately, but I couldn't even work construction.

At any rate, after my freshman year, I came home, and I got a job as pot-and-pan man in the Army mess hall. In that job you really worked. We started at five o'clock in the morning and worked until six o'clock at night. I made $1.53 an hour until three o'clock and time and a half after three o'clock. I used to look around and watch the black men working there. They had been there for years, and this was the real stuff for them. They formed assembly lines and mopped the floors, singing "them" songs, the blues. That was when I first got an appreciation for academic achievement. In my freshman years, my grades were average or below. However, when I went back to college for my sophomore year, my parents did not have to worry about my grades anymore.

I saw what a black man could look forward to without an education. Those folks were grateful to make $1.53 to $2.30 washing dishes and mopping floors, working from sunup until dark or almost dark. They were happy having that job because it supported their needs. When I left there in the evenings, I had to pass the swimming pool and see my white friends, all the same guys I went to high school with.

My father always said, "Dwight, what they do you can't do. They go work in drug stores; they go to work in the bank." When I came home, those jobs were not available to me. I had been a local football player in Aberdeen, but those jobs just were not available to black men.

So I worked as a janitor as I had in high school, and I continued to work in the Army mess hall. I would pass all of my little friends in my mess-hall whites. It was sort of a joke to those kids. But I didn't have any problem with it, at least I was working. The problem was that after I got home I would still have chores. I mean, I was home from college, and I got home from working from five o'clock in the morning until six o'clock at night, and I had to turn around and cut the grass and work in the garden. Cutting grass and working in the damn garden made no sense to me. That was when my dad and I really begin to have serious disagreements. That was my last summer coming home. I mean, work is fine, but there are certain limitations on everything.

Chapter 4: Academics

My father and I would have continuous conflicts centered on academics. He considered me academically lazy and an underachiever. He was so academically driven and so naturally gifted that it might have had an effect on my early childhood in terms of some type of retreating, retrenchment, or rebellion. When my grades were not up to par, punishment was always extra reading assignments and book reports. I was a voracious reader of comic books from early childhood, and later I delved into novels and nature books. I just did not have that academic interest at a young age. This became important in terms of the early part of my career. For example, I did not take the necessary business courses (accounting and economics) in undergraduate to be properly prepared for law school.

Just as this nation was dedicated to slavery, it was dedicated to keeping black people from being intellectually developed. The message of academic deficiency—a message that black people are inferior—was driven home to black kids from the time they were born. The message was delivered starting in elementary school, when instruction was automatically geared toward manual labor or servitude jobs, and especially when I moved into the white academic environment, when counselors automatically advised that I was supposed to be good with my hands.

"Get a skill. Get a physical skill," they said. The wording might have been different, but the message remained the same: whites were academically superior.

In my early formative years, in the second and third grades, I do not really remember academics. Maybe it was because of the pressure applied by my father. Maybe he was missing the boat in terms of where my gifts were, because his automatic assumption was that my gift should be mathematics as was his. Therefore, if I did not excel in mathematics or if I did not excel in the sciences, he harbored some degree of disappointment that I was not a chip off the old block. My loves were history and the social sciences. Maybe he thought I took after my mother's side of the family, which he felt did not fare as well in the academic arena. As far as my father was concerned, nobody was his academic and intellectual equal. My father's word for my mother and me was "stupid." But, then again, his favorite word for everybody was stupid. To some extent, my mother and I came to think our real names were "Stupid."

I remember one of my biggest confrontations with my father was in high school when I dropped out of physics and trigonometry. My father just went off! I mean, he just had no comprehension how I could attain admission to college without taking physics and trigonometry. I was trying to convince him I had no desire and no intent whatsoever to pursue mathematics, even though I may have had the aptitude to study higher mathematics and higher sciences. I had taken geometry; I had taken algebra; I had taken chemistry; I had taken biology; and the college requirements did not require me to have trigonometry or physics. I suppose it's relevant to mention here that my early years of schooling, as described in my report cards, were about girls, playing pranks, and everything else but study and focus. Nevertheless, I knew that colleges did not require me to have physics, so I didn't know why in hell I had to enroll in that subject.

Aberdeen High School, being close to the scientific base where my father worked, had wannabe mathematical geniuses running all around. These kids were splitting atoms, doing high-tech experiments in the ninth and tenth grades. In other words, Aberdeen High School was ahead of most schools in the state of Maryland in terms of math and science, except for the Baltimore Polytechnic Institute in Baltimore City. When I was at Aberdeen, I remember that a young woman (Sandra Sarune) got a scholarship to MIT in the tenth grade.

Being in a school associated with a military base, there was a large pool of scientific talent. At Aberdeen Proving Ground, there was the Human Engineering Lab, Developmental and Proof Services, and the Ballistics Research Laboratories. At one time or another, my father worked at all of these facilities, as well as other scientific laboratories. As a result of these facilities, the local high school in Aberdeen had a unique mixture, socially and academically, of local town kids and the kids of high-tech military and scientific personnel. This did not intimidate me. I just wanted to stay focused in terms of my ambitions without spreading myself thin trying to please my father. I made a decision, and that was that.

I remember from the second or third grade that I was always drawing when I wasn't playing around or "being bad" as my report cards reflected. I am talented in art, which is derived from my father and has been passed on by me to my son. My son, Alvin Dwight Pettit Jr., is a very gifted illustrative artist, which includes talent in painting and sculpture. He graduated from the Maryland Institute of the Arts in high school and the New York Institute of the Arts for college.

For me, rebellion was always there to a certain extent. I constantly had average or less-than-average report cards.

"Dwight has a low attention span."

"He is very inattentive."

"He bothers the other kids."

"What he thinks is a joke, the other kids don't particularly find funny."

"He is constantly busy doing something agitating."

I stayed in a confrontational situation with my father on report-card days. There were long and lingering times when I contemplated how I was going to get into the house without taking a verbal whipping, and how I was going to explain my report card when there was no way around it. I knew all hell was going to break loose, and the tongue lashing and punishment were certain to come. Nevertheless, I would not conform to the academic requirements that my father felt that I should follow. There was no doubt that he was right. This became a major factor to be played out later in litigation, starting with *Pettit v. Board of Education of Harford County*, 184 F. Supp. 452 (1960).

My constant rebellion surfaced in the third and fourth grades. I was taking IQ or achievement tests, which goes back to what white folks called *classification*. Without knowing this classification process was taking place, students were scored against certain levels of an academic scale. I was taking IQ tests that were going to have a profound effect on my life. Not knowing this, I was shooting spitballs or peeping under the table to look under some girl's dress or fighting or "bothering somebody" (as one teacher wrote), or I was drawing. I had no concept whatsoever of the relevance of taking standardized examinations.

At that time, they had a track system. For example in the fourth grade, the tracks were 4A, 4B, 4C, 4D, 4E, and Special. From the first through fourth grades, I was always placed in "general" (4C or 4D) classes with the so-called ruffians, hoodlums, rabble-rousers, and fighters. As the white community would argue later in my life, these tests reflected that I was less academically talented than other children my age. It would be argued that I was, in fact, not only noncompetitive with whites, but almost at the level of being considered retarded. This characterization would later be repeated in newspapers, courtrooms, and even once in a heated political campaign.

At Fleming Elementary in Turner Station, I had a very sweet fourth-grade teacher by the name of Miss Simbley. She was a large woman who looked as if she could have been my grandmother. She just loved and babied me to death. I could do no wrong. I could just sit in her class and draw all day long. One day, we had some type of special examination. It was not an IQ test, but it was some type of reading and comprehension test. I remember that we were all in the basement that day, and I decided to focus and fully participate. I also remember that I finished quickly and went back to drawing. As the papers were being reviewed, a little conference was held among the teachers. Then they went out of the room, and a few other people joined in. I do not know how it started, or why the spontaneity, but somehow I knew the conversation was about me. I knew that whatever the meaning of this test, there was some surprise or astonishment about my performance. The next thing I knew, they were telling me was I was being transferred to another section.

I had attended the first grade in Dundalk and the second through fourth grades in Turner Station. For the fifth and the sixth grades, I was enrolled in Bragg Elementary in Sparrows Point, and in the seventh grade I attended Sollers Point High School before moving to Aberdeen. Those different schools were due to educational logistics and my father's employment with the military.

As I recall, I reported to my new class at Fleming Elementary the very next morning. I ended up with a gorgeous woman as my teacher. She was very, very feminine and very eloquent. The class was made up of mostly girls, with maybe four or five boys; this was an A-Section class. Apparently, while monitoring the test in Miss Simbley's class, somebody had observed me, watched me reading and finishing before everybody else, and watched whatever else I was doing and surmised, "Wait a minute, something's wrong, this kid is in the wrong place."

All of a sudden, I was in 5A. I was with the smart kids, well, the so-called smart kids. The little girls who were in that class wore their little bows and their little, ruffled-lace blouses and had their little oiled legs with little white socks and the big ribbons on their braids. There was a world of difference between 5A and sections 5C–5D where most of the hardhead boys were enrolled. So there I was with Mrs. Dobbins, who I will never forget. I remember this gorgeous teacher leaning over to show me my Roman numerals. That large bosom was practically on my shoulders. The smell of expensive perfume enveloped the room. I said to myself, *I really like this.* Everything was pretty, and everything was different. I also realized that everything was now academically competitive. My stature in this section would be based on academic performance, not fighting skills. There was no more drawing. There was no more Miss Simbley to give me some paper and crayons. There would be no finishing early, just continuous work. I was now expected to perform with my new peers.

Plessy v. Ferguson, which said that the Negro and white schools were to be separate, but equal, was the law of the land. On the surface, the black schools and white schools at those times, both in Baltimore City and Baltimore County, were already equal for all practical purposes. Black teachers were sharp, gifted, and talented. The black school in Turner Station was relatively new and just as modern as the white schools in Dundalk. In Maryland, some political subdivisions were apparently willing to spend money equally to fulfill the legal requirements of lawful segregation in order to maintain said segregation. However, I cannot conclude that those expenditures were in fact totally equal in all areas.

My first exposure into real academic competition was in the fifth grade. I was still battling with my father, but all of a sudden it was from a different perspective. I discovered I was academically empowered regardless of what the previous so-called IQ and achievement tests said. All prior classification data was out the window, and I was starting over. However, this thing between my father and I was still very much present. I had been rebellious about school rather than trying to fulfill his expectations. To me, my dad was really a genius. He was the genius who was competitive and so much into his academic world. He enjoyed academics and excelled off the charts. His attitude said, *Look, white folks, you think you are intellectually superior, but here I am as a black man. Any test or challenge you give me, I am going to achieve it and score at the highest level.* I would eventually adopt this same attitude.

Whether it was academic endeavors, job hunting, or the bar exam, I believed that I could score at the top level, and I could do so anytime I chose. By this, I mean I found, as I went through high school and college, that I was able to reject the limitations placed upon me by those early standardized test. I found out that my academic ability was strictly within my power. It was almost as if I had a secret reservoir of mental talent that I could tap into at will. When I wanted to be in my shell, I could stay there happily. However, when I wanted to bring out my ability I could. It was almost as if I could reach down and bring out my father's genius. It was my choice. My mother is a very smart and gifted woman, but I think my father was academically gifted. These genes that I inherited from my parents could be turned on or off at will. It became a very fascinating ability because I could use it at any time.

I remember going on job interviews at banks and stores during the summer after my sophomore year at college. At one particular bank, the morning started with testing. There were perhaps 100 to 150 people testing for the job. As I recall, I was the only black person. The testing lasted all day until there were only two of us left. Of course, the white person got the job. I got an excuse. Although I scored higher, I was told that the white person was looking for a full-time job, a career, whereas I was just a college student seeking temporary employment.

Once my ability dawned on me in elementary school, I began pulling it up through the years whenever I felt it was necessary. For example, I took a physical science class during the spring semester of my freshman year at Howard University. This was a required course that was commonly known as a "wipe-out class," the type of class where they tell you, "Look to your left, look to your right, because those people won't be here after this semester." Howard was considered the academic mecca of the "Negro" community. Many of the university's so-called intellectuals did not accept athletes. I had played football in the fall and had already encountered some professors who resented athletes, in particular. In fact, I had already been placed on academic probation, and my grades had to be at a certain level to play football in the coming fall of my sophomore year. So all of a sudden, I was motivated.

Physical Science was taught in a small auditorium. There were about 150 people in the class. Some weeks into the semester, I went to Professor Scott and said, "I am aware that my grades are down, and I know that I haven't really focused and concentrated. What kind of grade do I need on the final exam to pass the course with at least a C?" All I was concerned about was getting a C. I still had not become academically aggressive, even though I was now in college.

Professor Scott said, "Mr. Pettit, your exams thus far have been below average." In perceived jest he said, "You would have to get an A on your final exam to get a C."

I responded, "An A? That's a joke."

"I'm not joking with you, son," he said. "There is no expectation that you can do it, but if you study hard and get a B, in all seriousness, you might get a C and pass the course. Now, I don't know whether you can get a D and be able to play football, but at least you might be able to get out of here and not have to retake this course." He was a very nice gentle man and a young professor who was very close to his students, or as close as possible with such a large class.

At the end of the semester, after the final exam had been taken, Professor Scott called back the whole class to deliver the exam grades. He reiterated how hard the exam was, given that physical science was a lot like high-school physics. He explained that everyone scored well below expectations because the highest grade in the class was an 87. He said he therefore dropped the curve so at least two-thirds of the students could pass. However, even by dropping the curve, one-third failed the final exam and thus the course. By dropping the curve, the high score of 87 would be graded an A. Professor Scott then said he wanted the student who set that curve to stand up. Because the papers had been machine-graded using just student ID numbers, Professor Scott did not know which student this would be, so he asked, "Will student number 624845 please stand?"

Well, that was my student ID number! I stood up, and like the professor, the entire class was silent, stunned, as if to say, "The football player?"

Professor Scott finally controlled his initial response, and as if fumbling for words, said, "Sir, aren't you the football player? I believe your name is Mr. Pettit. You came to my office. Are you also number 624845?"

"Yes, sir," I replied. "I'm number 624845." He then asked me to come to his office after class.

Later he said, "Well, young man, you scored the highest grade on the final. You aced the final. I had you all wrong. I am going to give you a B for the course." He went on to explain that he could not give me an A because of my earlier exams, but Physical Science would not stop me from playing football.

I would do the same thing on several other courses. In fact, my wife, Barbara, then my girlfriend, was with me and helping me with philosophy and logic during my junior year. Logic is an interesting subject. Like geometry, it is mathematical in many ways. There are a lot of mathematical principles and theories. Our logic teacher was an outstanding professor by the name of Dr. Winston K. McAllister. Back home in Baltimore City, Dr.

McAllister's brother was one of the biggest criminal lawyers in the city. In Dr. McAllister's course, if students aced the final at the end of the year, they would ace the course regardless of prior grades. Barbara was scoring eighty-sevens and nineties on every exam, and I was scoring in the seventies and eighties. I was passing, and Dr. McAllister was a big football fan, so I was not in a hostile environment. In fact, Dr. Mac (as we so affectionately called him) had been my employer during my summer job on campus as a counselor in the precollege program for high school students in the DC area. Dr. Mac made a game of the exams by teasing Barbara that he knew I would come through and beat her in the finals. She was so furious with him that it became a competition. She and I were, and still are, very competitive. We cannot even play cards or checkers without arguing. This competitiveness existed all through college. We took many of the same classes, particularly because I was able to get her registration processed early along with the football team. Thus, Barbara and I studied and went into the finals together.

In Dr. Mac's course, I said to Barbara, "Well, Bobbie, you know I can do whatever I want to do. So I've decided I really want to ace this course." I rubbed this in, and sure enough, to make a long story short, I aced logic. I will never forget it. During the final exam, I was seated behind her, and I kept hitting her on her shoulders because I could see she had a couple of wrong answers. I was trying to help. She thought I was trying to copy from her test paper, so she put her arms around her paper and told me to leave her alone. Dr. Mac heard this. He did not hear exactly what she said, but he looked around and gave me a look that said, "Do not get caught cheating." I knew that look. As much as he liked me, I should not push our friendship. The irony was that I was not cheating; I was trying to help *her.* I guess it was reverse cheating. Anyway, I aced the final with the highest grade in the class. I scored something like a ninety-eight. In fact, there were only three As in the whole course. Barbara received a B.

I had another professor at Howard University who was a very famous writer, Dr. Bernard Fall. At the time, he was one of the national advisors to President Johnson on Southeast Asia. Dr. Fall was later killed in Vietnam. Although I respected Dr. Fall academically, he was one of the few professors I hated with a passion, only because he hated me. He was a Jew from France who had been in the French underground resistance during World War II. Although most of the students in Dr. Fall's classes were white, he seemed to have a disdain for his black students. I do not know why he taught at Howard, which was predominantly black, given that he had what appeared to be such a prejudice against blacks. He just seemed to have such arrogance in his demeanor with blacks. Nevertheless, the man was brilliant, and his classes were fascinating. I took several of his courses—United Nations, Southeast Asia, and US foreign policy—and he never gave me higher than a C, even though I aced the exams. I developed a competitive relationship with him. If the exams were objective examinations, I would commit the whole section to memory and generally score 100.

Once, he actually stood up in front of the class and said, "This is actually impossible! There is no way in the world Mr. Pettit could have gotten everything right on this exam when the rest of you in this class scored in the 60s and 70s. There's no way in the world he could score a perfect paper!"

Dr. Fall would stand right in front of me and, on three or four occasions, actually tear up my papers and throw them in the trash can, declaring the exam null and void. In his mind, either I had cheated or I had been given the answers. He was such a self-centered, arrogant ass. When he arrived for class, students would stand up and applaud.

He once came into class with makeup on his face, saying, "Yes, I just left the White House, and I told Lyndon we should consider bombing the Chinese. However, because of the population, we would have to drop so much nuclear tonnage that the nuclear fallout would drift across the Pacific Ocean and kill off half the population of Los Angeles. So I told the president this was not a viable option." He was saying this while he was wiping off his makeup.

On another occasion, Dr. Fall announced, in a very derogatory manner, "I just left Walter Cronkite, and I have to come back here to lecture this class. And Mr. Pettit, of all people, scored 100 on the examination I gave you last week. A perfect paper! I find that totally, totally impossible and unacceptable." Such was his general arrogance.

My wife can attest to the fact that Dr. Fall did the same thing to me, not only with objective examinations, but also with a written paper. In my junior or senior year, I had to write a paper for one of his courses. After the assignment was completed, Dr. Fall invited the whole class to his home for a class session and dinner; he had this fabulous house in northwest Washington, DC.

When he got to my paper, Dr. Fall announced, "Mr. Pettit wrote a fantastic paper. It is so well written and articulated that it is an academic triumph. The only problem I have is that I cannot find the book or books from which he plagiarized it, and I searched for twenty-four to forty-eight hours."

He went on to say, "Now, Mr. Pettit, just like I never accepted those examinations when you had ridiculous scores, I am not going to except this paper. So, I'll tell you what I am going to do. I cannot prove that you've plagiarized, but I am going to give you forty-eight hours to write me another paper. If you plagiarize twice, I know I'll find the second book of source."

My wife and I went back to my apartment, and I wrote a second paper. Bobbie typed it over the weekend. On Monday, I gave him a second paper. This time nobody else was there, it was just he and I. He read the paper, looked off, and walked around his desk. He hit the desk and then walked around again. He stopped and returned to his chair. Leaning back, he just sat there and reflected. I could see the signs of disbelief come across this man's face. He had chosen the subject this time to make sure, according to him, that I did not plagiarize.

He turned his back to me and finally said, "Mr. Pettit, I don't understand it. To be quite candid with you, it appears that in some kind of way you have the ability to do this. I do not like you; I do not like what you stand for, and I do not like athletes. I will not give you an A, you will get a B. I am going to take off ten points because the paper is late."

I said, "Dr. Fall, it's late because you made me rewrite it. You threw away my first paper and made me rewrite it. That's why it's late, sir."

"Mr. Pettit, I am going to give you a B, and I suggest you take it and be happy."

A great professor was Dr. Gardner. He taught humanities and was one of the most verbally gifted people I had ever met, aside from my ninth-grade English teacher at Lemmel Junior High School, Ray Carpenter. Dr. Gardner had a great command of the English language. He was descriptively exotic in his expressions and quite historical. Being in his class was like being in a group play. He expounded eloquently on a range of topics, such as the Greek gods and notably Dante's *Inferno*.

As always, Barbara and I took Dr. Gardner's class together. He was just the opposite of Dr. Fall, who could not stand football players. When I came into class, Dr. Gardner would announce jokingly, "Ladies and gentleman, be quiet. The Greek gods have blessed us with Mr. Pettit's arrival."

I would sit down at the desk, embarrassed, and he would say, "Mr. Pettit, I was at the game Saturday, and I watched you as you uncoiled like a ballet dancer as you leaped down the field, soared to tremendous heights, and danced with the gods." He would go through all of these embarrassing descriptions.

He would say to the class, "I want everybody to keep quiet because the Greek gods need to rest. So, Mr. Pettit, you may put your head down on the desk, and you may drift off into the bliss of sleep because football practice is this afternoon."

Barbara would say to me, "I hate that, I hate you, and I hate him."

I took three humanities courses with Dr. Gardner. He was a fantastic human being, and his courses were awesome. Although I never got higher than a B in his class, I still have fond memories of this academic experience. He was a tough grader, but I learned about the humanities, Greek literature, and cultural history.

Chapter 5: If the Time Is Right

Turning on "the juice" is a gift of genes I still hold in reserve during trials. I can be average, but I know I can be above average. I have found that, in crucial situations, I have the talent not only to be good—I have a God-given talent to be very good. I mean, I can rise to an academic level that sometimes surprises even me. Maybe I suppressed it because of domestic turmoil in our house. Maybe I rejected it out of rebellion against my father. I may not have sustained it out of laziness, and maybe this is what my father saw. But, I can rise to the top as I choose.

I brought this talent to my bar examinations. But the first time I took the Maryland bar, I was failed on the exam. (This was the impetus for *Pettit v. Gingerich*, 427 F. Supp. 282, 1977.) This would be the first law suit in the nation to challenge state law (bar) exams. You will notice I did not say I failed the exam. No, I was failed on the exam. I knew, coming out of law school, it was a joke to take the Maryland bar, because they were passing only one or two blacks at a time. After the first failing exam results, I did a study and documented that blacks were passing at a statistical rate of less than 7 percent, while whites were passing at an eventual rate of 70 percent. Coming out of the University of Maryland, whites were passing at a rate approaching almost 90 percent. I compiled all of the statistics, and then I searched for a lawyer.

My lawyers in *Pettit v. Gingerich* were Elaine Jones, Jack Greenberg, and lead counsel Ken Johnson (now retired from the bench of the Circuit

Court for Baltimore City). When I first went to see Mr. Johnson, who at that time was with the firm of Gerald Smith and Ken Johnson, I said, "I am not just blowing smoke when I tell you that I passed the Maryland bar exam and that the only reason I was not admitted to practice law in Maryland was because of racial discrimination. I am telling you that I not only passed it, I blew it away." I was so confident, that as we got into the discovery phase of the litigation process, I challenged the defense to bring in the best grading experts in the nation and grade the exams of not only all of the whites that allegedly passed, but the whites who scored in the top 10 percent. I wanted all of the names taped over, and my paper mixed in with the rest. I wanted to have independent law examiners from across the nation, selected by both sides, to grade those exams. I told the trial team that I was willing to guarantee that I would be in the top 3 percent. However, I was passed on my third attempt, and the suit was dismissed as moot. I never learned as to where I ranked with those who passed.

At that time, I honestly believed that the legal and political changes coming out of the federal government and the civil-rights movement would create an immediate improvement in the conditions of black people and poor people in general. What I now understand is different from what I believed during the civil-rights movement of Lyndon B. Johnson's time and the affirmative action era of Richard M. Nixon. What I have come to understand is that by the middle '70s these movements were permitted and orchestrated, if not in fact created to some extent by the authorities. This is not to say I am a conspiracy junkie, however, I do understand that certain things are put in motion because they are allowed to be put in motion.

If you think back, Martin Luther King, Jr. to some extent was promoted in order to balance off the impact of the so-called radicals, or those considered radicals, such as Malcolm X, H. Rap Brown, Stokley Carmichael, Huey P. Newton, and the Black Panthers. He was acceptable to the establishment and therefore was given star status until his positions were unacceptable regarding Vietnam. The system helped to create him or allowed him to be created to a certain extent, because it was in the interest of the American system to have somebody at that point in time—during the riots and the break out of violence—to be talking about nonviolence. In a large part, the media promoted the civil-rights movement. The beatings in the South were brought to us on live television. In other words, for the larger majority of the American power structure, it was time for those things to happen—it was time for the Civil Rights Act and subsequent legislation. President Johnson was focused, and the agenda was pushed both by the government and the media. It was only when Dr. King challenged the establishment, the industrial military complex, and the war in Vietnam that all of a sudden he became unpopular to the establishment.

In the affirmative-action era of Richard Nixon, it was determined that minority business should be the focus of the African American community. Economic development and set-aside programs were created for the distribution of wealth, or if not wealth, at least the distribution of money through the poorer elements of society, meaning the "have-nots." Of course, this nation has never been about African Americans, but capitalism is all about the haves and the have-nots. If the have-nots are kept in a state of war with one another, they don't have the opportunity to focus on the haves. That, of course, takes us into police protection and such things as the property aspect of the system.

Fresh out of law school, I believed that elections in America were governed in terms of one's ideas, what one brought to the community, what one could offer the community, and what was in the best interest of the community. I had no understanding whatsoever that that was not the case and that those principals had nothing to do with American politics. First, American politics is governed by the monetary forces that choose candidates, anoint them, "media-rize" them, elect them, and then dictate to them. Money dictates those who will be elected. Second, the legal aspects of society are governed by the politics of the society, which in turn are governed by the economics of the society. We are allowed to achieve progress and win in those areas where the structure has deemed it is timely that those events take place. Victory, in terms of the civil-rights movement and the courts, was achieved because it was deemed to be timely and necessary to what, in fact, had already been decided and sanctioned politically. As with affirmative action in the Nixon administration, this was evident in the legislative process of the Johnson administration and likewise evident in the judicial results regarding *Brown v. Board of Education* and my school desegregation case and my father's employment case. Those were not individual victories; they were victories that were allowed to happen because the system found and decided that it was timely that those things happen.

Naïveté is the basis for the belief or premise that as an individual you can win legal cases that will effect positive change. You believe you really can come into our courts, as well as into our political world, bringing some individualism that will impact, for the good, those who are striving to elevate to a better station or to a higher level in terms of American society. You do not realize, until you reach a certain age, that your victories are victories that are allowed. You do not really understand that theory until you see the system change—when it is no longer timely for you to be victorious. Being part of the baby-boomer generation, I was predestined to win at the time I did. I was allowed to be on the winning side. Therefore, I came home to Baltimore City as the type of crusading lawyer who would only take cases that focused on the poor, the disadvantaged, civil rights, affirmative action, criminal law, and, of course, constitution law, in which I had been well grounded from my Howard University legal education. I believed this experience would be invaluable as I took on cases such as the Baltimore City cab drivers' union case; the "Turk" Scott case, *Scott v Watson,* a landmark civil-liability case in Maryland; and the "Boom Boom" Lester case, a case involving a black professional boxer who was losing his land on a county-property seizure.

In those early years, the first murder case I handled dealt with the possibility of the death penalty. All of these major, high-profile cases would come to me within the first five years of my practice, largely due to the national publicity that my father's case generated. It was a very exciting time because I was still acting under the naïve belief that I really could have an impact, that I really had the opportunity to change things and make a difference in that era of individualism. I also took the case of a Jewish woman in Hagerstown, Maryland, who was being deprived of her property. It was a seizure being fueled by the powers that be in Washington County, Maryland. During the same time, I also handled *Crocket v. the City of Baltimore,* which was a case that dealt with the constitutionality of the ban on for-sale signs. This case was preceded by a case out of Gary, Indiana, which went to the Supreme Court. In all of these cases, I had achieved some degree of success.

My naïveté had not disappeared during this time because I did not realize I was still on the wave of what was acceptable in American jurisprudence. It was still popular to bring and win civil-rights cases. It was still okay to bring constitutional cases and win, even if they were against the United States or corporate business. In fact, it was all right and sanctioned to bring about cases representing unions. It would be all right to defend the poor, the religious minority, the economically disadvantaged, or the other minorities. In the 1970s, this was still acceptable in America, and therefore, given my ability, it was okay to win those cases. So that created the false sense that I was achieving real change, rather than understanding that the system was allowing me to effect change on its terms.

I ran into the same thing in politics. The climate of America had not yet shifted to the Ronald Reagan years. As with my legal cases, I believed that I could not only bring about political change, but that I could get involved and actually get elected—because I was the better candidate. My naïveté was again fueled by that fact that my introduction to politics was just like my introduction to law.

As a lawyer, my first case outside of the SBA would be *George D. Pettit v. United States* 488 F.2d 1026 (1973). At age twenty-five, this would take me before the second-highest court in the country on monetary issues (then called the US Court of Claims), now called the US Court of Federal Claims. Like the law, my introduction to politics would be at the top, at the presidential level, by running into and meeting Jimmy Carter and becoming an intimate and intricate part of his campaign.

It just so happened that I was moving into areas where it was totally acceptable for me to be in the early and mid-1970s—because it was okay in America for blacks to get involved politically. It was okay for black activists to be accepted into the political system and for young black lawyers to be able to take on and win high-profile cases involving acceptable causes and politics. And even though I would do corporate work, having come out of the Small Business Administration, I also worked in property law and domestic law. However, my basic interest at that time was criminal law, forged in the area of the Constitution and civil rights. This emerging interest in federal civil rights and federal constitutional law would awaken me to the truth about our system. This opened my eyes. The light was clicked on.

Although I had been through *George D. Pettit v. United States,* supra, and gained experience through the SBA, where I had worked on affirmative action and developed some white-collar criminal experience, my first love was emerging as criminal law. As mentioned before, my first high-profile case (also my first capital and murder case) involved a codefendant murder trial in Harford County where a white colonel had been shot execution style. Charged were two young black males passing through, of all places, Aberdeen, Maryland. The colonel was abducted from a parking lot adjacent to a dance hall where he was attending a dance with his wife. He was taken into the woods, stripped, executed, and robbed of seventeen dollars. The defendants were apprehended in Virginia after they had abducted a white female as a hostage. Ironically, the white female would be the one who saved their lives. She kept them from being shot on sight, and she protected them when they were surrounded. They were then extradited back to Maryland.

Under Maryland law, the State could not make the capital case. They could not prove who pulled the trigger. To seek the death penalty in Maryland, the state would have to determine the trigger person. I was very fortunate that this case pled out. In most states, there is first-degree murder subject to the death penalty, first degree without parole, or first-degree murder where you have the opportunity for parole. My client pled to first-degree murder and received the opportunity for parole. He was very fortunate to be able to plead out to the first-degree murder charge, given a very conservative, predominately white county where he would have faced a white jury. At that time, he was eligible for parole in eleven and three-quarters years. I testified to this at a post-conviction hearing years later. Big cases like that would begin to come my way quite frequently.

I didn't really care for domestic relations. However, I did have the occasion to handle one major high-profile case before I left the domestic-relations area. It involved NFL football star Jim Parker. Jim Parker was an all-pro offensive tackle with the Baltimore Colts, a great championship team (1958–1959). I represented him in a divorce action in the early '80s (against his second or third wife) in Howard County, which is located between Washington, DC, and Baltimore City. What makes this story interesting is the Columbia, Maryland, Howard County location of the trial, where "Big Jim," as they called him, resided with his family.

Before trial day, one of the lawyers telephoned me saying, "Dwight, I think we better resolve this matter." He went on, "I don't mean to be offensive, but just as a matter of conversation, they don't like Negroes and Jews in Howard County. I'm just telling you because if we can resolve this, you may want to. I'm Jewish. We really need to resolve this before trial." That didn't happen.

I can't recall the judge's name, but as soon as he took the bench he said, "Before we get started, I would like to see Mr. Pettit in my chambers. This has nothing to do with the case." Once in chambers, the judge asked, "Do you think I can get Big Jim's autograph for my kids?"

I replied, "Sure, Your Honor, I don't think that would be a problem."

The judge indicated he didn't want it right then but said, "After the case, if you could arrange that for me I would appreciate it."

At that time, people in Maryland were fanatical Baltimore Colt fans. The Colts had been two-time world champions and were still in their heyday. Although retired, Jim was still a superstar. The case was tried, and the judge ruled in his favor for everything except alimony, and even reduced that. The wife was so upset that she called me all kinds of names. As I was walking out of the courtroom, I passed by the counselor's table and the two lawyers in the courtroom. To the one who had telephoned me, I said, "You know what, I don't know how Jews make out here, but Negroes seem to do all right." I found that to be very amusing, because what counsel had not done was consider the celebrity factor. Ironically, I would be on the losing end of this celebrity factor later in my career.

I had tried another case in Howard County prior to Big Jim's. That case involved a black child who just about lost his eye after being bitten by a German shepherd. The owners of the German shepherd were white, and we tried the case for three days in front of an all-white jury and a very interesting judge. He would later serve on the Court of Special Appeals for years. His name was Fisher, Judge Fisher. As in the Parker case, opposing counsel had a certain expectation about the judge. They were telling jokes when the judge—a very serious, very straight up judge—entered the room.

As the judge approached the bench, the opposing attorneys got up with a carefree attitude. "Well, Judge, you know, we represent the other side here."

The judge said, "Wait a minute, gentlemen. Let's step into my chambers." Once there he said, "First of all, gentlemen, this is a court of law, and as far as I am concerned, all people standing before me are equal." Then he said to me, "Mr. Pettit, let me say to you that I welcome you to my court." To the others, he said, "Gentlemen, I suggest the jokes, or whatever you're laughing about, must cease. Now let's go out and try this case."

I saw then that there were good judges, and there were bad judges. And every judge in the suburbs wasn't going to be a bad judge, and every judge in the city wasn't going to be a good judge. It is a fact that in our great nation, as we cross the lines of political subdivisions, counties, and cities wrought by the makeup of the state's population, justice changes, and it changes dramatically. Moreover, it changes unequally. Geography has a tremendous impact upon African Americans, but it helps to start with an unbiased judiciary.

My client in this case was a young black child who had been severely injured because of a dog bite. He almost lost his eye. Because it was an all-white jury, however, the other side was convinced we would lose the case. When the jury came back with the verdict in favor of the plaintiff, my client, I had an internal feeling of exuberance. But then, the strangest thing happened. The judge asked, "How much do you find for the plaintiff?"

I expected to hear a reasonable amount of money. The lead juror began to say, "25—" and I really believed I was hearing $25,000. I was shocked when I heard, "$2,500 for the child." Then, on top of that, all of the jurors came out of the box and passed by me with congratulations.

I said to myself, *Have these white people lost their minds? Do they really believe this tokenism is to be appreciated by a black American? Am I supposed to thank them?* I did. But, did they really believe they had done the right thing because they found for the plaintiff? Did they really believe we were supposed to show gratitude because they had done something grandiose, in their mind-set, while awarding my client pennies? I found the verdict to be inconsistent with the monetary award, but at the same time, I felt it was so interesting that they could believe in the deep caverns of their minds that they had rendered justice. If this had been a white child, in my opinion, he would have received at least $25,000. In fact, my thinking was that in most jurisdictions, my client would have probably been awarded at least $250,000. Even in Howard County, a conservative arena, surely it would be $25,000 and not just $2,500. I began to see a pattern in Maryland.

At any rate, one of my big first cases in the mid-1970s was a criminal case in the county during which the judge became very irritated with my demeanor and my style. Throughout my legal career, my aggressiveness would agitate some judges, particularly some white judges. I guess it was what they called arrogance.

This particular judge had the nerve to go into his "you people" bag. He was so involved with me that he made a major mistake. At one point, he got up from the bench and said, "I'm not hearing this case." But it was the State's prosecutor, not me, who had failed to file a document, and the judge's action resulted in a mistrial of the case. Because it was a major criminal case, the State tried to put the case back in. They couldn't because of double jeopardy. The prosecutor called to ask if I would allow this case to be set back in for the benefit of this judge, so he wouldn't be criticized for screwing up the case.

"The judge did what he did with a racist motivation. Let the case fall, or let the Court of Appeals decide." Anyway, as it worked out, my client benefited to a great extent. The case was dismissed and could not be brought back. She was ultimately acquitted, not on the evidence, but totally because of the attitude of this judge who was simply agitated that a black lawyer was in his court.

As fate would have it, I would later try a murder case in front of the son of this same judge. I chose to try the case without a jury because it was in the county, and it involved a very emotional issue. I thought the law was on my side and that a judge would be more compelled to follow the law than a jury. I can assure you, I would have won that case hands-down in the Baltimore City. At the time of the verdict, the judge made a statement that he wasn't sure what had happened. I had destroyed the State's case. The court wasn't exactly sure what had happened or what my client did or when he was supposed to have done it. Nevertheless, the judge said he was guilty of something, he just wasn't sure what. Now if ever there was reasonable doubt, this was it.

In the early days, I also worked in the District of Columbia and in Virginia. In one case, the target of a criminal investigation was a black person of prominence in DC. The authorities would set up a sting across the line into Virginia, because they knew they would have to deal with black juries in DC. Again, we're talking about the mid-1970s, and I was just getting my baptism in terms of the interaction between the American jurisprudence and my personal beliefs: beliefs nourished by my father's case, nourished by my integration case, and nourished by the fact that if you were right and the law was on your side, you should prevail.

What I had not yet understood was that my father won his case and I won my case because it was politically correct and acceptable for the time. In other words, in accordance with the prevailing political standard, the powers that be deemed it appropriate that civil rights for blacks should be court enforced. Blacks should prevail in terms of integration and the laws designed to protect them post-Civil War, post freedom from slavery, and post reconstruction—the Civil Rights Act of 1871, including 42 U.S.C. (1983), which was supposed to reinforce the emancipation and the Thirteenth Amendment to the US Constitution established years earlier.

At that juncture of my career, I had actually confused the politics of my victories with fairness. I believed that the justice ingrained in my belief system was also ingrained in the American system; if you were right and the law was on your side, you would prevail. I did not understand that if the political climate changed, it would not matter what the law was or what was right or wrong. All would be determined by what was politically correct and acceptable at that particular time. This theory and what I believe to be reality and truth, continue today.

I took a fraud case in Virginia that had received a lot of play in the *Washington Post*. A young man who was a federal official was charged with selling information that affected certain decisions within his agency. He was a bureaucrat—not a high political appointee, but rather a GS-12 or GS-13 civil-service worker.

We went before an older judge in the northern district of Virginia. As always, I had done extensive research and preparation. All of the defendants in the courtroom that day were black, and I did not see another black lawyer in court. The law enforcement officers were all white. I had never seen a judge make such a joke and mockery of the law. He chastised every black person who came before him with the "you people" references.

He said, "We are sick and tired of taking care of you people on welfare, and all you do is lie around and drink and make babies." He made obviously racist remarks to every defendant who came in front of him. This was something I had never heard before, not even from conservative Maryland judges. The conservative chief judge on the federal bench in the state of Maryland had brought me in his chambers and said he had nothing against Negros, but I had better be sharp and prepared when I came in his courtroom, because he did not tolerate incompetence. The white federal judges who I had appeared before may have harbored racial feelings or bias, but at least they were intelligent or aware enough to keep their feelings to themselves, even though it may have affected their decision or their verdict. Nevertheless, at least they didn't show their personal racial hostilities in court.

Finally, my client's case was called. I rose to face the judge. Because he was one of those joking type of judges, he would do his racial-stereotyping performance and then wait for the audience to respond with a laugh. It was not a courtroom; it was a circus. However, when I got in front of him, his face went into a very cold, stern stare. He looked at me but said nothing for a while.

Finally he said, barely above a whisper, that I was obviously not a local lawyer from Virginia.

I did have local counsel, Joe Wiggs (also a minority), but I recall he had not arrived in court that morning. I had prepared six motions: motions to suppress, motions to dismiss the indictment, motions to do this and to do that.

I said, "Your Honor, the first motion that I would like the court to address—"

Before I could finish what I was saying, he said in a very baritone voice, "Denied."

I said, "Okay. I have a second motion that goes to the heart of the indictment. I would like to quote you some law if I may."

The judge said, "Denied."

I anticipated a denial to my third motion, nevertheless I said, "Judge, this motion is a suppression of search and seizure of evidence, and I would like to quote—"

"Denied, Counsel."

Running out of motions, I considered how I should proceed: go on to the fourth motion, or rest, try this or try that.

I said, "Well, Judge, if you would just listen to this motion, I think this case—"

"Denied."

At this point, my client looked at me with some degree of alarm. This judge had not allowed me to get into arguments of any substance whatsoever. So, in the heat of battle, I had this brainstorm. I had two motions left.

Thinking very quickly, I said, "Your Honor, before you say anything, if I may, I would like to quote the Honorable Judge G. Harrold Carswell." I could see the shock on his face that this Negro was going to stand up in his court and quote a judge with whom he would be ideologically aligned.

Nominated for the US Supreme Court by President Nixon, Judge Carswell was considered one of the most conservative judges on the US Circuit Court. He had written a dissenting opinion in a case that I was now relying on. Judge Carswell's appointment was blocked in the US Senate, and this was national news because seldom had a presidential nomination to the court been blocked and this would be Nixon's second nominee rejection. However, during the Senate hearings much had come out revealing Judge Carswell's viewpoints and the organizations to which he belonged.

I continued by saying, "I have a feeling this court would be interested in what Judge Carswell had to say that has relevance to this particular case. And feeling like I do, I am sure this court would love to hear what Judge Carswell said before the court denies this motion."

Behold, this previously hostile judge got a grin on his face, ear-to-ear. I felt that he could not believe I had just gone where I went with him in open US federal court. A black lawyer was quoting a dissenting opinion from one of the most conservative judges in America. This tickled the living hell out of him, so he said, "Counselor, counselor, let's hear what you have to say." And for the first time, he allowed me to speak.

Now, Carswell was not someone I would normally quote. However, because of the ideology of these two judges, this judge began to absorb what I was saying in this particular set of facts.

The judge finally said, "Counselor, tell me again now, what did Carswell say?"

He got right into my presentation, and the courtroom picked this up because I begin to give Carswell compliments, "Distinguished like you, Your Honor."

The people in the courtroom began to smile and giggle as the judge laughed and complimented me. Finally, we went into a fifteen-minute recess. Here I was, an out-of-state lawyer, considered militant with my large afro and goatee, now someone who no longer seemed hostile to him. And I was not doing a jig. I was just going someplace academically and intellectually that he could relate to. I had pulled his chain. I was attacking him but in a way that was acceptable. I never said the man was not intellectual; the man was just racist. To be a federal judge, I am sure he had to be very intelligent. I was playing a brain game with him, quoting somebody obviously cut from the same cloth who had just been chastised across the nation.

When the judge returned from recess, he said, "Mr. Pettit ..." All of a sudden, I had a name. All of a sudden, I was a person. All of a sudden,

I was recognized as a lawyer. He said, "Mr. US Attorney and Mr. Pettit, I think you both had better approach the bench."

I thought, *Now he's going to take my head off.*

When I got to the bench he said, "Mr. Pettit, that was very creative. I don't know whether it was just your sense of humor or whether it was just your ability to enlarge this decision." He looked over at the US attorney and said, "Mr. US Attorney, I think we should resolve this case. I don't think Mr. Pettit should have to take this to trial. I think Mr. Pettit has raised a very valid point in this particular case, and I am prepared to dismiss the indictment." He continued, "Now, you'll bring it back I am sure and recharge. But, at this point and time, I'm tending to agree with the defense. I'm prepared to dismiss this indictment unless the United States can make Mr. Pettit a reasonable offer." He ended by saying, "I am going to take a half-hour recess, and I want the US attorney to sit down with this distinguished counselor, and I want you to see if you all can resolve this on a plea."

The case was over. I could not believe it. It was actually over. I had attacked him and the whole system without raising my voice and without saying anything demeaning.

I would never see that judge again after that day. My client was allowed to make restitution of $10,000 over six months. Of course, he was going to be out of federal employment, but he was saved from serving time for something like ten to fifteen years. When I got outside, I stood in front of the US federal court in Virginia and said to myself, "I'll be damned."

I had seen the real world in the court, and I thought, *It can't get any worse than that.*

However, it does, and it did; especially during another big case in my career, the Smith case, where for over a year and a half I represented a Jewish woman and her family in the mountains of Western Maryland.

But on that day, I felt truly—in the state that held the capital of the Confederacy (Richmond)—that justice had been achieved.

Chapter 6: Aberdeen

"Court Ordered Admission to Aberdeen High School"
*Alvin Dwight Pettit, a minor, by his parent George D. Pettit v. Board of
Education of Harford County*
184 F. Supp. 452, May 25, 1960

The above decision, by Chief Judge Rozelle Thomsen, was six years
subsequent to the *Brown v. Board of Education* case decided in 1954.
I had been denied admission to Aberdeen High School based on my
alleged low IQ, achievement test, and average academic history. My
case was taken into the federal district court by the NAACP's attorneys,
Juanita Jackson Mitchell, Thurgood Marshall, Jack Greenburg, and
Tucker Dearing.

Judge Thomsen, in ruling in my favor and ordering me into Aberdeen
High School, made the following statement.

> Under all circumstances, the infant plaintiff is entitled to the
> chance to make good in the tenth grade in the academic curriculum
> at the Aberdeen High School if he wishes to take that chance. Of
> course, the principal and the faculty of the school should advise
> him of whether he should enter the academic or the general course,
> and if he chooses the academic course, whether it would be wiser
> for him to enter the ninth grade or the tenth grade or enter some

other grade or course. The question whether his work justifies his continuation in that class or requires his transfer to another class is for the school authorities, to be decided by them without regard to the race of the infant plaintiff. Once again, I express my confidence in the good faith and ability of the superintendent and his staff of the Harford County school system. I will sign a decree appropriately worded to require the defendant to admit the infant complainant into Aberdeen High School at the beginning of the 1960–61 school years to the same grade and course as white children similarly situated and according to the same procedures that white children are admitted to that school. The principal of Aberdeen High School and other appropriate personnel may counsel the infant plaintiff to pursue such course of study as in the regular operation of the school they would counsel white children similarly situated to pursue. He will be required to conform to such advice to the same extent that white children similarly situated are required to conform. At no time should he be assigned to a course of study, graded, promoted, or demoted except in accordance with regular policy of the school to assign, grade, promote, or demote white children similarity situated.

The court was probably about as liberal as you could expect in that time and circumstance.

The judge noted that by then I had gone to three schools in three years: Sollers Point High School in Baltimore County; the "colored" school for Aberdeen, Havre de Grace Consolidated; and Lemmel Junior High School, where I was enrolled in the ninth grade, staying in academic parity by going back to Baltimore City. This meant three different schools in three years. At Lemmel, I was not even living at home. I was a boarder, commuting on the weekends. I was adjusting socially, and I had been elected president of the class, elected to the student council, and then elected chief judge of the school court—all in just one year.

Yet Harford County officials had argued that there was something wrong with me based on test taken in the third and fourth grades. The judge said this made no sense. The judge also said that by commuting on a weekly basis from Aberdeen to Lemmel, which was thirty miles away, I was essentially staying in a foreign place, without family, and still managing to achieve success at Lemmel. He noted that in addition to the commute, the separation from family, the academic requirements at Lemmel, and the pressure of being in the middle of a federal trial, I was not only surviving, I was sustaining and achieving beyond my peers. The court's order to admit me into Aberdeen High School meant I would be attending my fourth school in four years.

I call *Pettit v. Board of Education* the beginning of my family's legal trilogy. Later cases were *George D. Pettit v. United States* and then *Pettit v. Gingerich* (Maryland Board of Law Examiners), 427 F. Supp. 282 (1977). Without ascribing religion to this trilogy, I believe in the power of God's intervening hand, because each case was born from another. *George D. Pettit v. United States* was born from the fact of my father's integration of the county school. This was perceived as negative activity by his superiors at Aberdeen Proving Ground, which set in motion the retaliation discussed in *George D. Pettit v. United States*. A Confederate flag was displayed in my father's work place, "Dixie" was played when he came into the office, his name was omitted from scientific works and publications, and he was denied a promotion for fourteen years. If there had been a slight done to me by the earlier court, it was ameliorated in part by *George D. Pettit v. United States* when the court referred to me in a very complimentary way as the "plaintiff's able counsel" and appointed me to monitor the remand order and report to the court at ninety-day intervals.

In the fall of 1960, I was admitted to Aberdeen High School. I admit my biggest incentive to attend Aberdeen High School, probably more so than academics, was my desire to play football. The original problem for the Harford County school district was that I did not fit their desegregation plan. The elementary school had already been fully integrated, and minority students were enrolled in the junior high school. When I entered the eighth grade, they were integrating the seventh, when I would have been going to the ninth, they would have been integrating the eighth, and so forth. I was ahead of the plan. The "stair step" plan at Aberdeen High School was to integrate one grade at a time, and since they had to integrate, they determined it would first be a female student. The courts would allow them to do that, so the school board denied my admission, and no black males were admitted to the ninth grade or above until I was finally admitted by court order. Thus, upon my arrival, the high school was all white except for the three African American females.

Roslyn Slade entered ahead of me. She was a gorgeous girl, a senior. Her father was a colonel in the United States Army, and Mrs. Slade was more gorgeous than her daughter was at the time. The Slades had gone to court prior to me and had actually litigated this issue to some extent. When I entered the school, there was neither bonding nor friendship exhibited by Roslyn. I would meet Roslyn again as an adult in Baltimore City, but in school, she had more or less adopted a neutral identity, and, being older than I was, she existed in another world. Bessie Gant had been with me at Havre De Grace Consolidated and was admitted to Aberdeen High at the same time I was ordered into the tenth grade. Bessie was a nice girl, even now a lovely lady, but she was an evil, evil child in grade school (smiles). We used to argue like cats and dogs at the so-called colored school. However, we knew that even though we did not get along, we could be friends at the white school. But I was not going to push it. Sharon Joyner was another gorgeous girl, but Sharon was the daughter of a master sergeant, and she had a very strict mother. She was younger than I was, entering the eighth or ninth grade when I went into the tenth grade. She was a beautiful girl, but, of course, not allowed to go out or have any dates. Even though there were three black females in the school, there were no social relationships between us, which would have a profound effect on me during my transition at Aberdeen High School.

One thing that promotes the social-integration process faster than anything I've ever seen in American life is athletics. Much is known about black males and the impact of discrimination. Even though black males have been the most hated and more feared, if one is an athlete, if one can shoot the ball, throw the ball, run the ball, hit the ball, kick the ball, or knock someone out, it almost neutralizes the fact of color. It can bring about an instant change in someone's attitude and can create social acceptance overnight. In other words, athletics creates transition in attitudes and speeds up the entire integration process. We may be seeing a deep-seated resentment for professional athletes now emerging, but that is another whole study. I was very fortunate that I was blessed with three things: an above-average (I won't say great) athletic ability; an above-average intellect; and a reservoir of black men as role models, my father and uncles. It was a fact of life at my house that no matter what we were celebrating, boxing and sports were always going to start the day, followed by debates on politics and religion.

On the first day of football practice for the Aberdeen High junior varsity, I tried out for the quarterback position—not halfback, not end. Keep in mind, this was the school that had denied my admission on the basis of intelligence. The adults must have perceived this as the pinnacle of arrogance. After all, the quarterback was the leader of the team, the brain and heart of the team. Actually, it was not arrogance; it was just what I wanted to do. The head coach for the varsity team was Coach Smith, and Coach Schwartz was the junior-varsity coach. Coach Smith, a war hero, later became another very close role model in my life. He was a man's man, a tough, good ole white boy, straight out of the books: square jaw, blond hair, and blue eyes. He would kick us in the ass, call us sons of bitches, grab us by the neck, and so on. He was the perfect football coach glorified in American sports folklore (before things began to change regarding physical contact between coaches and players). Neither Coach Smith nor Coach Schwartz had nor dealt with any prejudices.

During the first few days of practice, I met a funny-looking guy by the name of John Almacy, a tall, thin, blond kid with sort of a hanging lower lip and a big nose. He was the first white person at Aberdeen High School who befriended me. Today John is my accountant and my close friend. In fact, he's been my accountant throughout the almost-forty years that I have practiced law. Back in high school, John was a little nuisance: a pesky white boy always laughing and playing. John's mother was German, and his father was an American Army sergeant. He had just come back from Germany, having spent the previous four or five years abroad, so he never appreciated the American dilemma of racism. In fact, he would later manage my first campaign. That was in high school when I successfully ran for vice president of the athletic association. His mom would design and help with my campaign posters. Everybody gave me the once over, but they didn't say anything to me. You could hear the boys talking, "There's the new kid, the colored boy." There were no blacks anywhere else in Harford County high school sports.

On the third or fourth day of school, John and I were in the locker room roughhousing and clowning around. He hit me with something, and I threw a wet towel at him. He ducked, and when he did, the wet towel hit David. David was the tough guy of the white kids.

I thought, *Oh shit.*

"I'm sorry, David," I said, "I'm really sorry." I had only been there a short time, but experience taught me how to determine the status order very quickly. I knew about the so-called tough guys, the guys people looked up to, and the guys to give space to. David very slowly turned around, and the whole locker room froze. I guess they had prior knowledge of something he had said he would do if our paths crossed. John stepped back when David walked over.

"Look here, boy; you hit me with that," he said, pointing at the towel on the floor.

My father had told me to keep the peace and not get into any hassles, so I said, "David, I'm sorry. I apologize. I didn't mean to do it."

David said, "You are going to have to pick up all these towels every day until I tell you that you don't have to anymore. You are going to be the towel boy for the locker room."

I said, "David, that's not going to happen. I apologize to you, but that's not going to happen."

My response was apparently not acceptable to David. He said, "If you can't pick up these towels, take your ass outside. I'm gonna take you out there, and whip your ass in front of everyone."

So I said, "Well, David, we don't have to do this."

But David said, "Oh yes, we do."

We went back and forth like this, but ultimately we went outside.

The irony of it was that all the parents were there to watch both football teams practice, varsity and junior varsity. Football was as big a thing in Aberdeen as it was in most small towns. In rural communities, the local high school team is considered as important (or more so) than a college or professional team. The Aberdeen Eagles were the same to these people as the Baltimore Colts were to Baltimore City.

So we went outside, and all the kids and parents crowded around. David was a very muscular kid and seemed much bigger and heavier than I. That didn't seem to matter to the crowd outside. No one, not the coaches nor any members of the teams, moved to stop what was about to happen, except my father. He had come to pick me up from practice with a young black kid by the name of Larry Stokes. Larry, who would become one of my best friends, was a big kid for his age. He was in a lower grade, but we played football together all of the time.

David put up his hands, and I commenced to doing the "Turner Station knockout" on him. I caught him flush with a left to the head, and then I hit him with two or three sharp right- and left-hand combinations. Down he went. In the "Turner Station stomp" we don't do like white boys and stop punching when the opponent hits the ground. I continued to throw punches. His father grabbed me from the back and screamed, "You'll kill him! You'll kill him!" And when his father grabbed me, my father grabbed him. Knowing my father, George, was enough for me to get off of David. David was totally unconscious, and people rushed to try to revive him.

We stood there for a few minutes while they called the ambulance, and we remained standing there while they tried to get the kid back to consciousness. In the meantime, the crowd started to close in around us. My father and I began to back out with Larry Stokes.

Lance Gracin, a star on the varsity football team, stepped between the crowd and us. He hollered to the crowd, "I saw what happened. David started it, and it was a fair fight, and if you want to get to this kid and his father, you'll have to go through me."

Well, Lance Gracin was a big Indian kid, all muscle, about five foot ten and at least 210 pounds. While Lance faced the crowd, we backed into the parking lot, got into the car, and drove off. We dropped Larry off on the way home. I remember that my father and I never said anything the whole way home, but I could tell he was just bursting with pride. It was a conversation that didn't take place. He had seen me go into a hostile situation; he had seen me dispatch this kid; and he had seen that part of himself, his personality, in me—all without displaying any fear.

When I got to school the next morning, the hallways parted like the Red Sea. "That's the kid that whipped David's butt yesterday."

Where before you heard little remarks like "nigger" this or that or the other, all of a sudden, all that had completely evaporated. Instead, there was, "Hi, Dwight. How are you doing, Dwight?" They were actually speaking to me.

As I approached my homeroom class, I heard everybody buzzing. I walked in, and everybody went silent. I heard somebody say to the teacher, "David transferred to another school." The kid had actually transferred out of Aberdeen High School. He enrolled five miles away at Havre de Grace—not the "colored school," Havre de Grace Consolidated, but Havre de Grace High School. Years later, David would actually come to me as a client. It was not so much that he had a legal problem; it was more because the story of our fight ran so many times in local interviews, papers, and local magazines, that I think he needed to purge himself, and the only way he could do that was to apologize and make amends. I know that when he reads this book he is going to say, "Oh shit, here I am again." I think he really needed to set the record straight.

Sitting in my office with David and discussing a case that really wasn't a case, I told him, "David, this is something that I don't think you can prevail on." It was a simple contract matter.

He said, "Dwight, I may not have a case; I just want to retain you even if I'm gonna lose. I want you to go into federal court and fight this for me." He had a construction business. I told him my retainer was $5,000. He immediately wrote me a check.

Even though the case was a loser, it was almost as if he had to get something off of his shoulders, something he had carried with him ever since he was a kid. Maybe it was the same weight I carried after my fight with Skippy Reid in Turner Station when I was the bully. As a kid, David had taken on an issue with the intention of reflecting the "adult" position—trying to do physically what the adults wanted to do. Maybe, without fully realizing why, he felt compelled to show demonstratively the community's disapproval of my entry into Aberdeen High School. At any rate, in spite of that disapproval, I was there. I had arrived and begun the matriculation of my tenth-grade year.

Despite the legal struggle to achieve enrollment, it had never really struck my psyche until then that you could be superior, yet you could be told you could not do something for no other reason in the world other than the fact that you were black (i.e., going out for quarterback). I mean, other people had experienced it, but, as a kid fifteen years old, that was the harsh reality—upfront and personal—of what my father had already told me.

Coach Swartz called me into his office about a week before the first game. He said I could play any other position on the team, but I could not play quarterback. I will never forget feeling the perspiration on my skin. I could feel myself turning blood red. I could feel myself choking up. I couldn't speak and later tears rolled from my eyes, yet I went back out there and allowed them to put me in another position. At that time, it was fullback. The interesting aspect about this was that they still did not have a quarterback, and they needed one right away because they had not prepared anybody for the upcoming game. When I got home, my father saw me coming, and I guess he saw it in my face as I walked toward the house; he knew that what he had already told me was so again. It was one of those silent moments. He did not say I told you so.

I played varsity under Coach Smith, but I never again tried to go out for quarterback. Coach Smith changed me to an end, and I played both offensive and defensive end. The year I entered the varsity, I still had to make the team even though I had a great junior-varsity year as a linebacker. This was a big-time football team in terms of Aberdeen, made up of varsity heroes Jim Goodson, John Basey, Dickie Wilkerson, and Lance Grayson. The Eagles were undefeated. They were legends. They were in the eleventh and twelfth grades, high school celebrities with letter sweaters bearing the big *A* that I was looking forward to having some day.

Coach Smith called the team in just before the opening practice of my varsity season. He looked around and said, "I've got something I want to say to you all right now." He pointed to me, "See this kid over here, Dwight Pettit? Some of you may know him from the junior varsity, but now this is varsity, and this young man is on this football team. And this young man is gonna play offensive and defensive end. I'm gonna say this just once right now. Any son of a bitch who doesn't like it, or if anybody doesn't block for him, or if anybody misses a tackle on purpose, or if I detect any of you letting down because this kid is on this team, I will kick your ass off this team so quick. So I'm telling you now, if you can't play with him, leave the damn field now."

Nobody had forewarned me. This was Smith doing this on his own. He stood there. Silence hit. He said again, "If anybody wants to leave, get the hell out now." He stood there about a minute and then said. "Okay, this is my football team. Let's go play football!" Unlike Denzel Washington in *Return of the Titans*, I did not have any black teammates; it was just me. I always get teary-eyed when I watch that movie because it brings back such real memories.

Coach Smith and I developed a good relationship over the years. Everybody loved and still loves him today. He just recently passed. About five years ago, I played in a celebrity basketball game at Aberdeen High School. I was asked to come back to be honored and to make a presentation to Coach Smith as one of the Hall of Fame coaches of Aberdeen High School.

One of my fondest memories of Coach Smith was when we played Wicomico High School on the Eastern Shore. The Eastern Shore of Maryland was just as racist as Mississippi or Alabama at that time. On game night I was probably the only black person in the stadium besides Mom, Dad, and the cleanup people.

Wicomico High was a large school with a powerful football team. They were running over us in the first half. In fact, on one play a big fullback literally ran up my chest and over the top of me. At halftime, Coach Smith cursed the whole team out. He kicked people in the butt, slapped people on the helmet, and he grabbed facemasks. He went off on everyone. When he got to me, he came to within six inches of my face and just stared at me with those crystal blue eyes. After about ten seconds, he said, "Son, you let me down." With that, he turned and walked away.

During the second half, I tried to kill anything wearing a Wicomico uniform. We came back to make it a close game near the end. As God would have it, with the clock running out, I intercepted a pass and went sixty yards down the sideline for the winning touchdown. Believe it or not, it was my birthday. As the team, the cheerleaders, and the band ushered me off the field, I took off my helmet, and all could see that I was black. I was sure I detected a sort of hush in the stadium. In the locker room, Coach Smith walked into the showers in his street clothes, getting soaking wet, gave me a big hug, saying, "Kid, you are all right."

Later, I said to myself, "The winning touchdown! On the Eastern Shore in 1963! On my birthday! You cannot tell me that there is no God."

In my junior year at Aberdeen, I went out for the wrestling team, competing in the 157-pound weight class. I was pretty damn good at 157, and I thought I would like wrestling. I won my first three matches. The team's first major opponent, however, was the team from Bel Air, Maryland. This was a formidable powerhouse. We didn't play Bel Air in football because the school was so big. They had over four thousand students. They were AA football, competing against high schools like Baltimore City College (a high school) and Baltimore Polytechnic Institute. Nevertheless, Aberdeen was scheduled to meet the Bel Air wrestling team in Bel Air.

When it came time for me to wrestle the guy in my weight class, the coach came over and said, "Dwight, you've been so good, we want you to help the team out and move up two weight classes." If you know anything about wrestling, going from 157 to 177 is an awesome leap in terms of competitive levels. This turned out to be one of the most brutally agonizing and depressing events in my whole athletic career. However, I was, in fact, competitive, until something popped in my chest. My opponent was the epitome of the "Great White Hope." He had muscles galore, blond hair, and an actor's face. Needless to say, after being dragged all over the floor that night to the roar of the crowd, and suffering a fractured rib, I ended my wrestling career at the end of that first season.

That would be the only night Harford County or parts therein would have the opportunity to witness my complete humiliation. I often wondered, was that sudden jump in weight class a coincidence, or was I sacrificed? I promised myself that I would never again put myself in that position—sort of like Muhammad Ali's apparent philosophy over the years. If there was a sport that I could not play or had not mastered, I did not play.

I was also on the baseball team at Aberdeen High. The coach was a man by the name of Kwiggs. In the afternoons, I also played baseball on the town's Babe Ruth League where I was an all-star every year, with a batting average above 400. I led just about every offensive category. But on the school team I sat the bench. The joke among my teammates was that because I sat on the bench all day during the school schedule, I must have been resting up for the night games. At the time, the slight appeared to me to be blatant and inescapable, yet when I came back to Aberdeen years later, Coach Kwiggs would come up and embrace me as if I was his long lost son. I would look at that man, and I would reflect and say to myself, "Are these people for real?" Here was a man who I felt at the time obviously slighted me, yet he had blocked out all recollection what so ever. Maybe it was subconscious or maybe it was someone else's higher decision.

It was the same with the basketball coach, who was also my history teacher. I don't recall that Mr. Dent ever spoke to me. However, it didn't matter because I was too physical for basketball anyway and would have always fouled out. At any rate, for me the stage was set, and the curtain was up at Aberdeen High School.

What is this whole racial-segregation thing all about? In America, what is this about? What is the major problem? What is the worst fear, the worst-case scenario, the worst thing possible that can happen? Is it about economics? Progress? Is it the dollar? Is it about hate? Or do we really concede that initially race in America was in large part about the white female? When I went to law school at Howard University, one of the first required readings was a North Carolina case where the court actually discussed the state's "reckless eyeballing" statutes. Under these statutes, you could be incarcerated for just looking at a white woman. Emmett Till, a fourteen-year-old, was killed and tortured for just whistling at a white woman in the South. So let's understand and not forget: we can talk about economics, we can talk about affirmative action, we can talk about ownership and land and property, but essentially, the strong political undercurrent for these laws was the protection of white females from mixing with black males. Aberdeen was the perfect example. They were willing to let black girls in the high school but not a black male. After my arrival, the racial barriers were very quickly cut by the mitigating grace that I was an athlete. I had knocked out one of the baddest kids in school and never again had to raise my hand in anger to another student from the tenth through twelfth grades.

At the start of my junior year, we had another black kid come into the conference (not the school). This new kid, playing for Laurel, was "all world." His name was Scott. He did the hundred-yard dash in 9.7, and it was rumored he had something like thirty-five scholarship offers. He was supposed to be going to Ohio State. Although I was on the opposing team, I was so proud of this opposing player. I think if Coach Smith could ever come close to saying the "*N*" word in his life, it would have been at half time.

He said, "I don't care what y'all have to do to that son of a bitch—" he stopped, and he looked at me, then repeated, "that son of a bitch. Break his leg, bite him, do what have to do, just stop him."

This kid could fly. He was the quarterback; he was the wide receiver; and he was the running back. In every play, he touched the football, and every time he touched the football, he just electrified the stadium. I was a junior at that time, so I don't recall whether I started in that game or not, but it was a tremendous experience to see another black athlete on that field in that environment.

Life was good in school; I had passing grades, and I was playing ball. Or at least until the little girls started their dance. Once a guy is accepted for his athletic ability and the ability to defend himself, here come the little girls. And then the equation generally changes. I had already talked to my father about this, and I already understood the meaning and seriousness of this whole scenario. I already understood the implications of doing something wrong or getting into trouble. My dad had sat me down and said, "Dwight, I don't care what you see, son, or what the other kids do. Those are white kids. You can't do what they do. And don't get caught up in your own popularity because you're playing ball. They will grow up and work in the local store, they will own the banks, they will own the businesses in the community, and they will go to college. The same kids you party with and drink beer with tonight won't know you in two years."

I'll never forget what was later said by the mother of one of my best friends. A few of us were drinking beer one night, including Bob Cinderoni, a fullback on the team that following year. (That's all white boys drink—beer.) We went over to Bob's house, and as soon as we came in, his mother, who was a very sweet lady, said to him, "Bobby, if you keep hanging out and drinking beer with Dwight Pettit, you know what's going to happen; you're gonna end up working for him." Although I am sure there was no racial intent, this was said as if that could be the worst thing that could ever happen.

Bob said, "Well, so what's the big deal?" And to me, it was not offensive at the time.

But what my father said replayed in my mind. "Dwight, you can't do what they can do; even if you think you are one of the boys and you think everybody loves you. They are white; you're not."

By the time I finished my junior year of football, I was Mr. Popularity. When I walked down the hallway, the kids were all over me. It was the tradition during our junior and senior years to autograph each other's yearbooks. There were always ten to fifteen kids lined up for my signature. Everyone wanted me to sign his or her yearbook. Not only was I a star athlete, I was elected vice president of the athletic association, a big deal at Aberdeen High. I had arrived. My father and Uncle John rewarded my achievements by giving me this really slick Buick convertible with big white tires known today as gangster whitewalls. Later, after the convertible, my father rewarded me again. One of the sergeants in the community, Wille Harris, was a mechanic who had this gorgeous little Thunderbird with Playboy rabbits on the fenders. He sold that Thunderbird to my dad in my senior year for me. A lot of people in the community were proud of me.

In spite of my popularity and flashy cars, I was very aware of the danger. I was very much aware that I could not have a white girl in my car. I was very much aware that I could not be in a situation such that I could be accused of something. I was very much aware, as girl crazy as I was, that despite all of the love and affection offered to me, I couldn't partake of it. The danger took the form of the state police or Aberdeen police, but was even greater with the military police (MPs) on the base, because they had me constantly under surveillance, and those MPs, in many cases, were Southern white boys.

I was also very much aware that at school dances, I could not dance with a white girl. My buddies, including John, would remark from time to time that the guys began to wonder if I was strange. Of course, this was said in jest. I'll never forget one night at the drive-in, one of the girls was going to do the football team. In those days, there was always some girl willing to have sex with all the guys. So, from the drive-in, we all went out into the woods.

The guys lined up and took turns, and when it was my turn I just said, "Hey, you know, fellas, I just don't want any." The funny thing about this event was that they had played around with the girl in a patch of poison ivy. Come Monday morning, you could identify everyone who had rolled around in the woods just by watching the "scratchers" walking around.

As for me, everyone said, "Okay, Dwight, obviously you didn't."

The beginning of my senior year, I was also elected vice president of Teen Town. This was an interesting phenomenon because Teen Town was a social organization for the kids on the base. We actually had a budget we could use for dances. My participation with Teen Town gave me the opportunity to spend a lot of time at the Officer's Club, including the swimming pool, which brought me in contact with a lot of teenage white females, who, to say the least, were very aggressive. The experience of leaving Turner Station at the age of thirteen and living a sort of spartan existence while commuting to Baltimore and attending Lemmel, resulted in the fact that I really had no social life. Then, at Aberdeen High, I refused to date or even go to dances with white females because I felt a responsibility to my parents for all the sacrifices they had made so I could go there to school. I didn't want to get into any "I told you so" situations. I didn't want to embarrass my family or the "Negro" community. I was thus ever-mindful that I was being closely watched. I was also aware that although white females might initiate social contact, they would be the first to holler rape in order to escape social ostracism or criticism from their own community. Nevertheless, because there were no black (at that time "Negro") females with which to socialize, I took advantage of the opportunity to spend a lot of time in disciplined social relationships with the girls at the Officer's Club pool or Teen Town.

At the beginning of my senior year, the Aberdeen PTA called a meeting, and they made a decision that every class I was in would be sexually segregated. The girls had to sit on one side and the boys on the other. I called these the "Pettit Rules." Because five or six girls used to come up and lock arms with me as we walked as a group down the hallway, holding hands was banned. Whereas, once the girls (particularly cheerleaders) would go up and get football players their lunches, the new rules prohibited this. All of these rules of social behavior were announced, all of a sudden, throughout the school.

At the time, I had one little white "telephone" girlfriend. I didn't have any social relationships with the sisters at the school. Betsy would not go out with me, Roslyn was older, and Sharon wasn't allowed to go out. Being too far away from the black community where the other black kids lived, I developed a little friendship with Kathy, a classmate in Spanish class, prior to the male and female separation rules. Her father was a big doctor in town. Suddenly, however, I got a call from him. I won't say it was a threatening call, but it was a call with a clear message for me to leave his daughter alone. But, if someone was bothering his daughter, it certainly wasn't me. We were just good friends.

I got into trouble just once. It was during my junior year. I threw a table at a kid in Spanish class who was teasing me about my Spanish. Principal Potter brought me down to his office and said very calmly, "Dwight, this is not you. You've been here for two years, and you've been a good kid. I want you to go back to your class, and I don't expect to hear anything like this ever happening again." He never did.

It was a strange three years. I had a good time playing football; I had a good time going to social affairs (without dancing); and I had a good time drinking beers with the guys. But during those years of my puberty, I had no social life in terms of dating, which is not saying I would have been much more sexually active otherwise. I didn't even do the little stuff that we did at Turner Station with the lights out in the basement and the little "grind" up against the wall. That didn't exist for me in high school. I didn't go to my prom. I just refused to go to certain social activities because the white girls would ask me to dance, and I did not want to be rude. I knew the repercussions that would develop just by dancing. I knew it wouldn't be a good idea to even get in the car with a white girl and go to the ice cream parlor.

I also knew if the local police didn't pull me over, the MPs would. I don't know whether I would have been beaten, mugged, or killed because I didn't put myself in any situation for it to happen. Whenever the police stopped me, I had guys in the car or I was alone. I was stopped so often that my father actually had to make a protest on the military base about my being harassed by the MPs. I was pulled over less often by the Aberdeen police, because I think they only had two police cars in the town, and not as often by the state police because the captain knew I played ball. But I was pulled over constantly by the military police, especially as I went on the base to Teen Town or to the bowling alley or the pool. I knew the ramifications of accepting requests from girls for a ride home after Teen Town; offers to "make out" were too dangerous. When my dad came up for football games, he would see the girls all over me and just walk away shaking his head. Later, he would always say, "Son, be careful."

One of the annual events at Aberdeen High was the powder-puff game. The senior girls played the junior girls in a football game on the night before the homecoming game. It was tradition that the president of the athletic association coached the senior girls, and the vice president coached the junior girls. Since I was the vice president, this meant I had to take twenty-five pretty little white girls and mold them into some semblance of a football team. First off, I had to show them how to put on the pads and the uniforms, how to get down in a stance, how to tackle, how to catch the ball, and so on. It was bad enough with the regular practice every day, but the black kids would also come up to watch these activities, and I could hear them, "Yeah, that colored boy is really crazy. That boy is going to get killed being out there with all of those white girls." The night of the powder-puff game, I had the girls in the locker room, giving them a pregame pep talk. I told them how we could win and how they had to go out there and play hard, hit hard, and get tough ... rah, rah, rah. I was hitting them on the shoulders and happened to look up at the windows. In the locker room, the windows were a floor above ground level, and the gym floor was dropped. I saw all these little black faces peeping through. It was so unbelievable to these kids that this black guy was in the locker room with all of these white girls.

While at Aberdeen High I was the vice president of the athletic association, president of Teen Town, a football player for three years, and the student elected "most congenial" by my classmates, yet I was never the recipient of awards when they were given out by the faculty. Actually, I didn't expect any. I just remember sitting there during every awards ceremony—observing, not receiving. Ironically, in 1977, I was invited back by the administration and the students to be the senior-class graduation speaker which is of course the same school that the legendary Cal Ripken graduated from the following year. In 2006, I would be inducted into the Aberdeen High School Hall of Fame, joining such luminaries as Ripkin, Army Major General Michael Stevenson, Erin Henderson of the NFL and others.

Dwight with the AHS Football Team

ADP carrying the football for AHS

WELCOME—It is with great pleasure that Aberdeen High School welcomes its returning alumni and the Elkton fans to the 1962 Homecoming football game. The Eagles have a distinguished record this year and will find in Elkton a worthy opponent for this important game.

As the game progresses, we hope the alumni will identify this contest of skill and determination with the best games they have witnessed during their school years and will join in the cheering for the 1962 Eagles.

Above all, may fair play and good sportsmanship reign supreme, and may the best team emerge victorious.

Head coach Jim Smith, (left) former Temple University football ..., is completing his eighth season as mentor of the Eagles. During that time he has seen his teams ... a 44-21 won-lost record. A newcomer to the coaching staff, Don Gilmer (right) comes to Aberdeen ... 4 years of playing halfback ... Appalachian State College in ...th Carolina. Both coaches have ... their long hours and hard ... pay off as the Eagles have ... a winning 1962 season.

Coach Smith

ROW 1: D. Pettit, T. Robinson, J. Cronin, D. Terry, P. Murphy, W. Ramsey, J. Stewart, B. Hughes. *ROW 2:* P. Wilkinson, S. Dixon, K. Warrel, L. Ward, D. McDevitt, U. Poetzchke, B. Gunter, A. Norman, N. Pritchard. *ROW 3:* J. Harrington, L. Thayer, G. Humpherys, L. McDowell, J. Homer, J. Webster, C. Hurd, M. Smith, B. Swallwell, A. Dean. *ROW 4:* S. Kupferman, C. Cruit, D. Piper, F. Lescalett, G. DeHaven, B. Smith, J. Feldman, P. Everett. *ROW 5:* B. Baicy, J. Kessler, J. Rudd, R. Simar, K. Riddle, G. Peroutka, S. Stine, T. Thompson, M. McCoy. *ROW 6:* J. Rudd, R. Emmons, B. Jacobs, A. Pedgrift, C. Siebert, D. McDonough, B. Rutherford, L. Tedrow, D. Holwager.

ADP Vice President of the AHS Athletic Association

nes involved in athletics,
ering in Varsity football,
vrestling. He is the first
baseball in the County
ters "politics" with his
President of the Aberdeen
hletic Association. During
is begining his social
a major force in the in-
ating and entertainment
ng the movie in Aberdeen
y had segregated seating.

The 1962-63 Athletic Association Officers: D. Pettit, Vice-President; J. Cronin, Secretary; W. Ramsey, President.

Athletic Association Officers

Aberdeen HS Class of 63

Dwight delivering commencement in 1977 at Aberdeen High School

JUNIOR VARSITY

FIRST ROW: S. Agapalaglou, J. Pedganay, C. Lawson, D. Pettit, G. Peroutka, D. Day, S Kupferman, H. Cooper, T. Robinson, B. Okin, M. McCoy, T. Osborne, B. Smith, W. Crocker, Coaches: E. Schwarz, Rosenberger. SECOND ROW: R. Bryant, J. Almacy, B. McDonough, B. Jacobs, D. Demaree, P. Bartz, R. Emmons, B. Linday, THIRD ROW: G. Robinette, D. London, L. Gravely, J. Smith, F. Lescalette, O. Beniask, F. Williams, R. Worrel, L. Christopher, K. Haldeman.

Junior Varsity

Teen Town Officers

WRESTLING

The wrestling team is one of the newest organized sports at AHS this season, but already is has established much enthusiasm and interest in the student body.

AHS was the host this year to the Tri-School Tournament in which AHS, Bel Air High School, and Havre de Grace High School participated. This event was the peak of the season, and the schools displayed fine sportsmanship and athletic potential.

AHS bravely met teams both from the Harford County league and out-of-county leagues, with undaunted spirits. The spokesman for the squad claims ". . . a successful beginning and a thoroughly enjoyable season."

Wrestling Team

ROW 1: C. Terry, T. Smith, C. Connelly, J. Hall, J. Kessler. *ROW 2:* K. Riddle, S. Phillips, T. Thompson, D. Terry, D. O'Brien, M. Perlman. *ROW 3:* M. Welsh, D. Summerall, D. Pettit, T. Robinson.

Dwight with AHS Baseball Team

Chapter 7: Howard University

The foundation of America's black culture and academic excellence in the 1960s was still Howard University. There are many other great historically black colleges and universities (HBCUs)—Hampton, Morgan,(known nationally for its school of engineering), Moorehouse, Spellman and Fisk University to name just a few—but Howard was number one because of its worldwide diversity and reputation. A cadre of black leadership at that time—judges, doctors, and lawyers—were Howard graduates. Howard and Meharry had the two premier black medical schools in the nation, and Howard and North Carolina Central were the leading black law schools. E. Franklin Frazier said Howard University was "the hub of the black bourgeoisie."

And so, arriving at Howard, I had great expectations, built up in my mind from childhood, of an opulent campus with rolling lawns of lush greenery, magnificent towering trees, and gracious old buildings. But when I got to the entrance on a city block called Georgia Avenue, I found the neighborhood tough guys—known by Howardites as "the block boys"—roaming this little piece of land that spanned about a quarter mile in width by perhaps a half mile in length.

This was Howard University?

I stood there, looking around for more. Across the way, I could see a lake or reservoir, and I hoped it was part of the university—that maybe that valley or that hill was part of the actual campus. However, it turned out to be a District of Columbia water purification plant. I was shocked.

Howard is a very urban school. It doesn't have a campus the size of Morgan State or A&T University or Fisk. As a football player, I have been to all of them. Howard University sits there in the middle of the city, in the middle of northwest Washington, DC, or more to the point, the heart of an urban environment you might call the ghetto of DC. At that time, if you stepped off the campus, you stepped off at your peril. So there I was, back in my fight-and-survive mode, because you had to go through the community to get to most of the dormitories. In fact, it was common to see Howard students walking quickly back and forth across the street—not because they were anxious to get to class or the dormitories, but because they were walking fast instead of running to keep from getting beat up by the block boys.

So here I was, in this great and historic foundation of the American civil-rights movement.

I was fortunate to have arrived during the summer, earlier than most students. I had taken some college-preparatory courses and stayed right into football practice, which began before all of the students arrived. Imagine my surprise when the first thing I encountered at this esteemed black institution was, of all things, prejudice—within my own community, within my own race. I have a light complexion and freckles, but I had no racial thoughts whatsoever about being light-skinned, brown-skinned, or dark-skinned.

When I showed up on the field for the first practice, several of the darker-skinned brothers looked at me with hostile glares as if to say, "What are you doing here?"

To myself I thought, *What do you mean what am I doing here? This is a black school; I'm back with my peers; I'm back with my people; and I'm back in a black environment. I'm happy to be here at Howard University. Why is this a hassle? Why is this a problem?"*

The response was, "Light-skinned niggers don't play ball." Shit, here we go again, this was unbelievable to me.

As Joel Mongo, the team prankster, would say, "Light-skinned niggers stay up on campus; they profile and be pretty boys." Guys who looked like me weren't supposed to be on the football field. In 1963, there was a caste system at Howard! After maneuvering through a white high school, breaking through athletic racial barriers, and accepting years of turmoil, I got to Howard University, and again I found myself on the outside looking in—on the football field of all places.

Howard University was really the core of the African American bourgeoisie. The color of a person's skin was noticed just as much as it had been in the white school from which I'd come. Howard had institutionalized skin color as a social classification throughout its history. The homecoming queen during my freshman year, Margaret, was a blue-eyed blonde, as "white girl" as any you'd ever want to see, yet she was "Negro." I was told she had trouble traveling home to South Carolina with her boyfriend. Apparently, when they traveled home on the train, they could not sit together because he would always have to go through the pains of explaining that she was black, not white. While he was trying to explain, he was in very serious danger.

Growing up, I was immune to color issues within my own race because my father never allowed me to be color conscious. Thinking back, the only person I knew who talked about a black person's color was my paternal grandmother. You have to understand that my father's mother was as black as coal, while his father was as light as any white person. On my mother's side, both of my grandparents were somewhat light or brown-skinned.

One of my early memories of my paternal grandmother was that when I was a little kid she would always say, "Come here, boy, and give me a kiss." Any time I was slow in doing so, she would say, "Oh, so you don't like your black grandmother. You want to leave and go to see your white grandmother. Isn't that right, boy?"

I used to think that was such an unfair thing to say to me. My slow response was simply because I did not want to be "mushed" all over, not because she was black. I was not a kid who liked to be kissed. We were never a kissing type of family, except for my father. He was just a "mushy" man and loved me so much.

When I was around eleven or twelve years old, I sat him down one day and said, "Dad (I never even used the word Daddy like my kids did and still do), we need to talk about something."

He said, "What, son?"

I said, "You know, this kissing thing has to stop. I know you love me, but this kissing me has to stop. I'm getting to be a big boy now." I believe he was offended to some extent, but he understood my wishes. After that, he began to just pat me on the head, pat me on the back, or give me a hug. I have never been mushy with my own kids; it's just not me. My grandmother thought I had a color thing, but she was very mistaken.

After I married my wife, who is dark, we went to see my grandmother for the first time as husband and wife. She had been ill, and other family members were standing around her bed. She had heard about my new wife, but she had never seen her. She really didn't recognize others in the room, but she looked up at us, and she said, "Oh my goodness, there's that li'l ole Dwight Pettit." She called me by my full name. "I'll be doggone; is that your wife, Dwight?"

I said, "Yes, Grandma."

"I'll be doggone," she said again. "You got you a little black girl." A smile came across her face and the faces of everyone in the room. It was a warm and memorable moment as she lay in her sick bed. She laughed and hugged my wife, and I hugged and kissed her.

As a child, I always had to fight because I was light or red with freckles. I guess this was probably the same experience for Malcolm X who carried the nickname Red. For a while, I was messed up in the head because I was the same color as the white folks, but it didn't matter because, as the saying goes, "a nigger is a nigger," regardless. The relentlessness of being in the white environment for so long took its toll. I remember in high school, walking around with my lips pressed together because I thought they were too large. As a young adult, I was foolish enough to try a Jheri curl for about a month. I actually let a pretty, young woman almost burn up my hair putting in the process.

Throughout high school, and then at Howard, I considered my peers to be the football players. I didn't really associate with the other kids coming into the university.

The first guys I met were the football players. Those were the guys I wanted to hang out with. The team picks and positions for the year had not yet been made, but I already considered those guys my associates. Soon enough, however, I noticed that after practice, the guys got together, hopped into cars, and went off to places to hang out. I was excluded. It was just like at Aberdeen High School in the beginning. I was again by myself. This had more of an impact on me than the shocking experience of being discriminated by whites. Was I supposed to go back up on campus and form associations with persons of the same complexion? Was our society so messed up that I was supposed to make associations only with light-skinned people? I later noticed the same phenomena occurring with certain sororities at the time. If you were a light-skinned female you were identified as an Alpha Kappa Alpha sister. If you were brown or chocolate you were a Delta Sigma Theta sister. I found myself right back in the same bullshit I had just been so happy to walk away from. Nevertheless, I once again cut through everything by using and honing my athletic talent and ability. As I made my entry into the world of college football, I became successful and accepted. I still go back for homecoming and meet up with the same guys—who to this day, still affectionately refer to me as "Bleach," my college football nickname.

Because of football, I had the opportunity and good fortune to meet my wife within my first few weeks at Howard University. Barbara Nell (Bobbie) Moore was coming into a dance just as the team and I were leaving. She was a very gorgeous, young woman with great curves and a little bit older than I was. At that time, I was seventeen, and she was twenty. As she passed by us, the whole team turned around and watched her walk up the steps. Without saying a word, we all turned and went back into the dance. I was chosen, as the freshman in the group, to go over and say something to this dark, lovely girl. Of course, the upperclassmen expected her to snub me, but she pleasantly accepted my offer to dance.

Well, as I later found out, she accepted my offer because she was quiet and very shy. She thought that if she danced with the least menacing of us, someone smaller in size and obviously shy, that would preclude the team from further harassment. Admittedly, the team was rowdy: hollering, screaming, making a whole bunch of noise, and more or less dominating the whole dance. I danced with her, and she accepted my company, and we were together the whole evening. Later, I walked her to the dormitory and asked if I could see her again.

She looked at me and said, "Do you know who I am?"

I said, "I know that you told me you are Barbara Moore and you're from Newark, New Jersey."

She said, "Well, I'm the freshman queen, and I'm the Omega bunny, and I'm ..." She went on as if she had obviously just graced me, a freshman, with the honor of dancing with her, and spending a couple of hours with her. In other words, I was really out of my league, and my presumption exceeded any possibility that I could ever take her out.

Being arrogant in my own right, I retorted, "Do you know who I am?"

She said no, so boldly I said, "Well, come to the stadium on Saturday and find out," not even knowing whether or not I would play Saturday or even dress for the game.

That week we were playing Virginia State, a very strong team. To put this into proper context, football at Howard when I arrived in 1963 was an athletic joke. The team had not done anything for several years. To the student body, these were a group of guys who liked going out and getting mauled every Saturday. Introducing oneself as a football player evoked laughter and smiles, not the kind of adulation or admiration I was used to. Freshman girls were supporters because they did not know any better. However, upperclassmen didn't think Howard football was something to put money on. At any rate, I was not yet fully aware of this when I stuck out my chest and asked Barbara to come to the football game on Saturday.

Howard had not beaten anybody in a year or so except, as word would have it on campus, "the lame, the blind, the deaf, and the dumb." I do not mean to be offensive to the disabled, but this was being said after Howard played Gallaudet College, the highly esteemed college in the District of Columbia for people who have hearing and/or speech impairments. Gallaudet was the only school the Howard football team had beaten in a year. At that time, because black athletes couldn't universally or easily go to white universities as they do now, Morgan State, Florida A&M, and Grambling were black athletic powerhouses, and Virginia State, Maryland State Eastern Shore, and A&T were a close second on that scale.

To be honest, I was allowed to make the team. I initially tried out for the quarterback position, which was not one of my better ideas given my lack of requisite experience and the ample supply of talent on hand from around the country. So, before I was cut from the team altogether, I told Coach Sease that I was in fact a receiver in high school. I made the last cut by the slightest margin.

I sat on the bench during the first game with Saint Paul, and I did not make the traveling squad for the second game against Cheyney State. We came home for the third game against Virginia State, and I was allowed to dress for the game. I wore a discarded tackle's uniform and a helmet that swung around my head because it was too big. As an end, my jersey was supposed to be numbered in the 80 series, but I was wearing a tackle's jersey with the number 70, and the jersey was all the way down to my knees. I really looked like a clown, and this was the game to which I had invited this gorgeous girl. The quarterback for Virginia State may have been Baltimorean Reginald L. Lewis, who is widely known as the former chief executive of Beatrice Foods, which was the largest black-controlled corporation in the world at one time. At the time of Lewis's untimely death from brain aneurisms, Beatrice Foods was worth billions of dollars. He had attended Virginia State and played quarterback for the Trojans around the same time that I played for Howard.

The stadium was full and rocking. I was happy to be there, even though I was not starting. All you could hear in the background was this deep growl of Virginia State Trojans fans repeating the nickname "Trojans" in the stands. My stomach was in knots as I sat there on the bench. Virginia State was rolling. It was a hot day, and every time Virginia State hiked the ball, they went fifteen or twenty yards a clip. The dust was boiling up, and Virginia State kept thundering down the field until they scored the first touchdown. When Howard got the ball, Coach leaned forward, craned his neck toward the bench, and said, "Do I have an end?" According to later stories, all of the ends leaned back. The coach leaned back and said again,

"I need an end." All of the ends leaned forward. (Again, these were stories told years later in jest.) Nobody wanted to go out there; it was turning ugly quickly. The Virginia stands were in full force, and the Howard stands were just partying; they knew what was getting ready to happen. It was going to be 50 to 0 very quickly.

At this point, I was so intent on the game that I had not leaned forward, and I had not leaned back. After the third or fourth kid had been carried off the field, Coach Tillman Sease came over and grabbed me by the back of my jersey and pulled me upright. Coach Sease was in many ways like my high school coach: a fantastic man. But in temperament, style, and philosophy, he was the total opposite of Aberdeen's Coach Smith. Coach Sease was the nice-guy type who let his assistants be the ass kickers—or at least that's the "good cop, bad cop" approach he used.

So when Coach Sease pulled me up, he asked, "Son, you want to play ball?"

"Yes, sir! Yes, Coach!" I was really excited.

He said, "Take a knee."

I got down on one knee, and he looked me over: at six foot two inches and 160 pounds soaking wet, I was all skin and bones in an oversized jersey and lopsided helmet. Finally, he started to push me out there, but then he grabbed me back and looked again at those players from Virginia State. They were huge linemen—260, 270, and 280 pounds. The running backs were maybe 205 to 220 pounds. Coach Sease looked back at me with this expression of pity on his face as if to say, "I can't do this to this kid. It's inhumane. There's no way in the world I can throw this scrawny kid out there to those monsters."

So we go through this ritual for like ten minutes, where he's pushing me out, grabbing me back, throwing me out, and then grabbing me back. Finally, he said, "Sit down, boy."

This went on some more until finally Coach Sease asked, "Son, do you really want to play ball?"

"Yes, Coach!" The drums were beating, Virginia was rolling, the stands got louder, and then they scored a second touchdown.

Coach finally let go of my jersey and gave me a push, "Boy, get in the game at right defensive end."

I went into the huddle. We were on defense. My teammates looked at me like, "Oh shit, this is bad now. He sent the little white boy out here." We broke out of the huddle, and I went to my position at right defensive end.

Virginia State turned around and actually came up to the line of scrimmage without a huddle. The quarterback looked out on the line, spotted me, and someone said, "Look at this little white boy out here on the left side. Take the kid out. Hut one, hut two ..." They thought it was funny, a 160-pound red boy lined up at the right defensive end. The mighty Virginia State line pulled off the line of scrimmage and started an end sweep toward me, bringing everything—tackles, pulling guards. They were intent on just wiping me off the planet Earth. They hit the corner, and the dust swirled; the big back was rolling behind the big guard in front. All of a sudden, there was another swirl of dust. While people were partying and laughing in the stands, Virginia's left side of the line suddenly went down.

I heard the loudspeaker say, "Ladies and gentlemen, Virginia State has just been stopped in the backfield. We can't see who made the tackle at this point, but it looks like it is a number 70. For the first time today, ladies and gentlemen, Virginia has been stopped in the backfield. We still cannot see who made the tackle. Wait, yes, it appears to be number 70, but we cannot find his name in the lineup."

Virginia State lined up again and came back the same way off the ball. Boom ... the swirl of dust ... the big linemen swirling down ... the big back ... boom, another swirl of dust.

The announcer again, "Wait a minute, ladies and gentlemen, the tackle has been made again in the Virginia State backfield. We're trying to get a read on who this is—the kid is from Aberdeen—Petet ... or Petreat or Petite. We don't know who the kid is. He's a freshman." You could hear the paper rustling over the loudspeaker as the announcer started going through his rosters, trying to find out more about number 70.

Virginia went back into their huddle. They could not believe it; everybody was quiet. The whole stadium got quiet, especially the Virginia State side. Virginia came back to the line of scrimmage, this time with a play in mind. The quarterback looked over to the left and checked off, "Hut one, hut two …" Again the line came toward the left side, pulling out the guard, fullback, the big back with the ball, and … boom, at the line of scrimmage, the swirl of dust.

Yelling this time, the announcer said, "Ladies and gentlemen, I do not believe it!" Nobody believed it. "Virginia State has been stopped again by this same kid in the backfield! The tackle is being made two or three yards in the Virginia State backfield. We got a read on him now, he is listed as 195 pounds, but obviously, that's not correct. He is from Aberdeen, Maryland. His name is Dwight Pettit."

That was the beginning of my Howard University football career.

Virginia State could not believe what had just taken place. I had stopped them three times in a row in the backfield. They came back out, and because it was fourth down, they kicked the ball. The sideline and the stands were delirious. The defensive team began leaving the field, but the coach pointed his finger at me to indicate, "Stay there." I stood on the field by myself until the Howard University offense came in. Our quarterback Staley Jackson (now in the Howard Hall of Fame as Dr. Staley Jackson) came up to me, "Hey man, can you catch as good as you hit?"

I said, "Let's try. Throw me the ball."

He called my play, and on the first play from scrimmage, Jackson went back while I cut across the middle, deep at Virginia State's twenty-yard line. Jackson threw the long pass, and I caught it at the fifteen-yard line—a fifty yard pass, getting hit at the five-yard line. Howard University went crazy.

"Ladies and gentlemen, the kid is now on offense. He's seventeen years old, and he's from Aberdeen, Maryland. His name is Dwight Pettit. He is now on offense, and he has just brought Howard University into scoring distance inside of Virginia State's five-yard line."

The whole stadium went wild. We went on to score, and Virginia did not score again for the rest of the day. The final score was Virginia State, 14, and Howard University, 7. The Howard University football team discovered itself, and football was reborn.

All the guys who had barely spoken to me began congratulating me.

I was a genuine local athletic college star at seventeen years old. That's when my college football nickname, "Bleach," was born. As it turned out, the 1963 football team went on to win its last five games, after Morgan State, of course, and the 1964 team went on to become one of the greatest teams in Howard's history, both athletically and academically. I remember such guys from that era as Kenny Price, Wayne Davis, Kenny Jasper, Dick Oliver, and Johnny Mercer. They are some of the guys that I still have a bond with and talk to today.

"Bleach," the name given to me by teammate Joel Mongo, was the combination of the color thing and the racial thing, topped off with affection. Mongo, known far and wide as "the Mong," was the Richard Pryor who had yet to be discovered. He gave everybody nicknames. Zellie Dowe, a pass receiver who could have gone pro if he had so chosen, was nicknamed "Golden Wheels." Madison Richardson, one of the top surgeons in the United States today, was nicknamed "Killer Monsoon" and "Mad Dog." He had two names because of his passion. Edward Pinkard was also known as "Pinky" because he was dark and had pink lips and blue eyes. As the team became more prominent, Mongo assigned names to all of the stars.

Every time I return to Howard for homecoming with my wife, all of the guys get together and tell football stories, invariably including a "Bleach" story. Most are off the charts, filled with more legend than truth. They have me doing things that I do not remember doing. They recall to mind the beginning of my football career at Howard and, most importantly, my romance with Barbara. Now she is affectionately known by those who know her best as "Bobbie," but back then, at Howard, the football team called her "Black Beauty." I was on cloud nine at that time. I was taking heavy courses on my academic schedule, but I discovered the spoils of college football. In one week, I had made the *Washington Post* with the caption, "Howard University Lead by Freshman End." All of a sudden, I had achieved campus notoriety, which meant girls, popularity, and parties. All of a sudden, Howard football was not quite a joke anymore. We had played Virginia State to a standstill, and suddenly, walking across campus, everybody was talking instead of laughing.

My roommate, Sam Norman, adopted me because, according to him, when I traded Baltimore City for Aberdeen, I had become "country." Sam was a slick guy from Trenton, New Jersey, a sharp guy who was always immaculately dressed to a *T*. He had all the girls. He was determined to remake me in terms of my dress and style. First, he told me I had to get rid of my white bucks. I mean you just did not wear white bucks at Howard University back in the '60s. I also wore buttoned-down tab collars, but no tie. Tab shirts are back in style now, but in those days, tab collars buttoned up without a tie was not considered within the black dress code. Sam was also determined to remake me socially. I had the ability to meet girls because I was a popular football player, but according to Sam, "Man, you can meet them, but you still gotta learn how to talk to them. You gotta have a rap, some conversation. You gotta have some game, some talk, and stuff like that." I became Sam's protégé. He was determined, and the whole dorm knew. It was his main mission to make me into a lady's man or at least transform me out of the country and back into the urban scene.

Our next game was against Delaware State, and I was a starter. I did not have anything close to the game I had against Virginia State, but I still held my own playing both offensive and defensive end.

Following that game, Captain Bob Willis remarked, "The Bear comes to town next week." The Morgan State Bears were simply awesome. They had remained unbeaten for three years. In its backfield, Morgan had Leroy Kelly, who would later become all-pro for the Cleveland Browns; on defense there was Willie Lanier, later an all-pro linebacker for the Kansas City Chiefs; Dobbins, all-pro in the Canadian League; Savage and Pompey would become all CIAA; and Raymond Chester, who would go on to play for the Baltimore Colts.

Captain Willis was emphatic when he told me, "Boy, you will grow hair on your chest when you meet the Bear next week." I found out what that meant when the Bears went on to crush us 53 to 8. I think I was helped off the field at least three times; it could have been more, because I lost count somewhere along the way. I had never seen nor felt anything like it in my life. I had never seen people that big who could move that fast. It was an awesome display of football power. I believe to this day that if Morgan, with their size and speed, had been allowed to play any school in the nation, whether it was Alabama or Nebraska, they would have been competitive. Their speed was unbelievable. Although we were trounced by Morgan State, that was the last loss our team suffered in 1963. We were not beaten again in the conference until the fifth game in the 1964 season when we once again came face-to-face with the Morgan State Bears, this time on their home turf in Baltimore City. For that game, I led the team into the stadium in the city where I began. I do not have to tell you how emotional that was for me.

The 1964 football team of my sophomore year was inducted not only into the Howard University Football Hall of Fame, but also, according to Coach Sease, into the NCAA Academic Hall of Fame. In my opinion, the '64 team can rightfully be counted among the great all-around football teams in American college history. Note what I just said, I did not say Howard University's history. I said one of the great teams in American history (athletically and academically). The 1964 team was a nonscholarship team because Howard was not giving out athletic scholarships at the time. The student body went on to hold protest demonstrations for scholarship during the years 1964–1967 under the leadership of student council president Ewart Brown, who later became the prime minister of Bermuda. That football team produced more than five doctors, including Dr. Madison Richardson; at least eight lawyers, including Bob Willis and Bobby Mance; and a number of engineers, legislators, professors, teachers, academicians, and MBAs.

Years after we graduated, my wife and I were flying from Plains, Georgia, where we had been visiting presidential Democratic Party nominee Jimmy Carter. We got on the plane, and I looked in the cockpit as we passed by and there was Stanley Allen, our other quarterback, sitting in the pilot's seat. I'm certain this record of achievement by a football team rivals that of any other football team in the United States, including Harvard or Yale. The 1964 team produced leaders of national prominence including H. Rap Brown, who started summer training as a quarterback, although not finishing the season for reasons that would later become apparent. The equipment manager on that team was Cleve Sellers, later to

97

be the leader of the civil-rights movement at South Carolina State. As a side note, others at Howard at the time included Stokely Carmichael, Togo West, and Larry Gipson. Although not a participant in varsity athletics at that time, Larry Gibson (of Maryland legal and political prominence) later served as the joint force commander in ROTC and would become associate attorney general of the United States. Togo West would later become secretary of the Army under President Bill Clinton, and Stokely Carmichael, later known as Kwame Ture, would become a national civil-rights activist. All of these people, including famed singer/songwriter Donny Hathaway and actress Debbie Allen, were at Howard University at the time. But the team itself was phenomenal because of its impressive academic talent. Howard University was a magnet for those who came primarily for academic reasons and just happened to also be good athletes. This is something our young people need to know—you can do both. Athletics and academics can go hand in hand.

Morgan State was at its athletic peak when Howard traveled there for the 1964 game. They had been undefeated for three years, and they defeated Howard 15 to 8, but only in the last few minutes of the closing quarter. The game was played in the pouring rain, with Howard fans screaming at the top of their lungs. It would be one of the only two defeats suffered by Howard during that season (the other was to Drexel Tech). Going forward, we shut out five teams, and football became socially acceptable. Football players were "in." They gained status on campus and demonstrations were breaking out in support of scholarships. The university became so paranoid about the sudden surge of the football program's popularity, perhaps fearing it would overshadow academic excellence, that they dropped Morgan State from the next year's schedule. As it turned out, we never again played Morgan during my remaining two years. (Morgan would later be re-added to the schedule.) Howard was invited at the end of the 1964 season to participate in a bowl game in Florida, but the university declined.

There is a picture on my wall recognizing the 1964 Hall of Fame team. It bears the caption, "This team of nonscholarship athletes posted one of the greatest records in Howard's history, losing only one CIAA Conference Contest, and was invited to the most prestigious Negro bowl games for

HBCUs at the time, the Orange Blossom Classic." Being at Howard University and on this team helped me rediscover myself socially and intellectually and repair the psychological damage done prior to Aberdeen High School. The repair had not been completed at Aberdeen High. Even though I survived academically, I was still there only by order of the court, not because of any open policy adopted by the faculty or administration. Howard University embraced my academic awakening. I began to realize and understand the lies I had been told and the injustice that had been done to my family and me. But for my father and mother, the injustices that too many African Americans suffered—and suffer—could have been crushing and never overcome. Others less fortunate have never had an opportunity to be academically, socially, and spiritually reborn. I did.

There was an academic paper referenced in *Pettit v. Board of Education of Harford County*, which contained the following statements:

"Nearly all studies agree that any environmental change raises or lowers a child's IQ, though not more than 5 percent or 10 percent. In most cases where really striking changes in a child's environment occur, the increment or decrement in IQ is greater and may reach as much as 30, 40, or more points ... Intelligence tests claim to measure native intelligence. Actually, they measure native intelligence as developed by the environment stimuli. Their proponents have sometimes argued as though intelligence ratings in the first place are inclusive of all phases of intelligence and not simply those phases that can be measured. In the second place, intelligence tests have been treated as though they tested the most important phases of personality and that other elements of personality do not really matter as much. The role of energy and activity has been minimized" (Henry S. Borgardous, professor of sociology, University of Southern California).

Another interesting quote in the memorandum filed and referenced in the case was that, "A very great majority of high school students, though not especially gifted, will do reasonably well if motivated and given the opportunity to choose work in which they have average aptitude. They will succeed reasonably well at that work. The nation is filled with successful doctors, lawyers, teachers, engineers, bankers, and businessmen whom the testing system would not have rated among the highest upon graduation from high school and would not originally have been deemed potentially qualified for the work they are in. When the records of graduating college students in the highest and lowest end of the class, as determined by scholastic indexing, are compared in retrospect to admission records, it is obvious that high scores at entrance do not guarantee college success in individual cases, nor do low scores doom a student to academic obscurity. Furthermore, all the major systems of testing admittedly deal with probabilities involving groups, not with facts involving individuals; that is, even if they should be reliable for considerable majorities within certain larger groups, they cannot be trusted for any specified human beings."

The studies referenced in *Pettit v. Board of Education* were cited in memorandums of law and briefs filed with the court. The issues of IQ and intelligence were explored extensively. There are serious questions as to the correlation between academic achievement and intelligence tests and/or success later in life. I argue that these tests unfairly supported the "track systems," particularly within urban educational environments. These tests were used in an effort to undermine and discourage, and in fact put our young people within a certain box of defined limitations. Their usage affirmed the debated issues of W. E. B. Du Bois and George Washington Carver—the argument by Du Bois being that we were being steered into the working class, the manual labor-orientated segment of society. Quoting again from briefs in *Pettit v. Board of Education*, "Even in the areas where we were offered academic studies, still the main goal was to in fact have us mentally conditioned to the fact that, as a whole, as a population group, we would still do the medial labor task of America and not aspire to the intellectual realm of society."

A friend and colleague of mind, a legal giant, Billy Murphy, once said on a talk show, "White America is orientated to being average and to being academically and professionally normal." In other words, if you are a white person, you are told you can achieve and succeed if you just do what is necessary to get by. You will be rewarded because you are white. You do not have to strive for academic excellence; You do not have to strive for being in the top five or, as W.E.B. Du Bois said, "in the talented tenth." If a black person strives for and achieves academic excellence and goes on to operate at the top level of his or her professional environment, for the most part he or she will be operating with intellectually average people. The black person will be more successful.

I reread my father's memoirs the other night, and he had said basically the same thing. What tore at him was the stress of being academically superior in terms of the sciences—physics, engineering, and mathematics—while his "average" white coworkers got the recognition and promotions. He did the work in writing the papers and books filed at the Library of Congress, but it carried their signatures. One white supervisor told him he did not need a promotion because "Negro people did not have the same expenses as white people." We did not live in neighborhoods with the same housing costs. Negro kids did not go to expensive schools. We did not have to belong to a country club.

I remember once as a child, my father said, "You know, Dwight, there are people that I am working with and working for that are not even college graduates. These are high school graduates with diplomas from Poly." This is not to knock Baltimore's Polytechnic Institute; Poly is a tremendous high school. My father's point was that there are people that were actually working as scientists and engineers without the necessary college credentials. On the other hand, my father not only aced calculus, physics, and formidable mathematics, he had actually taught these subjects at the college level. Then, in a white environment, his supervisors and bosses were people working at an average level with average credentials—being white was their main credential. Moreover, they controlled his destiny. Thus, he was tremendously frustrated.

Once I got past the diminutive size of Howard University, I found that it offered outstanding preparation for everything that I could imagine for a successful life. By my junior year, I was majoring in political science, with a minor in psychology. I do not know why I chose psychology when I should have pursued a minor in economics or business. I suffered in law school for not having done so. I also developed an interest in the military through ROTC. I loved Howard University then, and now, because I had the opportunity to interact with great professors and great minds in a great multicultural progressive environment.

During the summer of my junior year, I went away to officers' training school at the Air Force base in Plattsburg, New York. I embarked with new confidence, having studied under professors from all over the world in a supportive environment. I had shed the monkey on my back, including the insecurities incurred during my years at Aberdeen High School. Yet, when I got to Plattsburg, I was once again in a predominately white environment. Out of hundreds candidates competing to be officers in the United States Air Force, there were only three blacks (all from Howard University)—Van Brakle, Lipscomb, and me. We were there to be trained, graded, and ranked (first, second, third, and so forth) before returning to our individual ROTC programs. Everything we did was competitive, whether it was athletic or academic, or in individual, squadron, or flight competitions. Right away, I sensed I was again being perceived as arrogant, belligerent, and Black Power orientated—an activist and agitator.

In the Air Force, flights make up a squadron, squadrons make up a group, and groups make up a wing. The wing is the top level of command. Every week there was a major competition in a different area. The first week, we were supposed to design the flight symbol. I am artistically inclined, so for Flight B I drew a ferocious bumblebee wearing boxing gloves. It won first place. The next week was a track-and-field athletic competition. I came in near the top. The third week was an academic competition, and I placed in the top three. In marksmanship, I scored high. During survival training, Flight B ate well because of the fish I caught while everyone else struggled on a survival diet.

All of a sudden, there was a perceived difference in the attitude of the white officers toward me. The originally overt friendliness disappeared, as if they were thinking, *Who does this Negro think he is?* I was under the scrutiny of the officers, and I sensed hostility.

During the last week of camp, there was a speech writing and delivery competition, with the subject being "Why I want to be an Air Force officer." I was confident in my writing and speaking abilities and certain that I would win. The whole wing had to submit speeches. The next day, they declared my speech the best written. However, I was not to deliver it. It was announced, "The best speech was written by Cadet Lieutenant Pettit. Cadet Lieutenant Pettit, would you please stand up." The presenter continued, "The speech is just great, about being an Air Force officer, however, it has been determined by the senior command that we will change the rules. Lieutenant Pettit will not give the speech; instead we will give that honor to Lieutenant Lipscomb."

At least they did not select a white cadet. Lieutenant Lipscomb was a quiet black guy—a real nice guy, laid back, and … acceptable. Van Brakle looked like a white man with straight hair, but that was too obvious, so they designated Lipscomb. The next night, at the final dinner before we were dismissed to our respective schools with our rankings, Lipscomb delivered my speech to the wing. They did not justify this, nor did they have to. It could not be said aloud that this was racism because the speech was given by another black. Heard, if not said, was the message, "We are going to put you in your place. You won the art contest, you excelled in the survivor course, you did the athletics, and you were in the top academically, but we will be damned if we let you stand up and take over the whole dinner with your speech. The speech may be great, but we will be damned if we let you give it."

It was like the quarterback experience. This time I was not hurt, I was angry. I remember sitting there, fighting back the pain, thinking, *I will not let them destroy me.* I sat there quietly listening to somebody else just as my father had watched his works being delivered, signed, and published by white people. Now I was listening to another black kid give the speech I wrote to the wing. At any rate, I got through it, despite also not being ranked among the top five, possibly because of my attitude.

When I returned to Howard University as a cadet major, I was called in to meet with the military personnel. These were real officers who had mentored me. "Dwight, Major Lipscomb came out in the top three. We heard about him giving your speech, and we are very sorry for that. You and Van Brakle just about tied."

Appointing a wing commander or an army battalion commander within Howard University's ROTC was major stuff in those days on black campuses in general. Lipscomb was appointed joint forces commander, in essence commander of both the Air Force and Army. The appointment of the Air Force wing commander came down to Van Brakle and me, but I told the major that football was my primary nonacademic activity. I had no problem stepping back and letting Van Brakle become wing commander because he was looking at the military as a career. Van Brakle was thus promoted to colonel and the university's Air Force wing commander, and I was appointed lieutenant colonel and group commander. This was great because Van and I were tight. We would again cross each other's paths in our military careers.

ROTC was Van's life—and Lipscomb's life too. In fact, both of them would later go on into the active Air Force as commissioned officers, and I would go into the Reserves with a deferment to go into Howard University Law School. When I was later called to active duty, I encountered the same thing that the military had done to my father. It was an instant replay of his life. When my father went into the military, he tried to go in as a pilot in the Army Air Corps. He was denied that opportunity, and after attempting to file suit, he was shipped to England. I had a similar experience attempting to go into the Air Force, not only as an officer, but also as a lawyer in the Judge Advocate General's office, known as JAG. I was denied. Van Brakle unknowingly played a major role in this situation, and because it became a major internal issue, so did the FBI, the commander of JAG of the Air Forces, and the secretary of Reserve Affairs, a man by the name of Render.

Along with ROTC duties, I had a heavy course load on my academic schedule, and I continued relishing the spoils of college football. In my senior year, I shared an apartment with a roommate named Leon Johnson. He worked at night, so Barbara and I had this big two bedroom apartment all to ourselves. I was living in sort of a young single-man's paradise. Howard has always had a reputation of having beautiful female students. One afternoon, the football team was practicing, and we looked up when the band came down the field. There was a new flag girl who was really "developed." We had seen the cheerleaders and flag girls before but not the newest majorettes. This new flag girl, Sunny, had gorgeous big legs in white boots and "shortie" shorts. As the band marched past, heading to their practice area, the coach blew the whistle and said, "Freeze, stop the practice. Somebody is going to get hurt; just let this child get past." Every day they would actually stop practice so someone did not run into the goal post or something. We would just stop and let the majorettes pass. But this was just typical Howard University.

A wild adventure occurred after the homecoming game at Hampton. There was a picture circulating of me hanging off the balcony of the building called "the Wigwam," where the visiting team slept at Hampton. I was pictured in my number 82 jersey and shorts. I had gotten surprised with a girl in a restricted area by the security guard, and to avoid getting caught, I had climbed out a window and clung to a fire hose. Somebody had taken my picture. The next day back, Coach Sease called a meeting and said, "Anybody could have had on a number 82 jersey, so I'm not going to say it's Dwight." He looked around, and then continued, "We can't make out the face; it's dark, so we can't say it's Pettit. But I want to tell number 82 this better not happen again."

Coach Sease treated me like a son. Those were some great times. I just could not believe my good fortune. I cannot think of anything that I could have done in life that could have been more fascinating and fun than going to Howard University and having the opportunity to play football at a black university. In fact, in my senior year I received the Holland Ware Award for the all-around athlete and scholar at Howard University.

I was also a prankster. I was constantly a busybody on the lookout to start something. For example, at Morehouse College in Atlanta, we buried a drunken Mongo in the grass and leaves while trying to find our dormitory. I also led the hazing of a new kid who had transferred in from Norfolk State. The only problem with this was that McFadden was a six foot five, 250-pound tackle with absolutely no body fat. He practically wiped us out the night before a big game. On another occasion, when we were freshmen, everyone had to have their heads shaved. On this issue, I almost had to fight "Killer Monsoon" (Dr. Madison Richardson, now a top eye surgeon in the country). Monsoon, at five foot eleven and weighing about 200 pounds, had allegedly taken ballet in Los Angeles. When he came to Howard, he was a running back and was said to have a black belt in karate. It was said that Monsoon would actually get in the gym and do this ballet thing, but I tell you what, nobody laughed and nobody messed with him because he had those kinds of muscles. Monsoon had muscles everywhere. When Monsoon and Willis came to me to cut my hair (a freshman tradition), I jumped up and "sold wolf tickets" or, as they say, talked shit. Nevertheless, they cut my hair, because I knew it was the better part of valor to get my head shaved rather than take the ass whipping that the two of them could have administered. They were like two Arnold Schwarzeneggers.

I heard the next night that they were going to cut Leroy Jenkins's hair. Jenkins was a big ole country boy from Florida, standing about six foot four and weighing 215 pounds. Jenkins slept with a razor. They went over to him about four o'clock in the morning, creeping to his bed because they were certain that he was in a deep sleep. Jenkins in a slow Southern drawl said, "Madison and Captain Willis, I hear you muthafuckers, and I'm not even going to get up. But I tell you one thing, I got this razor here named Sally, and if you come over here too close, I'm gonna cut both of you too short to shit."

All we heard after that was those two crawling back to their beds, and that was the end of Jenkins getting his haircut. He was the only one that I remember who did not get his haircut that year. The next day the guys ragged on Monsoon, "We thought you were a bad son of a bitch from LA, but we didn't hear anybody getting their hair cut last night."

Black colleges and universities were great institutions, not only of academic life but also of athletic and social life in a network we no longer see today as grand, the black athletic network. Nowadays, we might see a game once a year on television coming out of the Orange Bowl in Florida where Florida A&M plays Grambling or Grambling plays Hampton or Southern. But in the days prior to integration, college football was the social-networking event of the educated black community. One would go to a football game in those days and see women dressed in stockings and high heels. Homecoming at Howard, as at other black schools, was a major traditions with queens and celebratory singing stars and bands. Can one imagine running onto the football field as we did at Hampton University to the sounds of Jr. Walker and The All Stars playing "Shot Gun" live. One has to understand that integration has diluted all of that.

I remember very clearly being in Tennessee for a two o'clock game between Howard and Fisk University that was attended by thirty to fifty thousand in the stadium. By the evening game at eight o'clock between Florida A&M and Tennessee, there were over fifty thousand people in the stands. Liquor flowed, and the people got primed for the after parties. The Florida A&M band would strut in with their "death march," taking a full half hour to get on the field. It was the real deal as shown in the movie *Drum Line*. The announcer introduced the Florida A&M backfield as anchored by Bob Hayes, the "fastest human alive, creating the fastest backfield in the world—pro or college." (That year Hayes would represent the United States in the one hundred-yard dash at the Olympics.) Hayes's legs were insured by Lloyds of London. Next, they introduced Dick Nolan from Tennessee State as the second fastest human alive at 9.2 in the hundred, followed on the field by Claude Humphries, who would later be drafted by the Atlanta Falcons at six foot five and 325 pounds. He came out high stepping, wearing white spats. They said he did the one-hundred-yard dash in 10.5, which most of the white running backs could not do at the time. In my opinion, this was awesome talent, all concentrated in these small black schools throughout this nation before integration had had a profound impact.

I believe athletics were a major vehicle in the movement toward integration. Many people do not understand or appreciate this. One has to realize just what Jackie Robinson did in baseball, for example, or what Jesse Owens did in the Olympics in terms of Hitler and white racism, or what Joe Louis did when he knocked out Max Schmeling.

Of course, we all know what Muhammad Ali did in terms of breaking down religious and racial barriers. Although he was a boxer, his impact in terms of social progress, black pride, and the Vietnam War was immeasurable. Ali was my idol. I had the tremendous honor to be called upon by the Muslims to hang out with the Champ whenever he was in Maryland. I was in politics, and the Muslims felt that we looked so much alike that I was always included in the Champ's schedule. In jest, I was scheduled to do three rounds with him in Baltimore City in 1977 in an exhibition. This was purely for fun. I joked with the Champ that he shouldn't get crazy and forget this was only for fun, not real. I told him I would be bringing my baseball bat just to be sure. Unfortunately, I had to withdraw from the event due to politics. I had been put forward by President Carter to be his U.S. Attorney for Maryland, and the event because of Muhammad's religion and activism could have been controversial. It was one of the major disappointments of my life that I did not participate in that exhibition, and I don't have pictures of me in the ring with "The Greatest."

In 1963, Daryl Hill (now a friend of mine), would be the first African American to play football for a major white Southern school, the University of Maryland. In 1970, Alabama would play host to a heavily black southern California team. That game would begin the major transition of athletic integration of the schools in the Deep South. That would greatly speed up the overall integrations process started by the court action of *Vivian Malone and James Hood v. Alabama.* I also remember when Alabama, coached by the famous Bear Bryant, would play Nebraska in 1972 for the national championship. A black kid by the name of Johnny Rogers, who would receive the Heisman Trophy that year, ran circles around Alabama. The next day Alabama's famed coach, Bear Bryant, would come out and say (and I'm not quoting him but paraphrasing), that he couldn't compete with that kind of speed. The next thing that would happen would be the total integration of these Southern schools and the recruitment of black athletes across the South. This in no way undermines the credit due to James Meredith and Medgar Evers and the civil-rights warriors who made the ultimate sacrifice in the integration of the University of Mississippi and other Southern institutions.

There were still only a very few blacks in the student bodies of these schools, but there were blacks on the football and basketball teams, if nowhere else. It was a sad commentary that while we fought the George Wallaces to achieve integration, it was the need of major white universities to recruit black athletes so they could be competitive that helped break down barriers.

Playing football gave me the opportunity to establish a social life, and it allowed me a taste of the black experience I had missed during high school. It gave me the opportunity to travel around the country, to be able to see other universities such as Fisk, Morehouse, Spellman, and

Hampton, and to gain experiences that took my education to another level. I look back at my college days in contrast to high school where I really had no social life because of the racial situation. At Howard, I met athletes who could have gone to any college in the country, and I had the opportunity to participate in major socially historic events. Howard was among the first universities to stage on-campus demonstrations. In fact, while in law school I had the opportunity to be legal advisor for students during protest movements. It was an awesome experience to be in this environment. As *Playboy* magazine said, Howard University was "the breeding ground for the black revolution." It was almost like being in the "mecca of black society," as W. E. B. Du Bois described it in his biography about his experience at Hampton.

Looking at the effect of integration on the infrastructure of today's black economic community raises serious questions. Integration is a double-edged sword. We had our own businesses, our own hotels, our own restaurants. We lost all of that when we were assimilated into the mainstream. So now we look at Baltimore City, where we have a couple of black-owned bars. We do have a couple of restaurants (maybe two), we do not have any hotels, and we do not have any African American holdings in long-term economic developments. However, I am pleased to note that we do have one black-owned economic institution founded and still existing in Baltimore, which is the Afro American Newspapers.

The NAACP was here a few years ago for its national convention, but there were no black establishments where they could assemble, lodge, dine, or be entertained. This was the unfortunate, but hopefully not a permanent, result of the integration process. At Howard Law, the lineup of professors was awesome. I had benefited from some of this as an undergraduate, but I experienced the full measure of this in law school. Barbara and I were married by that time, and she was the main thrust of the family financially because she was able to get a summer job at the embassy of Senegal and a teaching job at Shaw Junior High School in the fall. I was lucky enough to land the perfect job as a clerk and guide at the National Archives while in law school. John Jones, one of my buddies on the football team, lined me up for the job. For three years, in the evenings and on weekends I answered questions and sold duplicates of the Constitution, the Bill of Rights, the Emancipation Proclamation, and other historical documents.

In the years from 1967 to 1972, I met and made another set of friends: Pickett Thomas, Harry Goodman, José Barnes, and Ernest McIntosh. Pickett Thomas and I ran together while I was at the National Archives, and Goody introduced me to another side of Washington, DC—the real side.

By my senior year, I was in class by day when not substitute teaching, and I was at the National Archives by night. The flow of tourists was slow in the winter, so I had nothing to do but study and read the law. The National Archives, like other buildings in Washington, was very majestic and imposing. I was the only black there, other than the uniformed Secret Service officers. White tourists stopped, stared, and took pictures of the black men lecturing and protecting our most cherished historical documents.

One day I got a letter from the national archivist himself. It read, "Dear Mr. Pettit, I understand you are doing a great job in the main hall. I am pleased to hear that we no longer have problems on the cash register." Before John and I were hired, there had been a problem of missing money. The letter continued, "But the tourists come to see the documents, not you, so could you please tone down the color and style of your clothes. Thank you, the National Archivist of the United States."

Dwight at Hampton University

Dwight-ROTC Cadet

Howard University Defensive Line (1966)
as painted by, Alvin D. Pettit, Jr. (2000)

Barbara and Friends 1963

Barbara on OMEGA Court

Dr. Staley Jackson and Clyde Mason at Homecoming

Zellie Dow aka Golden Wheels at the Homecoming

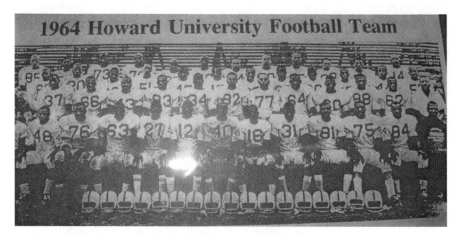

Howard University 64 Team

Kappa Brothers – Art Thompson, Leon Johnson, Clyde Mason, Fred
Charleston, and Henry Edwards (aka Nightmare) at Homecoming

Chapter 8: Love and Marriage

I met my wife as a freshman, and we dated throughout our four years at Howard University. We were sort of adopted by the campus because while I played football, she was the Omega freshman bunny, the freshman queen, the football sweetheart, and sweetheart for two or three other organizations. We were able to take classes together, so our relationship was observed on a daily basis, even during the time we had our temporary breakup.

Keys Restaurant was a fabulous little restaurant when Barbara and I started dating. For twelve dollars, you could get two short-rib dinners complete with beef ribs, gravy, mashed potatoes, string beans, corn bread, apple pie à la mode, and ice tea. I made sure to save up enough money to take Barbara to that restaurant every Sunday. This put me first in line to assure I had the date with her versus all of my competitors. They wanted to take her to fraternity parties, but I was going to take her to eat. That was the beginning of forty-nine years of being with this same woman and forty-five years of marriage. We were together then and thanks to the good Lord, we are still together today. Moreover, we still go back to Howard's homecoming each year. She is the star, not me.

One day she said, "Dwight, I came to Howard University to get an education, number one, but also to get a husband. I'm twenty-one years old and you are eighteen. I didn't come here to fall in love with a kid running around with a football. I came here to meet a doctor, lawyer, or somebody to establish a meaningful relationship with and look forward to graduation and a future—marriage." I was able to convince her that even though I was a kid, I was very mature. Our relationship blossomed, and the whole university watched it grow. They watched us get engaged and date through our senior year.

Our wedding was unbelievable. The football team, Omega Psi Phi, and my fraternity Kappa Alpha Psi were prominently in attendance. It was probably one of the craziest weddings that would ever be recorded in the unwritten history of Howard. Not only did most of the football team go to the wedding, the wedding as they say was "off the hook." It was in Newark, NJ, while the city was burning in the mist of the 1967 riots. The National Guard was on duty throughout the city. I had worn my Air Force uniform up to Newark with my lieutenant bars, so when I arrived for the rehearsal the night before the ceremony, the National Guardsmen saluted me. They didn't know whether I was there as an off-duty officer or as a United States Air Force officer involved in the occupation of the city. The next day, our wedding motorcade had National Guard escorts, and we entered and exited the church through a line of National Guardsmen with bayonets drawn.

Barbara, Dwight and Alvin, Jr.

Family 1975

First Child

Joe Slaughter, Larry Stokes, Dwight, Clyde Mason,
Joel Mungo, Wayne Davis and Barbara

Nisha and Alvin

Tommy and Adel Moore (In laws)

Chapter 9: Fraternity

I did not pledge anything during my freshman, sophomore, and junior years. I had no interest in a fraternity. I did not doubt that fraternities were a great stepping-stone for some of those who came to college and had nothing else to help present themselves to the campus community, nothing else to promote their college social life. This gave "nerds" (including me, but for football) instant transformations. Some guys, who couldn't even get a girl to smile at them, would pledge a fraternity, become an Alpha, a Kappa, a Q, or a Sigma, and all of a sudden become the slickest guys on campus or, in some cases, downright obnoxious. Either way, they had access to girls. They became an active part of the academic social family. Well, of course, me being me, I felt I didn't need this status. Football gave me instant status. By the time I was a senior, I was a group commander in the Air Force ROTC, and I had my gorgeous girlfriend, Barbara, who was considered by many to be the first chocolate girl who would have been homecoming queen if only she had placed her name in nomination. (She didn't, so Charlotte Fleming became Howard's first brown-skinned queen of my era.) At any rate, the last thing I thought I needed was to pledge a fraternity.

In the middle of my senior year, I had finished all of my required academic courses, so I decided to have fun during the final spring session. This was again about me going back to being academically lazy. I had a tendency to become very lazy, very quickly. I took football 101 (an actual course), ROTC-military science and advanced swimming. What the hell,

I didn't have anything else to do, so I let my roommate Clyde Mason and some other people talk me into pledging Kappa Alpha Psi.

Now I'm a Kappa, and I'm also a Mason. I became a Mason as a gentleman through a religious and historical but orderly, legitimate process.

Kappa, well that's another story. I'll put it to you like this: I've played football against the roughest and toughest; I've been in basic training in Officers Candidate School; I've gone through brief military survival training; I've been on the streets of Turner Station, Washington, DC, and Baltimore City; and I cut my teeth in a white environment where I had to fight my way to prominence through a racist and hostile atmosphere. Nevertheless, I have never experienced anything, nor will I again voluntarily experience, anything like pledging a fraternity at an HBCU.

Being a commander in ROTC and a known athlete on campus, one cannot imagine the hostility I encountered. "Who does this joker think he is? He's a football player, he's this, and he's that. This is my opportunity to kick his ass." I think my pledge period, like everything else that has happened in my life, was totally confrontational. First of all, you should never pledge when your roommate is already a member of that fraternity. That was stupid. And you should never pledge as a senior. You should only pledge while still in your freshman or sophomore years, when you are still low key, under the radar, and nobody knows you. You should never pledge as a high-profile senior.

I've seen litigation and represented folks who were involved in lawsuits about hazing. My line brothers made me the president of the line, the "Notorious 19" as we came to be known. I saw things that were totally unbelievable, things supposedly to bring about some type of bonding, friendship, and brotherhood. How could someone treat me like that: beat my ass until the muscles in my butt disintegrated and my ass hung down where my thigh should be, and then expect fraternal devotion? How could they beat my chest black and blue until I had no pigmentation left whatsoever, and then slap my blindfolded face until my cheeks were as red as cherries, and expect all this to be about love, bonding, and eternal friendship?

It got so bad, so confrontational, in my pledge period that I actually led my pledge brothers off-line for about two weeks. The dean at that time, Dean Black, heard that I had been badly hazed, and he tried to find me for an inspection. Although I hid out from the dean because of my loyalty to the fraternity and my desire to save the frat from suspension, I wasn't going to allow the fraternity to hurt me or my brothers.

I pulled the line off the night they hung one of my brothers with his necktie until he passed out, and another one was thrown down some stairs. The liquor was flowing; they were kicking everybody's butt. They were beating on us while we were blindfolded.

I was still a football player, and it got to the point where I took the blindfold off and said, "Okay, enough is enough. If anybody touches anybody else, it's on!" Among my pledge brothers were a black belt, three football players including myself, and a basketball player. I continued, "When I say the line is off, the line is off, so that means if you touch us now it's a free-for-all."

After a few exchanged expletives, my brothers and I went off-line. Bobby Graves, the polemarch (frat president), said, "Who are you son of bitches afraid of? Are you more afraid of Kappa Alpha Psi or Dwight Pettit?" Well, my brothers weren't afraid of me, but they knew I was correct in holding to my principle. So the Kappas put the word out on the East Coast that there was a freckle-faced son of a bitch who thought that he was badder than Kappa Alpha Psi. To me, this created a life-threatening situation. I'm not exaggerating: Kappas came in from all over the East Coast looking for my brothers and me. My line brothers literally had to hide me out for a period of about ten days. I remember laying on my stomach up on the roof of Howard's Fine Arts Building on a cold Saturday afternoon. The temperature was twenty degrees. Looking over the campus I saw groups of Kappas searching with sticks and paddles, looking for "that son of a bitch Dwight Pettit". Because it was a Saturday, there weren't many other people on campus besides the Kappas looking for me. I felt my life was literally in jeopardy over a fraternity.

The word finally came that if I didn't bring the line back, there would be no line made that year. When they couldn't find me, other means of communication opened up, and we finally sat down for negotiations. Meeting with the powers that be of Z Chapter at Howard University, I agreed to bring the line back on if they acted within a certain degree of civility. It was understood that if the agreement was breached, I would take the line back off. If they acted normally, the line, including me, would take as much punishment as deemed reasonable.

At any rate, our line returned, as agreed. The first night we went back to the Kappa House we immediately noticed there were a lot of cars outside—many more than just those belonging to Howard's Kappas. After we walked in, they immediately closed the door behind us, blindfolded us, put us in a couple of the cars, and took us out to the DC stadium, which was across the street from a golf course at that time. When we got on the golf course, I heard cars coming from everywhere—I mean cars and cars and more cars were pulling up. Apparently, all of the out-of-town Kappas were still in town. When they told us to strip down to our underwear, I thought to myself, *What have I put myself into now.* Then they began to sing Kappa songs, and though still blindfolded, I sensed that we were surrounded by a vast sea of people, no less than two hundred, singing over our heads.

Amid the singing, I could hear some voices talking.

"Where's that chump Dwight Pettit?"

"Where is that son of a bitch?"

After a while, I could hear them tap one of my brothers, and then another and another, and tell them they could leave. I could also hear my brothers saying they didn't want to leave, but they were dragged off, put into cars, and driven away. Finally, it dawned on me that I was in the middle of the field in my underwear, all by myself, on my knees, and surrounded by two hundred or three hundred men, with probably two hundred unknown to me and from other universities that Howard had no responsibility for and vice versa. In other words, any one of them could have done something ridiculous, foolish, or illegal, probably without any accountability.

It was four or five o'clock in the morning, and my ass was really on the line; I was in the middle of nowhere and half naked, so I did some serious praying to my God that nobody out there would be foolish. Suddenly

I sensed them moving very, very close, hovering and kneeling down all around me. I expected to be struck or kicked at any moment. I was sure they were going to make an example out of me. With the singing now closer to me, the dark of night took on a majestic somberness. I was scared, I was cold, and I had no idea what was going to happen next.

The pledge period was designed to check your mental status and determine whether you were tough enough to hang in there or if you were stupid enough to do dumb stuff. I simply wasn't going to do certain things. As the night began to give way to morning, the singing began to fade, and I began feeling space as they started backing off. I could hear people getting into the cars parked about fifty yards away, some still singing as they drove off. When all fell silent, I pulled off my blindfold and discovered that I was alone on my knees, in the middle of the field at five o'clock in the morning, with my clothes on the ground beside me. At that point, if there was a spiritual connection in terms of fraternities, I was experiencing it. I had been Kappa reborn. I didn't and couldn't imagine a gun to my head like the prisoner of war in the movie *The Deer Hunter*. There was no comparison to war, but I believe that psychologically a comparison could be drawn. The fear of the unexpected and unknown was relevant to the circumstances.

I came back on campus the next day, and all of my line brothers were looking for me. Word was out that I had been through the ordeal, and the big brothers had questions for me.

"Are you going to be a good Kappa now?" was the question.

I shouted with enthusiasm, "Yes, big brother, I will be a good Kappa!"

I took what I should have taken as the president of the line, so now we could all "go over"—"Cross the burning sands." Maybe going through the hazing I had just been through was the same for everybody, but for me it was tough. I asked myself why nothing came easy in my life. Everything I did had been confrontational. It was as if I was being prepared for something later on down the line. I needed to be hardened to confrontation or to be hardened to other distractions.

The five-bedroom apartment I shared with Clyde Mason and three other football players during my junior year was located on Georgia Avenue, above Highs Ice Cream. Clyde was an off-the-charts mathematics genius who ultimately graduated with a bachelor of science degree in engineering from Howard after successfully amassing an almost straight 4.0 GPA. He later received a master of business administration from Wharton School of Business. In addition to brains, Clyde was a big, five-foot-eleven, strong man weighing in at 225 pounds. He had a Cro-Magnon neck, such that his head and neck seemed to be one piece on his broad shoulders. He was a great football player. We are close friends today, or as close as two former roommates can be living in two different cities. My other roommates included Leon Johnson, who had the little yellow Mustang that I used to borrow to run up and down Fourteenth Street looking at the prostitutes all night; Harold Dobbins, who was a tremendous athlete; and Alan Henry. Our apartment became quite famous, or infamous within reason, as a popular hangout. Football parties and Kappa parties were always held at our apartment, and girls were always dropping in. Our place was among those known more for the social life than academics. It was the black version of the movie *Animal House*.

One night, Leon and I decided to give a party. All of the in crowd was there. Although I did not become a Kappa until the following year, we served "Kappa Punch"—a mixture of Wild Irish Rose wine and grain alcohol. It smelled like formaldehyde, but it had a sweet taste once mixed with lemons and Kool-Aid. The girls got blasted—in fact, everybody would be wiped out that night. I was a little toasted and pretty much into the party, playing the records while my girlfriend Bobbie danced. It had gotten to be a big party with probably 150 to 200 in the apartment when Bobbie came over to me and said, "Dwight, I hate to tell you this, but you need to ask a guy out there to leave. He keeps grabbing me on my butt."

Well, everybody at Howard knew Barbara was my girlfriend, and that just couldn't happen. I'd had more than a few drinks, and it didn't immediately occur to me that she was talking about someone who wasn't a student. So, when Bobbie led me over to the biggest, meanest-looking, muscle-bound, six-foot-three guy weighing at least 220 pounds, I thought to myself, *Damn!* That son of a bitch, obviously not a student, looked as mean as you ever want to see in life.

"That's him," Bobbie announced. At this point, fear overcame the drink, grabbing my body and mind. I knew all about the block boys who existed in the world separate and apart but all around Howard. The block boys ruled the streets. Whenever I walked down the street, I always carried a Coca Cola bottle, not because I liked drinking Coke that much, but just in case I had to use it as a weapon. However, the block boys never bothered with me. They would see me coming and just say something like, "Hey, number 82. Man, that boy can play." The guys on the streets always had something good to say about me, so I never had any confrontations even though I had to walk almost ten blocks back and forth from campus every day. They would beat up or rob other campus kids, but I never had those kinds of problems.

But now, in my apartment, I looked up at this guy—all the way up—and said with feigned bravado, "Man, I don't know how you got in this party, and I don't mind you being here, but it's my apartment and it's my party, and I would appreciate it if you don't grab my girl again."

He looked down at me, and he said, "Motherfucker, I'll grab you."

Along with the music, the whole party stopped. Everybody was like, "Oh shit, this big son of a bitch, whoever he is, is getting ready to kick Dwight Pettit's ass."

With Bobbie standing there beside me, there was nothing else for me to do, nothing else to talk about, nothing else to discuss. I made an instant decision that I would have to hit the son of a bitch right then, because if I let him hit me first, the ball game would be over.

So I didn't bother saying, "Well, man, [this or that]," "Put your fists up," "Man, I'm going to kick your ass," or "Man, let's fight." Instead, I just hauled off and hit the son of a bitch as hard as I could. And I didn't stop. With each punch, my high school ring cut into him. Just like in the movies, he went from wall to wall, gushing blood everywhere. People started screaming, and the girls started running. I kept hitting and hitting him, but he was so big, he wouldn't go down. We got into the middle of the room where I kneed him and hit him over the top with a right, and he went backward and down. He was still conscious, so I got on top of him and gave him at least four or five more shots to the head. His blood splattered all over the white shirt I was wearing.

Finally, he looked up and said, "Motherfucker, let me up."

For good measure, I hit him four or five more times until he appeared unconscious. Only then did I get off of him.

The other block boys who were there with this guy, picked him up off the floor and started for the door. One of them stopped and said something to my roommate Clyde. I hadn't realized Clyde was there until I heard this guy say to him, "Man, he fucked him up. Y'all fucked up my man."

I heard Clyde say, "What do you mean? What happened?"

The guy turned and Clyde said, "Chump, get off of that shit. Your ass was here all along. You saw his ass get whipped."

The guy said something else I couldn't hear, and then Clyde hauled off and hit him. *Bam!*

That's when I realized there were five block boys in the apartment, not just two. My other two roommates were not there. That left only me, Clyde, Leon, and Bobbie in the room. We found out later that people were hiding in closets and under beds. The fight became a scene out of the Wild West, with chairs broken over people's heads. One guy hit Clyde with a Coca Cola bottle that opened up the whole left side of his head. Blood splashed, but Clyde never buckled. He was like Cro-Magnon man, a 220-pound lineman who just turned around like a zombie, grabbed the guy in the crotch and by the neck, picked him up in the air over his head, and threw him down the stairs head first. Then Clyde turned on the guy I was originally fighting with, later identified as Johnny Simon, and backed him up between us until Johnny dove over the banister and ran out the front door into the street. Bobbie called the police, and although we were only a block from the police station, they never responded. Eventually all of the block boys were gone, as well as everyone else—including Clyde, who was taken to the hospital for stitches. This left just Bobbie and me in the apartment. Bobbie and I filled bottles with water and lined them up at the top of the stairs so we could throw them down the stairs in case any of the block boys decided to come back. For good measure, Bobbie yelled aloud for anyone outside to hear that we had a gun. Actually, we only had a plastic water pistol. With all the punches that were thrown, I was the only one that didn't have a cut or anything else to show. When Clyde got to Freeman Hospital, now known as Howard Hospital, he discovered Johnny Simon was already there getting stitches. Clyde contacted the police and had him arrested.

The old days were not like they are now. Back then, if you were good with your hands, you were respected. Good athletes were respected. If you could fight, you were respected. Nowadays, the better you are the more likely you are to get shot. The word was that while Johnny was getting sewed up, his crew asked him, "Do you want us to go back up there to Georgia Avenue and kill that nigger?"

Johnny reportedly said, "No, don't kill him. I was messed up. She was his woman, and I was wrong. Don't kill him."

I found this out only later in the courtroom. I realized then how close I had come to not being here now. I learned that Johnny Simon was the light heavyweight or heavyweight boxing champion while at Lorton Federal Prison in Virginia, and he had just been released only two or three weeks earlier. My roommate Leon was from Arlington, Virginia, where Johnny Simon lived, and Leon had tried to be one of the boys by inviting Johnny Simon to our party. Johnny and his henchmen planned to make our college party their special occasion for the evening.

The trial was set for downtown DC, and all of my friends, those at the party, came out to testify for me and against Johnny Simon. However, as soon as they brought Johnny out, wearing a black shirt, the comedy act began. One student after another suddenly developed amnesia. They had either a class to go to, a professor to see, or this or that to do somewhere else. The courtroom just about emptied out.

A lawyer came up to me and said, "Young man, I'm the lawyer for Johnny Simon. He wants me to tell you that if you go through with your charges, he's going to violate his parole, and he's backing up a lot of time. He was in for attempted murder. If you would drop the charges, he would be very appreciative."

I talked it over with Bobbie and decided to drop the charges. Later, Johnny Simon walked over to me and clamped a big paw on my shoulder. I said to myself, *Oh shit ...*

But he said, "Hey, man, I really appreciate what you are doing for me, man. Can I take you out and buy you a beer?"

I said, "Really, Mr. Simon, it's not necessary."

He urged, "No, I insist we go for a beer."

I let Bobbie go back with the other students, and Johnny and I went for a beer.

He told me, "I had a lot of fights. Man, I done fought a lotta guys on the streets and a lotta motherfuckers in jail. I'm a boxing champion. You ain't but a ball 70 [170 pounds]. You're as fast as a little sonofabitch as I have ever seen."

I said, "No, Mr. Simon, that's not really what happened. See, Mr. Simon, you were drinking, and I really apologize. I know I couldn't have really beaten you if you were sober." I sat there, but at that moment, I felt as if I was talking to Sonny Liston, and I wasn't quite as big, confidant, or arrogant as Muhammad Ali.

That whole episode became another story about my junior year in Washington, DC. Everywhere I went after that, whether on campus, to noncampus parties, to street parties, or to nightclubs, I was referred to as the kid who knocked out Johnny Simon. They would say, "Not only does that little guy know how to play ball, he's the little guy who knocked out Johnny Simon." Until then, I had not realized Johnny Simon was a living legend in the District of Columbia.

I was no longer just the ball player—now I had a pass to the streets of DC.

In my senior year at Howard, I moved from Georgia Avenue to Harvard Street, between 14th and 16th streets, just a few blocks from the hub of D.C.'s nightlife; the land of nightclubs, prostitutes and hustlers. With my street cred, I hung out and partook of the nightlife. I cruised the streets in Leon's yellow Mustang convertible throughout my entire senior year.

All along Fourteenth Street, for fifteen blocks down to U Street, the sidewalks were lined with the most beautiful women in the world: Caucasians, Asians, Hispanics, and of course blacks, all half naked, breasts out, and wearing miniskirts showing their butts. If you had ten dollars you could have anything you wanted on the streets of D.C. Now Leon and I never actually had an extra ten dollars after buying gas so, the issue was academic even if we had been so inclined to make a purchase. But all the girls, pimps, hustlers, and dealers knew me. I hung out in the streets, the strip joints, and in back-alley after-hour clubs, never doing anything illegal but always there. When I walked into nightclubs like The Blue Canary, people would say, "Hey, 82!" or "Hey, Dwight!" I was always playing and bullshitting with the girls. It was a whole different world, in a cool way. All the girls on the strip adopted me as the young college kid who was part thug but not a pimp. If one of them got into trouble, I offered advice. If somebody threatened to beat them up, I was a peacemaker. As a result, I was always welcomed without money in the clubs and strip joints. I was in another world.

Reflecting on my senior year, I felt academically awakened; I was an athlete, and I was thoroughly enjoying the popularity that goes with all of that. Moreover, my romance with my girlfriend was secure. She was Ms. Everything. The question on campus was whether she was going to be homecoming queen. It was her choice. The only thing I did in my senior year that was an adventure was pledging Kappa. Other than that, I made up for the years of social exile at Aberdeen High School. Not only was this a time of academic matriculation, study, and discovery, I felt reborn after coming out of a white school. I had been re-Africanized, re-blackened. I was released from the white bucks, the tab shirts, and the crew-cut hair that I had adopted while in a white school. I was back in the streets and back in fashion, just as I was in Turner Station. I wore slick clothes (to the extent I could afford them) and had a wavy haircut. I had "the look," and I drove a slick car (albeit Leon's car). I felt as though the Lord had lifted me from one world into another and another and back again. Going from the black world of my childhood, to the white world of my youth, back into the educational environment of Howard University, and then into the streets of hard-ass DC, I had been totally redefined, reshaped, remade, and reborn again by differing cultural experiences.

I was also the product of the academic process of Howard University, the athletic process of football, and the street life of Washington, DC. Moreover, the street life of my early adulthood was not the same as my childhood; it was ten times faster. These were the formative experiences taking me into law school (where I would be broken down and rebuilt again), through the riots, and through civil disobedience and academic matriculation.

Impressions or rather misimpressions are intangible concepts. When I entered Howard's law school, there were also those who viewed my academic profile negatively because I was an athlete. A few of my undergraduate professors, including Dr. Bernard Fall, were just down on football players, down on athletes, and down on black people. I nevertheless prevailed, but I got a second major shock to my psyche in law school.

This was apparently not a unique situation. While recently on vacation in Aruba, I met Judge Richard Jackson, a sixty-seven-year-old black Philadelphia jurist, a friend of Leon Jones and Trumell Valdera, who are my wife's closest friends. Judge Jackson was not only a Kappa but also a 1965 graduate of Howard School of Law. We enjoyed a discussion of Kappa, and we compared the psychological blows and scars suffered in law school as well as the pride in our accomplishments at the institution. Our recollections were so identical that I realized—thirty-four years later—that mine were not isolated experiences.

Chapter 10: Homecoming

Athletics, and football in particular, were always my vehicle for close male bonding. A lot of the ballplayers come back for homecoming. I have missed a few homecomings, and I have missed some of the guys. But going back, even after more than forty years, I know I'm going to see anywhere from seven to ten of the guys from the 1963–67 teams. They come from California and Florida and everywhere in between. Before we go to individual parties and restaurants, we always first get together for laughs and drinks, generally beer. We're getting a little too old for hard whiskey. We tell war stories about who made what tackle or who caught what touchdown, and we create plays in our minds rather than the ones that really happened. The stories get grander and grander. Watching Ray Lewis and the Baltimore Ravens the other day, I saw Ray in the middle of the circle leading the dog chant, "what time is it! what time is it! it's game time....whoff, whoff, whoff, whoff, whoff."

We had a similar chant at Howard, "Eat the big dogs!" We were like the Alabama teams of the '50s and '60s, smaller than other teams but fast and quick. By small, I mean we had a big defensive line but a comparatively small offensive line, averaging 200 to 215 pounds as opposed to 240 to 250 pounds like most teams. Before breaking out of our huddle, we'd all growl and holler, "Eat the big dogs!" Then we'd get up to the line of scrimmage, and as Harold Orr (a burly guy who's now a doctor in Los Angeles) got into his three-point stance at the other end of the line from me, he would growl, "Pettit?" and I'd respond, "Yeah, Harold?" and he'd yell, "*Eat the big dog!*" and I'd yell, "*Eat 'em!*" We would do that just before the count, before the play would go off, and really get into the other team's heads, especially when they knew we were bringing it.

That was the type of bonding we developed. The highest form of bonding actually happens in the military, but my basic military officer's training lasted just six weeks, too short a time to foster the same type of male bonding normally developed when assigned to a combat unit. I never had a chance to bond that much with the Masons, because I came into the Masons as a young man while running for Congress. My mentor was Samuel T. Daniels, the honorable, high, most Worshipful Grand Master. He basically just waved the magic wand and walked me through the Masons.

However, with Kappa Alpha Psi I bonded very closely with my eighteen line brothers, even though I didn't have a close bonding relationship with the fraternity itself. Two of the guys on my line were also on the football team. Henry Edwards, nicknamed "Nightmare," was the fullback. Years later, I bought a big ferocious-looking German shepherd for my kids, and I affectionately named him *Nightmare* after Henry. Another guy on my line was Agee. He later became an assistant US attorney in DC, and we ended up squaring off in a case involving a murder that happened, of all places, at Howard University. I saw Agee recently at homecoming. He's retired now and in private practice. Harold Barnett, a muscular pretty boy out of Chicago, was also one of the Notorious 19. He used to look at Barbara all the time and say to me, "Why you? How could you be the one? And how could you keep this fine woman?" I thought of Harold as sort of a younger brother because he was light-skinned with an attitude about being light-skinned. He also reminded me very much of myself, because you could tell he came up in the rough part of Chicago. He was part thug, and being light-skinned and red, he probably had to be a super bad thug. He came from money, and word was that his daddy was very much into the action in Chicago. Shingler, whom I would later remeet as vice president of a bank now in Baltimore City, was a big basketball star at Howard. At six foot five, Shingler (nicknamed Shing) was taller than I was, so arranged by height on the line, he was number nineteen and I was number eighteen. He was a tremendous all-CIAA basketball player.

Chapter 11: Halls of Howard Law

Barbara majored in French, with a minor in Spanish, and thankfully, with her help, I managed to pass Spanish 3, which was one of my last requirements for graduation. I had not taken Spanish since high school because I hated it; it was a real struggle for me. However, it was imperative that I receive a passing grade of at least 65. My problem was that my Spanish teacher at Howard, Senora Portuanda, did not speak English. Without Barbara's help, this would have been an insurmountable problem. I hedged my bets by sometimes carrying a football to class, pointing to it as I explained to Senora Portuanda, in my stumbling Spanish, my need to get at least a D in her course. Ultimately, I got my D and passed, so by the time I started my senior undergraduate year at Howard, I had taken all of the required courses for my major in government and my minor in psychology.

It did not occur to me until later that I had not taken any economics or business-related course work. Instead, I cruised the first semester of my senior year and second semester taking only those classes that allowed me to pledge a frat, lie on the grass, and hang out. I carried a boom box even before "boom boxes" became popular. I was having so much fun that at one point I told Barbara that I had thought about staying an extra year just to hang out.

She scratched that idea. "Fool, you need to graduate, get out of here, and grow up."

When Barbara graduated from Howard and got a job teaching French and Spanish at Shaw Junior High School, I entered Howard University's School of Law, not truly aware of what was about to hit me in the world of higher academics. I presumed that if I could master Howard's undergraduate degree program, I could do the same in their law school. That is not a notion I would now presume. I immediately faced courses such as Legal Accounting, Business Law, and Commercial Transactions. These courses were designed to weed out "presumptuous" students.

At the age of twenty-one, I was one of the younger people in law school. My classmates were generally older because, after the undergraduate studies, they had gone on to pursue professional careers or to receive advanced-level degrees before pursuing the study of law. Those like me, coming straight from the undergraduate level, made up less than half of the starting class. At Howard, there were two sections, with one hundred students per section. After the first year, each section had been reduced to perhaps fifty students, ultimately graduating even fewer.

The students who had majored in business as undergraduates had an advantage early on. In my Legal Accounting course, Professor Jerome Shuman just looked at us and said, "Here is the accounting book; here is the law book. Ladies and gentlemen, I suggest that you take the accounting book home and learn accounting on your own. I will teach you the law." In other words, the professor was not there to teach each us the basic principles of accounting; he was only there to teach us the application of accounting to commercial law cases in the law casebook. It was up to us to know what a debit and credit were, along with the basic intricacies of accounting. From the beginning, I found that I was in academic hot water: straight business law and commercial law were one thing, accounting was another. Passing this three-credit course was imperative. Failing Legal Accounting, and possibly something else, would result in being put out of Howard Law very quickly. There was no academic probation if one dropped below 70. That person was automatically out.

There were professors who roamed around the hallways of Howard University School of Law almost as if they were emperors or senators in their chambers. The students would breathe in their every syllable and word. The law school was almost a world unto itself, separate and apart from the university. Like the Howard University College of Medicine and the College of Pharmacy, it was down in a place called The Valley where few went. Undergraduates went down to The Valley, what they called Death Valley, only if they had to take a physical science, biology, or chemistry course. Death Valley was the home for scientific graduate students and the law school. The law school was the cornerstone in the embryonic stages of the civil-rights movement and was the home of Thurgood Marshall, Charles Houston, James Nabrit, and many other great lawyers and judges.

I really didn't know about white law schools, but I assumed, given that there were so many lawyers across the country, that they would have an ample supply of talent to draw upon—enough to pull in all kinds of professors, ranging from mediocre to great. At Howard University, it was much different because prior to the affirmative action and recruitment programs of the 1970s, African American students had few other places to study the law and become law professors. By extension, African American law professors had few other places to teach except African American law schools, and there were only a very few of those: North Carolina Central, Texas Southern University, and Howard University, with Howard being "the big dog." So here we were, looking at all of these would-be gods, both black and white. The white professors in undergrad school, like Dr. Bernard Fall, were big fish in our little pond, and the black law professors, having gravitated to a black institution because they were not allowed in general to teach law at a white law school, were the top in their particular professions nationwide. Howard had a faculty (of both blacks and whites) that was the cream of the crop, favorably comparable with Harvard and Yale.

During my years at Howard School of Law, 1967 through 1970, the lineup looked like an academic all-star team. It seemed that every professor had written the book on the subject that he or she taught. For example, in Contracts, we were assigned the Newton Pacht contract casebook written by Howard professor Newton Pacht. Professor Jerome Shuman taught Corporate Law. He was a big, burly, young genius, perhaps thirty-five or thirty-six years old at the time, who also taught at Georgetown Law. He had made his money in the stock market, bought a huge house off Sixteenth Street, DC's "Gold Coast," and drove a Rolls Royce to work every day. Professor Patricia Harris, who taught Constitutional Law and was a protégé' of Linden B. Johnson would go on to be the first woman appointed to a major presidential cabinet seat. (She was appointed by President Jimmy Carter as Secretary of HUD and Secretary HEW). Dr. "Red" Morse, considered to be one of the academic scholars of his time., also taught Federal Jurisdiction, Corporation Law, and Civil Procedure. Dean Miller and Dean Clyde Ferguson were considered giants in criminal law, and Tim Jenkins is now seen on national television talk shows as one of the progressive leaders in the legal profession. James (Jimmy) Cobb, who taught Business Law, died not long ago—he had founded and was chairman of the board of the first black bank in Washington, DC. Spencer Boyer, one of the top tax attorneys in the country, taught Tax Law and accounting. The judge who taught Trial Practice was a US district judge, and I did my trial argument in front of a Court of Appeals judge. The list goes on and on, and I am omitting many names. Nevertheless, the entire faculty comprised the "Who's Who" in African American jurisprudence. They were giants.

Particularly notable during my time at Howard Law was Professor Herb Reid, who was recognized on the national stage because of the case *Powell v. McCormack* argued before the United States Supreme Court. This would be a landmark case on the powers of Congress to seat or expel its members. Congressman Adam Clayton Powell had been expelled from Congress, and Professor Reid was one of the lawyers who took the case to the nation's highest court. In fact, Professor Reid was preparing his case while I was taking his Constitutional Law course. After presenting his argument before the court, Professor Reid came back and lectured to the class the same day. His lectures were always insightful, if not unique. He would come in and sit at his desk, protrude his tongue out of his mouth, put his left hand to the left side of his face, and then just sit there looking out the window for fifteen minutes or so. The class of fifty students would also just sit there, all intensely silent, as if looking at something that was divine. Nobody would breathe, the silence would be deafening and any voice heard would be sacrilegious. Finally, Professor Reid would speak with a blurred tongue. He talked with a lisp. He would look out of the window and say, "The constitutional premises that we shall discuss today will revolve around the Fourteenth Amendment to the Constitution of the United States of America." He would talk for about five minutes and then stop. Everybody would start applauding even though he had yet to say a damn thing. By the end of the class, he would have talked for about twenty minutes. Then, suddenly he would stop and walk out. Everybody would rise and give him a standing ovation. I think this adulation was more for his achievements than for the lecture. As I went through the day, I would go from one great lecturer into a class that was being held by one greater. I had never experienced anything like it. I thought I had seen it in undergraduate, but in law school, I really had entered the hallowed halls of academic heaven.

However, to be very clear, among the many lawyers who passed through Howard's doors, some practicing, some teaching, there were a couple of fools. One of those fools in particular was Professor Chick Chisholm. I had the misfortune of landing in Professor Chisholm's class because I had no choice whatsoever. Allegedly a renowned (albeit allegedly disbarred) New York City defense attorney, Professor Chisholm was living off his notorious reputation and ego. He was a total idiot. To look at him, one could say he was considered a pretty boy: brown-skinned, straight hair, and slim, with so-called white features. He talked with a distinctive mixed drawl. He laid his words out in sort of a hanging fashion, almost a mumble that he defied you to understand. You were supposed to be able to cut through whatever he was saying and decipher the information. I began to observe that not only was he a clown, but we were supposed to be amused by and appreciate his warped sense of humor.

Chisholm looked at me on the first day of class and did the same thing that Dr. Fall had done, saying, "Boy, I don't like you." He spoke to me dismissively, almost in a Moms Mabley voice, "I know what you were in undergraduate, but you are not law material, son, and I will put you out of here." He went on to give me a failing grade of 60 in his Civil Procedures course. Given that 64 was the established failing grade, his action was a vicious and malicious attempt to get me summarily thrown out of the law school. He came very close to doing just that, except for the fact that he had made it known how he felt about certain students for no particular reason, which emboldened a couple of other professors to give a point or two to my advantage, saving me from being dropped. I later repeated and passed Civil Procedures over the summer at Catholic University. I went all the way through law school aware of the peril of having to repeat him. He would say to me in the hallway, "I got you in your first year, boy, and you're still here. I'll get you in your last year." And, true enough, in my last year I drew Chick Chisholm for Federal Jurisdiction, a major required course.

Riots began to occur across the country during my second year of law school. In DC, riots erupted after the murder of Martin Luther King Jr. I was able to get into the streets during the looting and shootings. Howard University law students were recruited to give legal services to hundreds of people who were being arrested. We were given armbands and IDs and put right into the streets. Fires were burning, windows were being broken, and people ran past with televisions and whiskey. President Lyndon Baines Johnson called for sanity while I rode around with the troops and provided counsel to people in the courtrooms. It was a fantastic experience on a live stage.

I always say that going to school in DC was a great experience, in large part because it was the location of the halls of Congress. I met Senator Robert Kennedy in an elevator. I went to a fabulous party in Georgetown when John Jones, the person who got me the job at the National Archives, was invited by a Kennedy staffer. It was a party hosted by one of Ted Kennedy's aides. Only in DC could those types of things happen where you could go to a committee hearing on Capitol Hill, go to work at the National Archives, and go to the Library of Congress to research. DC is a hell of an educational place. I also had the opportunity to matriculate at Catholic University's School of Law because I had failed Professor Chisholm's class. It was a blessing in disguise, because I was able to see what another law school was like in comparison to Howard.

Unrest began to take place on campuses across the country, with undergrads staging demonstrations for varying reasons. Again, Howard was in the lead in this national period of student unrest. At one point, the university was under siege and closed down. I had the opportunity to serve as counsel and one of the student legal advisors representing the students in negotiations with the president of the university and the US Marshal's office. This was unbelievable firsthand experience, watching the university under siege. The students went into the administration building and closed it down under the leadership of Joel Mongo, my ex-football teammate.

While all of this excitement was taking place, I still attended my law-school classes, was a substitute teacher at Hamilton Junior High School, and worked nights at the National Archives. At Hamilton, I was known as "Big Red," and I kicked butt. Discipline was different then than it is now. Now, I would probably be fired or put in jail for assault. Those junior high kids were big kids. Nowadays you have to pat them on the shoulder and say, "Johnny, go to class, be good, and do not swing at the teacher anymore." In those days, I just picked up the guys and shook them or grabbed them by the collar, and everybody said, "Okay, Big Red, we got it." Those were their formative years—and mine too.

Going into my last year of law school, I had gotten into the groove. My grades had been improving dramatically; I was making As and Bs in most courses. I was doing everything right. At first, my professors did not recognize me from Joe Blow, but I finally became socially acquainted with them, mostly thanks to my wife, Barbara. She always stole the show in social situations, helping to ingratiate me with my professors and others. I remember once at a law-school dance, the professors gave her the trophy as the prettiest girl there without even a vote. She always was, and still is, my safe pass. When all else failed, she could get me in the show. However, I knew and dreaded that I was ultimately going to have to take Federal Jurisdiction from Chick Chisholm. At that time, the interim dean of the law school was a man named Diggs, a nice, approachable gentleman. Prior to the start of the registration period for my last year, I met with him, and I explained my concerns.

"Dean, while I've been here I've worked hard. I have a wife, and, in fact, we are getting ready to start a family. If I have to take Chick Chisholm for Federal Jurisdiction, I know that everything I've done these past years will have been wasted. I know he intends to fail me no matter what I do."

Diggs looked at me, crossed his legs, and said, "Son, I can't do anything about that. We don't allow students to select professors. You are in Section 1, and Chick has that section for Federal Jurisdiction. There is nothing I can do to take you out of that class, so you may as well do the best you can to pass his course."

"But, Dean Diggs, there is no way I am going to pass his course. It's not going to happen."

"Well, son," he sighed, "there is nothing that I can do for you."

Nevertheless, every day after that, I sat in the hall outside of Professor Diggs' office. Whenever he walked by I would throw up my hands as if to say, "What am I gonna do?"

Finally, one day Dean Diggs opened his office door and reluctantly said, "Come here, boy. Come on in here. You're getting on my damn nerves; you're just sickening. I can't come to my office without you sitting out there just moping and crying. Here, I'm going to change this damn thing. Don't say a damn thing to me. Here is your change in schedule. I'm crossing Chick Chisholm off. Dr. Red Morse is now your professor for Federal Jurisdiction. Just get the hell out of my office, and I don't want to see you out in the hall sitting in front of my office anymore."

All I could say was, "Oh God, thank you!"

He threatened, "I don't want to hear that, I don't want to hear thank you or anything of the sort. Just get out of my office."

And with that, I was registered into Dr. Red Morse's Federal Jurisdiction course. It was one of the courses that equipped me the most for the work I've done in civil rights. I was determined to prove Chick wrong and even more determined to justify Dean Diggs's action and prove myself worthy of his confidence. I went on to post one of my highest grades that year. I was near the top of the Federal Jurisdiction class with a final grade of 88. The decision made by Dean Diggs opened the gateway. I was going to graduate from Howard's School of Law.

Every time Chick Chisholm passed by me in my senior year, he just glared. "You got away," he would say. By whatever measure he considered worthy, he had intended that I was not going to be a Howard lawyer. I guess I was supposed to kiss his ass ten times a day and laugh at the Moms

Mabley jokes he told for twenty minutes before each lecture. They weren't funny, but everybody would laugh. Maybe I didn't laugh hard enough.

There was a hierarchy of students at Howard's law school, which included those with a pedigreed family history such as a father who was a lawyer, judge, or doctor, or those who simply had money or who were exceptionally gifted. It was a very competitive atmosphere. We had guys like Bobby Mance, who played football with me as an undergrad. His father was a big-time doctor in DC. Dickey Tynes is now a multimillionaire who stopped practicing law years ago and has a janitorial service that was initially contracted under DC mayor Marion Berry. Speaking of Marion Berry, another Howard lawyer already mentioned is Herb Reid who represented Adam Clayton Powell and would become Berry's chief counsel. There was Bob Washington out of Newark, New Jersey, who dressed so sharp that they nicknamed him "The Senator." Joe Wiggs from Virginia would later handle a big fraud and government bribery case with me in federal court. These guys and others would stand outside, decorating the front of the School of Law in their three-piece suits as the undergraduate girls walked by in The Valley. They came to law school looking like lawyers—like they were already cut and destined, already ordained. They came with money, driving Vettes and GTOs. They were the elite of Howard Law. After class, they would talk with the professors and exchange great legal principals and thoughts. It was a social circle I didn't even try to join. I couldn't be at that level because when class was over for me, I had to go to work, do some substitute teaching, and then get my tail down to the National Archives at night. These guys were the future giants of the legal profession, freshman lawyers before they even graduated.

This was the academic environment of Howard University's School of Law. I harbored no envy, jealousy, or animosity; this was just Howard Law, one of the greatest law schools in the nation. I believe that even with the trials and tribulations I faced, no other school could have prepared me better for the journey I was about to embark upon. Howard Law actually demoralized me, dehumanized me, and stripped me bare. As an undergraduate, I could only marvel at the gods of law, the emperors of the black aristocracy, and the lords of black academia. As a graduate legal student, I really saw it in full bloom. And so, I would graduate from Howard Law among these giants, having been remolded, rebuilt, and reborn until I was a member of the academic elite. I had twice become a member of a family with a national and worldwide history.

Not only is Howard University the largest African American university in the nation, but at that time, it had the largest percentage of foreign students in the world. Coming out of Howard School of Law meant we were not just among what Du Bois termed "the talented tenth," we were also counted among the talented 1 percent. In contrast to white law schools, Howard taught not only contract, corporate, and criminal law, it also provided a tremendous platform in constitutional law and federal jurisdiction that played, and plays, a pivotal role in the civil-rights movement. As Howard lawyers, we were engraved with a commitment to the African American community like no other lawyers. Because of this, Howard University lawyers are readily recognizable. It is not arrogance nor combativeness nor a confrontational demeanor, it is more a compulsion to never shy away from those things that our people need. Howard lawyers are well trained to tackle the cause of civil rights and to take cases on behalf of society's disadvantaged: the have-nots, the persecuted, and the prosecuted. Whereas it is a natural inclination to make money, Howard lawyers are trained to be such an advocate for the persons adversely affected the most by "the system," that it almost takes you away from the root of your economic survival. This is the stamp of being a Howard University lawyer. I believe that unlike any other place in the world, no matter what you do academically you always come back to the fact of the greatness of the Nabrits, the Houstons, and the Thurgood Marshalls. The pictures of these great litigators grace the walls of Howard Law. For that matter, there is even a picture of General Howard, the founder of Howard University, who, as a white man, fought vigorously for black causes.

Howard instills and requires a focused mind-set. You have a responsibility as a black lawyer, an African American lawyer, like no other responsibility, like no other profession, like no other individuals walking the face of the planet. You come out of there as if you are specially ordained. It's like the inspired preparation you receive as a minister, priest, or ecumenical ambassador. You are prepared. You actually walk with a degree of arrogance (as I have been told) and with a degree of academic superiority. You truly emerge believing you are the best at what you do. As your parents told you, you had to be better. At Howard and at Howard Law you are trained for excellence. As a Howard graduate, you are trained to take it to another level; it is instilled upon you that your road is going to be rougher, your mountain is going to be higher, and your river is going to be deeper. Therefore, Howard Law has to fortify you as a lawyer, as a professional. It has to fortify you more than it does graduates of its other professions, because as a lawyer you cannot bury your mistakes like a doctor or file away your numbers like an accountant. You are going to be worldwide and on stage. They tell you at Howard Law that you cannot walk out and become an embarrassment to Howard Law. "You cannot go out spreading ignorance around the world. if there was any potential of you being an embarrassment to Howard Law, it would be a huge wrong". That is their mentality. That is their philosophy.

Today I am quite proud of the fact that the former dean of this great institution is a Baltimorean, Kurt Schmoke (Baltimore's former mayor), sharing Baltimore City's historical roots with Supreme Court Justice Thurgood Marshall, a graduate of Howard Law.

While society might ask, "Dwight, why did you want to be a lawyer? You could have become a doctor or a dentist or a teacher or a preacher or a mortician." These were all acceptable allowed professions for black men and women in society, because white society didn't really want to treat, teach, preach, or bury, much less interact with or touch, black people themselves. But to become a black lawyer or a black accountant, two fields dealing with society's legal system and economics, was taboo, so very few men and fewer women rose in such areas. I remember Occupation Day back in elementary school. When asked, I said, "I want to be a lawyer." That drew laughter because our people in the '50s and '60s were just not conditioned to this possibility. Being a lawyer then was something no one should reasonably aspire to be.

Even my father later told me at one time, "Dwight, maybe you should consider going into the military. You are a commissioned officer in the

United States Air Force. Why go to law school? When you come out they probably will not let you pass the bar." This was a realistic consideration by many people, even from a fighter like my father. I remember the dean of Howard Law, Dr. Miller, asked me in my last year of law school, "Son, where are you going to practice?"

I said, "Maryland."

He sort of looked at me and laughed, "You know that it is a joke for anybody coming out of Howard to pass the Maryland bar. They just won't let you pass. They might let blacks pass if they went to the University of Maryland, but coming out of a black law school, they just won't pass you."

The Vietnam conflict draft deferment that was in place during my undergraduate years continued through law school, and although I became a commissioned Air Force officer, my service in the Air Force Reserves also translated into immunity from the draft. As I neared the end of law school, the issue before me, given that I had not yet passed the bar exam, was whether I would go into JAG (Judge Advocate General) service or whether I would go into private industry. I would later be admitted to the Nebraska Bar in 1971.

By that time, Richard Milhous Nixon had become president. I remember the night he defeated Hubert Humphrey. I sat up all night until Nixon was declared president of the United States. I cried that night, but not as bad as when John Kennedy was killed. (The question is always, "Where were you when they shot JFK?" We were on a bus heading to Livingston College for a big football game the following day. The game was canceled.) I cried again when Martin Luther King Jr. was killed and when Sirhan Sirhan killed Robert Kennedy. These events had a tremendous effect on me and all Americans. We all shared a lot of tears during those tumultuous years.

I went into a negative state of mind when Nixon became president because I was such a fan of Lyndon Baines Johnson. I firmly believe that Johnson was one of the best presidents, if not the greatest, for African Americans. Lincoln did what was political, and Eisenhower and Kennedy did what they had to do, but Lyndon Baines Johnson, a Southern Democrat from Texas, actually forced through legislation championed by the likes of Martin Luther King Jr., Clarence Mitchell Jr., and Whitney Young. He signed the 1964 and 1965 Civil Rights Acts, and put teeth in the civil-rights movement. Then there was Nixon, pictured with Sammy Davis Jr. (not to disrespect Sammy) hugging him around the waist, smiling. I thought that was such a negative picture because I found Richard Nixon to be distasteful at that time. Never would I imagine I would have the opportunity to work in his administration and that he would turn out to be very different from the image that was projected.

During 1970, my last year at Howard Law, I attended Employment Day. Because of Nixon's big push for affirmative action, all of the big corporations were there. Still in its embryonic stage, affirmative action was a concept birthed during the Johnson administration that came to fruition in the Nixon administration. I didn't see it coming, but my first job out of law school would be in the Republican administration of President Richard M. Nixon. I was recruited by the Small Business Administration to serve in the national office. In fact, I was only the second black hired as a trial lawyer in the Office of Litigation, one of the national office's three legal divisions. My boss in this division was Bob Webber, a Republican good ole boy out of Kansas who told me right off that he opposed affirmative action. Nevertheless, he hired me because of affirmative action. In speaking to Mr. Webber, one day I said, "With all due respect, Bob, if not for affirmative action, you all would have never come to Howard University, and I would not have even been considered. You undoubtedly would have only gone to Harvard, Yale, or Georgetown, where the sheer number of white candidates would have outnumbered the qualified black candidates. Some of them might have even been more qualified, but with so many whites in the crowd, a black person would not have had an equal chance. So, because of affirmative action, you came to Howard University, and you got the opportunity to interview well-qualified persons of color. This was an opportunity that wouldn't have been available before."

That is what affirmative action did. It gave us an opportunity to compete, to be interviewed. It did not give less qualified people something they did not deserve. It gave African Americans the opportunity to be at the table. If it had not been for affirmative action, Exxon, General Motors, AT&T, the Justice Department, the Small Business Administration, and others would not have been at Howard Law. Because of affirmative action, they were, and Bob Webber, the general counsel of the Office of Litigation, hired A. Dwight Pettit.

I had beefed up my studies in law school to make up for what I had not done as an undergrad. I took every kind of business and accounting-related course available, including Commercial Law and International Commercial Affairs. I was not going to repeat the same mistakes. As the Lord would have it, being hired by the Small Business Administration once again threw me totally into the world of finance. However, this time I was a bit more prepared, albeit not as prepared as those who had majored in economics, business administration, or accounting. All of a sudden, I was swimming in a sea of white lawyers with strong economic backgrounds from Harvard, Yale, UCLA, Georgetown, and the University of Virginia. I was on another playing field on another level. Everybody had been the valedictorian of his class, the cream of the crop, the top of the top. At that time, the SBA had about 175 lawyers across the country. The only other black attorney who had been hired was Leon Buche who was now in the Washington, DC, district office. The main office where I was hired was the national office that had about 60 attorneys. The only other blacks in the national office were the secretaries and there were no female lawyers period, black or white.

On day one, Bob Webber called me into his office and gave me his "young man, we're going to get you started" speech and then handed me a stack of folders containing my assignments, which included tasks relating to the Uniform Commercial Code, economic and financial transactions, and investigations. I was numb. In essence, what we did was not only the review of financial packages and banking institutions' foreclosures, but also all of the research for litigating white-collar crimes for the Department of Justice. Whenever the DOJ was going to prosecute someone for stealing money or bank fraud, we had to prepare the foundation and do the paper chase. We had to research and document all bank paper, including checks and how the checks traveled. I had to learn a completely different language.

Instead of returning to my assigned cubicle, I went straight to the library after leaving Bob Webber's office, thinking, *God, what have I gotten myself into this time.* I sat there in a corner, surrounded by commercial law books and awash in beads of sweat, not knowing where to start. I knew these white folks had an expectation of my intellectual demise. I did not think Bob had a racist bone in his body; he was just a good ole Kansas white man who had never met an academically qualified black person before coming to the Small Business Administration. However, I could not say the same for the other whites. They kept peeping over the bookcase as if to say, "What is he going to do?" and "How long is he going to last?" Again, my fat was in the fire. I had been thrown totally to the wolves. But, having been thrown there by Howard School of Law, I was prepared for the fire—even though I did not know it. And again, God was in the library with me.

I must have sat in the library a long time because I remember my shirt was soaking wet from sweat, and I had to finally take off my suit jacket. Bob Webber was so much into making me feel comfortable that I believe this was the reason he came by the library and told me, "Dwight, I'm going to be away for a few days. I've got to tour some of the offices around the country. I want you to take my office until I get back." Although he was the associate general counsel, not the general counsel, Bob had a fabulous office overlooking the White House, with a huge desk, a full library of books, and the support of several secretaries. I know the white folks were looking at me as if to say, "Has Webber lost his mind?" After having been hired only one week before, I was sitting in Webber's office, behind his desk.

One morning, I was so intent on trying to understand and comprehend what I was reading, that I did not immediately hear the voice calling out to me until it got louder, "Excuse me, Dwight?"

When I turned around, I saw this young white guy, Eric Benderson, looking at me. I had been introduced to him once before because he was one of the guys on Webber's staff. He sat down next to me and in a whispered voice said, "Dwight, I know what you are going through, man. I came out of Georgetown Law. When you first get here, this place really blows your mind; it's really demanding. They talk about private corporations being demanding, but this is really demanding. Government here is not laid back and relaxed. It's really like being in a private firm. They really throw a lot of stuff at you in the beginning. This is a young agency that has to prove and justify its existence. It's not like working for Justice or Commerce where you can get lost in the numbers. The Small Business Administration is such a new agency that they're always trying to cut its budget, not to mention affirmation action and loans to minorities. This being a Republican administration, a lot of people don't want to see the Small Business Administration exist. So, we work in double-drive because we are always in Congress or court proving ourselves. Dwight, let me help you. I can help you. I can show you where everything is. I can show you all the short cuts, where the bridges are, and what you need to read and where to go and look."

Unexpectedly, this young man literally adopted me, because he saw another young man struggling. Eric became my guide and my information bank. He was very smart. I later learned he was Bob Webber's right hand. Whenever something came from Congress or came from the White House, you would hear Eric's buzzer go off, and he would say, "Dwight, excuse me, but the boss wants me."

Eric would run into Bob's office, and I would hear Bob say, "Congressman [so-and-so] just called, and we gotta do [this or that]" or "I got a briefing due in front of some senators, and we need to do [such and such]." Eric was the shark that would always go out and get the information—even though Bob had a staff of fifteen or twenty in the Office of Litigation. Webber always turned to Eric, who was really a dynamic and budding star. I began to work hard and feverishly to try to keep up. I knew I had the ability, I knew I could do anything I wanted to do, and I knew Howard University and its School of Law had doubly equipped me. My insecurities quickly fell away. I always love telling about the time, seven months into my employment, when Eric's buzzer and my buzzer went off simultaneously. In other words, there were by then two stars in the office. We became Bob Webber's legal beavers, his legal superstars.

Rookie lawyers had to do all of the personal tax cases for the agency. I did not know this when I came on the job; nevertheless, I was assigned to do employee income taxes in the first year, and this sharpened my skills. I also found out about all of the black executives appointed by Richard

Nixon out of Chicago, Illinois. I met some great people who tried to get me to become a Republican, like Connie McHiggins, who was a director of the Small Business Administration's Equal Employment Opportunity Division; Art McZier, who was the SBA director for minority enterprises across the nation; and, of course, Winfred Smith, who would later become my boss at the Washington, DC, district office of the SBA. Also, there were high-level blacks such as Robert J. Brown (special assistant to President Nixon) who came out of black politics across the nation.

I had no idea these people maintained positions of such power, or more specifically, that they wielded the power of the distribution of money on a national level under the secretary of Commerce.

I stumbled into a black world that I had not known existed. This was a Republican world, all about money. They were not that much into civil rights, per se. Rather, they believed in the power of economic development in the black community, and that this would lead to gains in civil rights. If one had money, businesses, and economic independence, if one owned something and were about something in terms of making money, this was the entrée into mainstream society, and integration would take care of itself. In essence, the vehicle for integration was not so much the law as it was the dollar bill.

Connie McHiggins would ask me to head up an investigation of equal employment within the agency. I was, by then, a trial attorney and tax attorney for the agency, so this new assignment broadened my experience and responsibilities beyond the borders of my division. People like Connie McHiggins and Art McZier were impressed. The word traveled through the establishment that there was a black lawyer in the Nixon administration who came out of Howard Law who was not an affirmative action bust, who was a good lawyer who had not folded. They found out that this lawyer had not only been hired, but he was accepted and moving within the white establishment of the agency. The blacks higher up in the Nixon Administration began to meet and adopt me. As the head of EEOC's internal investigations within the entire agency, I was given the directive and budget to review all of the SBA's six hundred personnel records, hold hearings, and make findings of fact and determinations.

Once I became active on the national scene at the SBA, I interacted with a broader hierarchy of professional African Americans, who doubted me at first. With me being a black attorney, some of the blacks were somewhat standoffish about whether I would be conservative, especially because I had been ordered to head the equal-employment investigations. I met some great people in the agency including Neil and Bruce, who were staff employees. These guys were among the SBA personnel who hung out during lunchtime in front of the government buildings to discuss politics and world affairs.

In the evenings, I had several social circles. There was Harry Goodman and his world of weekend-long parties and Pickett Thomas and longtime friend Delores Zimmerman, known as ZZ, who was DC's gorgeous Ms. Socialite along with Ms. Heady Nelson. Through Heady, my wife and I would meet and join with her and Isaac Hayes at the opening of his movie *Truck Turner*. And ZZ would keep us informed of DC's social calendar. Of course, I had the continuing social circles of Kappa, which included my main running partners, Ernest McIntosh, José Barnes, and the infamous DC socialite Charles (Lobo) Taylor. I played touch football on Saturdays with the government league and finally had a chance to play quarterback on the SBA touch football team. This was serious football at that time, because we played big teams such as the State Department, the justice department, and the Commerce Department that were manned by former college athletes, former pros, or semi-pros who had transitioned to working for the government.

On top of my tax work, equal employment investigations, and everything else, Bob Webber brought me a case out of Colorado dubbed "The Big-4 Case." This was the first case in the nation to test the Nixon affirmative action decree setting aside certain monies for minority businesses. This would later be known as the "8(a) Program." Under this program, promoted by Nixon, first preference went to minority firms even though bidders might have included white general contractors, as the Supreme Court had ruled that you could not set aside money just for African Americans. This would later be distorted because whites would come in and set up black fronts under white ownership to get federal money. In light of these challenges, I was called in to help write, in conjunction with the Justice Department, the parameters and definition of a legally defensible affirmative-action opportunity program. We came up with a concept to withstand legal challenges: economically deprived. Those who are economically deprived should arguably partake of the benefits of the federal government's affirmative-action programs. This helped to save the programs (although diluted), because economically deprived included women, Hispanics, African Americans, white Appalachians, Native American Indians, and other people who were being deprived. The irony was that as one of my first major assignments in the Small Business Administration, this affirmative action rewrite called upon me to defend affirmative action for an administration that blacks had considered hostile. It was mind boggling to me that Richard Nixon, who blacks despised so much and had fought so hard against his election was throwing out money like water. If you had a company, you got paid. Richard Nixon created a bank lending initiative for minorities, called MESBIC, because SBA could not otherwise loan money fast enough directly. Nixon gave seven million dollars to Floyd McKinsick to open up Soul City in North Carolina. Floyd got the money, but I do not know what happened to Soul City. When I became district counsel for the SBA district office in DC under Director Win Smith, a strong black administrator who in fact was the only black SBA director in the nation, I approved Marion Berry for his second loan upon direct orders of the White House to Mr. Smith after Berry had defaulted on his first loan. At the time, Marion Berry ran a company (Pride Incorporated) that distributed trash cans bearing advertisements on them. Berry, who had his head on right and never forgot where he came from, was a black activist marching on his way to becoming the mayor of DC, despite the fact that he was an alleged womanizer who hung out at all of the clubs on the Strip. Everyone who had anything to do with Berry got rich. The second SBA loan that I approved for Berry allowed him to refinance and save Pride Incorporated, which ultimately allowed him to come back and run for mayor. I am very proud that I had a small part in that. I did not argue with my boss Mr. Smith because the White House, the Nixon administration, had ordered it. I was actually in the bowels of an administration that was very much about economic development for African Americans—the total opposite of what I had been programmed to believe. Yes, I am talking about Richard Milhous Nixon. Where Johnson saw legislating for civil rights, Nixon saw economics. This thrust me into opportunities to work with the Justice Department where I was groomed in preparation of major bank-fraud investigations. Mr. Webber would get an award from the Department of Justice for one of my cases, a major white-collar crime prosecution. He got the award; I got the promotion to a GS-12. He was associate general counsel, but I got the accolades within the office, thus defying all the expectations of the old boys' crowd who believed I would come in and fail.

Chapter 12: My Military Career

I enjoyed three tremendous years at the SBA—years of learning and valuable experience. But one day, while still there, I got a strange phone call from my mother. She was very upset, and she said, "Son, I know you were involved in things during the riots and demonstrations and everything, but, son, what have you done now? The FBI called, and they want to see you in Baltimore City right away. They left a number at the house, and they want you to call them."

I was stunned. The FBI? Back in law school, along with many other classmates I had picketed the Department of Justice. Also, I personally knew people involved in the civil-rights movement at the time, including H. Rap Brown and Cleve Sellers. They were the young national black leaders back then and during my years in SBA.

When I got to the FBI office in Baltimore City, they addressed me as lieutenant, and asked me to sit down.

The agent said, "Lieutenant, we have a proposal for you. As you may know, the director, Mr. Hoover, has been looking for Negro agents, and we have done a background check on you. We have reviewed everything about you, and Mr. Hoover would like to see you become an FBI agent."

To say I was shocked was an understatement. I asked for a further explanation.

"Well, Lieutenant, what we had planned was that you would go into the Air Force with your current commission as a first lieutenant. But, you won't really have to put on an Air Force uniform. Instead, you will become an FBI agent and draw both salaries, one as a lieutenant in the United States Air Force and the other as an FBI agent. You will be sent for training as an FBI agent, and, you're going to like this part—"

I interrupted, "What's that?"

They continued, "All we want you to do is hang out in DC."

I looked at the pictures on the wall, and that was when it dawned on me what they wanted me to do. I had gone to school with Stokely Carmichael and H. Rap Brown, I had participated in some demonstrations, and I had the big bush, so they wanted me to be a stool pigeon. They wanted me to infiltrate the Black Panthers and other black militant organizations. They wanted me to put on jeans and hang out in the nation's capital by the Potomac River, Lincoln Memorial, or Washington Monument like a hippy or beatnik or whatever, or down around Capitol Hill. They wanted me to be a conduit of information back to the FBI against my people. They wanted me to be an informant.

For that, I was going to be doubly compensated, including all of the military benefits of an officer. I was just a GS-12 in the SBA at the time, so I could not readily imagine what this offer would earn me. I couldn't make the calculation in my head that fast. But I didn't need to.

I looked around the room and I said, "Gentlemen, I am really honored, and you can tell Mr. Hoover that I am deeply moved by this trust." I did not want to be too sarcastic because after all, I was talking to the FBI. "But some of these people you have up on the wall are friends of mine, especially Mr. Brown up there. He was my quarterback in college. I am sure you know that. I think I hear what you are saying, and I think I understand what you are saying, but please tell Mr. Hoover, 'Thank you, but no thank you.'" I got up, exchanged pleasantries, and walked out. I later called my mother and father, and I told them that I had not done anything wrong. I explained that the FBI just wanted me to be an agent for them, which was an offer that I refused.

About two or three days after I got home, I got orders in the mail that read, "Lieutenant Pettit, you are hereby called into active duty."

I said to Barbara, who was standing in the room with me, "Well, it looks like I am not going to be at the SBA much longer. We are in the middle of a war, and the United States Air Force is calling me to active duty."

Then I read the rest: my orders told me to report to Denver, Colorado, for training as an intelligence officer. I said to Barbara, "Whoa! Wait a minute, what is this shit, an intelligence officer? Those sons of bitches told me that if I passed a bar I could go into the Judge Advocate General's office as an attorney. By then I had been admitted to the Nebraska Bar. Now all of a sudden they are going to renege on me? Nope, that is not going to happen."

Barbara replied, "What do you mean, 'That's not going to happen'? You are an officer, and you have to do what they say. You have to do what they tell you to do."

I was really, really pissed off. They were going to make me do what I refused to do for the FBI. All it took was for the FBI to make a call and tell the Air Force that I had rejected their offer and the Air Force should call me to active duty. Now they were going to make me do involuntarily what I would not do voluntarily. They were going to compel me to be an informant for the military.

On Monday morning, I put on my pretty little Air Force uniform of starched, crisp, summertime khakis, my lieutenant's bars, my sharp cap, and my sunglasses, and I marched right down to the Pentagon. I just walked into the Pentagon.

I snapped off my salute when I was greeted with, "Lieutenant, who are you here to see?"

I said, "I am not exactly sure who I should see, but I think that I want to start with the Department of the United States Air Force."

I was admitted into the Pentagon in full uniform and started knocking on doors, oblivious to what I was doing. I knocked on doors to the offices of the secretary of defense, the secretary to the Air Force, the secretary of this, the secretary of that, and finally I hit a door that said "Secretary Render, Secretary of Reserve Affairs for the United States Air Force."

I told the receptionist in this large office that I wished to speak to Secretary Render, and in answer to her question "What about, Lieutenant?" told her I preferred not explaining at that point.

As it turned out, Secretary Render was just coming out of his office, and he asked me directly, "Lieutenant, what's the problem?"

I nervously introduced myself as Lieutenant Alvin Dwight Pettit, and he could readily see I was stressed out.

Secretary Render said, "Well, Lieutenant, come on in here, and sit down, son; let me know what the problem is." I had actually gotten into somebody's office!

I said to him, "Secretary Render, thank you so much for seeing me. I have been called to active duty, which is not a problem. However, I went to law school, and I passed the bar, although not yet in Maryland; I expected to be brought into the United States Air Force in JAG." I went on to tell him what happened with the FBI, and he said, "Well, son, why didn't the Air Force bring you into the legal division? I heard they need Negro lawyers. Hold on a second." He reached over and grabbed the phone. "Get me the Judge Advocate of the United States Air Force."

I thought to myself, *Oh shit!*

He said into the phone, "General, I've got a young Lieutenant Alvin Dwight Pettit down here, and I don't understand what is happening. Come on down to my office, and call General [so-and-so] and General [so-and-so]. Tell them to pull some files. I want to get to the bottom of this."

It didn't take long before his office was packed with senior officers. He said to them, "Now this young man told me that he's a lawyer, he graduated from law school, and he's working for the federal government. You called him up to active duty, and you want to make him an intelligence officer instead of a lawyer. I thought y'all needed Negro lawyers."

One of the generals said, "We do, Mr. Secretary. But, we took 50 percent of the Negro lawyers that applied for JAG, and Lieutenant Pettit was not in the 50 percent that we took."

Secretary Render said, "Oh, okay, Lieutenant Pettit was not in the 50 percent. So, Lieutenant Pettit didn't make the grade or what?"

The general glanced at his file. "No, he made the grade. He was near the top at officer's candidate school, and he was in the top third when he came out of law school. We took 50 percent of those that applied."

The secretary said, "Well, how many Negro lawyers applied, and how many did you take?"

The general answered, "Two applied."

"Oh, so out of two lawyers, you took 50 percent, meaning you took one. Is that right, General?"

They were so embarrassed. I could see them turn red. When there was no answer, Secretary Render continued, "So you're telling me that you had two Negro lawyers, and both of them applied to be JAG officers in the United States Air Force. You took one, and that's what you are calling 50 percent? Well, who is this other one, and how much more is he qualified than Lieutenant Pettit?"

The general said, "Well, sir, he's really not any more qualified. The only difference was that he was the wing commander at Howard University, and Lieutenant Pettit was the group commander at Howard University. Lieutenant Van Brakle was chosen to go into JAG, not Lieutenant Pettit. Lieutenant Pettit was qualified."

The secretary said, "I'll be damned, Lieutenant Pettit is qualified in every way."

I interjected, "Well, Mr. Secretary, I was playing football at the time, and I agreed that Lieutenant Van Brakle would be wing commander and I would be group commander."

The secretary said, "And that's the only distinction between them? As bad as you all need Negro lawyers? How many lawyers do you all have in the United States Air Force, Negro lawyers?"

"Well, two or three, sir."

"And you had these two top young men from Howard University, and you won't take Lieutenant Pettit. Okay, gentlemen, I see the picture. I heard it. You are all dismissed."

You could feel the tension in the air. He said, "Lieutenant, I am very, very sorry. I am glad that you brought this to my attention, and you will hear from my office."

There was a telegram waiting for me with I got back to my desk at the Small Business Administration. It was a notice of military discharge.

It read, "Dear Lieutenant Pettit, you are hereby being discharged immediately from the United States Air Force for medical reasons. It has been determined that you have left ventricular hypertrophy of the heart."

I thought, *What the hell is left ventricular hypertrophy?*

I immediately went to Mr. Webber and told him I had met with the Air Force that morning and suddenly found out I was half-dead and needed to see a doctor right away. I ran straight to the doctor's office and showed him the telegram.

"Doc, what's the matter with me. I'm still a young man."

After examining me, he said, "Mr. Pettit, there is nothing wrong with you. Evidently, you and the Air Force have had some type of political collision. There is nothing wrong with your heart. You have a little bit of an enlargement of the left ventricle on the side of the heart that pumps, as do most athletes who train and run a lot. It is not an abnormality; it is within range. This is not the kind of thing that disqualifies you from military service. You are an athlete, and in fact, I believe you passed the physical as a pilot. Son, believe me, there is nothing wrong with you."

I thought, *Well I'll be damned. Those sons of bitches have discharged me. I would not do what they wanted me to do, and now I have embarrassed them, so they are going to discharge me. I'll be damned.*

I went home and showed Barbara the telegram and doctor's report. Within just one week, I had gone from being an FBI recruit to being an intelligence officer, and within the past twenty-four hours, I had gone from being an intelligence officer to getting a medical discharge—albeit an honorable discharge.

When I got to work the next morning, my mind was still blown. I read the letter about my discharge over and over. "Honorably discharged" it said: a medical discharge. I knew my papers would be forwarded, and my military services ended.

Damn, this is happening. But what if I'm drafted? Can I still get sent to Vietnam? I reflected on what had happened to my father when he wanted to be a pilot prior to the creation of the Tuskegee Airmen. They drafted him and sent him to England.

What in the hell is going to happen to me?

I sat there in my office, doing nothing, until Margaret (Mr. Webber's secretary) said, "Mr. Pettit, you have a call. It's the United States Navy, Admiral Zumwalt's office." Well, right at that time, Admiral Elmo R. Zumwalt was on the cover of *Time* magazine. He was a tough, tough, white guy who had just been appointed by Nixon to be the chief of naval operations. One of his stated goals was to rid the Navy of racism and discrimination. He wanted more black naval officers and more black CO personnel.

I picked up the phone, nervous as hell, and before I could say anything I heard, "Lieutenant, this is Commander [so-and-so]. I'm with Admiral Zumwalt's office."

I think I said something like, "I understand. What can I do for you, sir?"

"We heard what the Air Force did to you. Admiral Zumwalt wishes to send his greetings to you."

"Thank you, sir." I did not know Admiral Zumwalt knew I existed.

The voice on the line continued, "Yes, a lot of people have heard about you in the last forty-eight hours. You have done a lot to sort of ... well, rock the Pentagon. Admiral Zumwalt is looking forward to meeting you. Secondly, Admiral Zumwalt wants me to extend to you the opportunity to become a JAG officer in the United States Navy. Admiral Zumwalt asked me to tell you that you and your lovely wife, Barbara, can pick any naval base in the world for your assignment. You will not be brought in as a first lieutenant, but at the naval equivalent of a captain. I would also like to inform you that there is only one other Negro officer in the Navy's JAG office. You will be our second. The admiral is looking forward to meeting you and Mrs. Pettit. We need to set up a press conference, and we would like to get your answer today by phone. The Admiral would like to go public with this as soon as possible."

I think the commander had more to say, but I could not help interrupting, "Wait a minute. Are you saying I'm out of the Air Force?"

He said, "Yes, sir. You're out."

"But did you see the problem with my medical situation?"

"Lieutenant, that was total bullshit. We are sure by now that a doctor has told you that it was bullshit. It was a political decision because you embarrassed the Air Force. Admiral Zumwalt does not give a damn about that. As far as we are concerned, you are in excellent condition. We have looked at all of your medical history and all of your background, including your academic background. We also found out that you are a great lawyer in civilian life with the Small Business Administration. Our arms are opened to you."

My mind was now reeling, but I had to ask one more question, "Am I going to be drafted if I don't do this?"

"No. As to the Air Force you are out; you have been honorably discharged, and your service is done. You will be coming into the Navy at your own choice. There is no other obligation."

I said, "In other words, if I don't accept your offer, nothing will happen to me. I'm not going to be drafted, and I am out of the Air Force; I don't have to come into the Navy, and right now I am a civilian."

"That's correct, Lieutenant. We would love to have you, but there is no force or no coercion here. This is your decision."

It is amazing how fast a dumbstruck mind can become crystal clear. I said, "Please tell Admiral Zumwalt that I am honored, and I will convey this offer to Mrs. Pettit. I am sure she will also be honored. Please tell the admiral I am a very big fan of his and that I have been reading about him and what he's doing in terms of our armed forces and the nation. Tell him that I appreciate his offer, but no thank you, sir. I think I'm going to stay out."

There was a slight pause on the line before he said, "Well, Lieutenant, if that's your decision, we respect it, but we wish you would have joined the Navy, and we wish you the best of luck, sir. I will convey your message and your respects to the admiral. Good-bye, Lieutenant."

That was the end of my military service.

Officer's training

U.S. Air Force Officer's graduation class 1967

Chapter 13: Private Practice

I was admitted to the Maryland bar in June 1973, after extensive litigation, specifically *Pettit v. Gingerich* (Board of Law Examiners), 427 F. Supp. 282 (1977).

However, it would not be the court ordering my admittance, but the fact that I officially passed the examination. I assert without hesitation that I passed on the first take. Statistics had shown blacks passing at a rate of one or two per exam out of about ten or twenty taking the exam, meaning 7 to 10 percent of the blacks sitting for the exam passed, while whites passed at an overall rate of 70 percent. These statistics were constant except for one year, 1969, when five blacks were admitted. Most were from prominent political Baltimore City families or graduates from the University of Maryland Law School. Again, due to the tenacious litigation of my attorneys Kenneth Johnson and Elaine Jones, funded by the NAACP Legal Defense Fund, my case (being the first lawsuit of about twenty filed around the country) illuminated the issue. After filing my suit, I advised black legal graduate groups around the country as to how to duplicate the litigation. During the litigation, the State implemented the multistate exam (a national objective exam) as well as other safeguards to prevent pre-exam applicant identification.

Once admitted to the Maryland bar, I resigned from the SBA, and Barbara, Alvin Jr. (then five years old), and my daughter, Nahisha (then two years old), and I came to Baltimore City and moved to the Bonnie

Ridge Apartments. I opened my first law office at 800 N. Charles Street, Baltimore, Maryland, an old building undergoing renovation on the northwest corner across from the Washington Monument. Overseeing and managing the structure's redesign was a young white architect by the name of John Clarke. John personally showed me the property, and we became real good friends. The office suite I selected had stained-glass windows, dark wooden ceilings, and a huge fireplace. This was going to be a gorgeous building, but in the meantime, we dealt with scurrying rats, debris, power saws, noisy hammers, and all the other things that go with any major renovation. Through my attendance at bar meetings and dad's case, I had reconnected with my childhood friend Michael Mitchell, who was working out of the offices of his mother, Attorney Juanita Jackson Mitchell. Mike's father was Attorney Clarence Mitchell Jr., who was widely known on Capitol Hill as "the 101st senator." Mike's oldest brother was State Senator Clarence Mitchell III (recently deceased).

After I moved in the new offices, Mike joined me, my secretary Ingrid, with his secretary Angie, his future wife, as we would open the doors as Mitchell and Pettit. At the time, I was a public defender by day, and Mike was an assistant state's attorney, a prosecutor, by day. By this, I mean, under the rules of the state's attorney's office and the public defender's office, we were allowed to have a civil practice.

I ordered all of the furniture, including burgundy carpeting, a huge conference table, and a big mahogany wood desk for my office. We had everything a law office needed—except clients. We were so naïve. I was really under the impression that you could open up an office, stick out a shingle, and, being a black lawyer in a predominately black town, the clients would just line up out front. We sat there and sat there, watching the telephone, day in and day out. As I watched, the ten thousand dollars I had borrowed from the SBA began to dwindle. I finally made a call back to the SBA and talked to a gentleman who put me in touch with a man in Baltimore City by the name of Samuel T. Daniels, grand master of Maryland's Masons' Prince Hall Grand Lodge. After meeting with him, he gave Barbara a job and politically adopted me. Sam was also the director of CEBO in Baltimore City. CEBO was another SBA MESBIC. Sam became my mentor and I his protégée. He gave me some work collecting on defaulted loans, using almost the same experience I had gained with the SBA. This was the start of my legal practice in Baltimore City.

Between 1973 and 1975, we expanded our practice to include Aire Davis, who was later put on the Court of Special Appeals, and Roberta Gill who was one of the plaintiffs with me in the Maryland bar discrimination suit. The firm became known as Mitchell, Pettit, Davis, and Gill. Cliff Gordy, now retired Judge Gordy, came to work with us as an associate. When Davis and Gill left the practice around 1975, we reverted to Mitchell & Pettit and made the transition from Charles Street to 222 Saint Paul, a very popular building at the time. Our suite of offices was on the thirty-seventh floor, the top floor. Some very prominent lawyers also occupied that downtown building. Even before leaving Charles Street, we were known as a young, aggressive litigation firm; this was mainly because I had won my father's case, and Mike was a high-profile attorney and had contacts. We attracted highly watched cases. Michael was a brilliant lawyer and our "rainmaker," as they say in the law, because his family name helped produce the business. But, as it turned out, Mike was more "the Mitchell" and thus a busy politician, so it generally fell to me to prepare the litigation on the business he produced. But he would always join me at some point in time for trial.

Mike and I were on a high roll as trial lawyers. We thought at the time that we were right out of the movies. Mitchell & Pettit hosted big parties on the first floor of our building in the Longfellow's Club that was eventually owned by John Clarke. The club had the same vibe as the bar in the TV show *Cheers*. We socialized seven days a week. We were the brand new lawyers in a vibrant town going through a political revolution. We were going to be super lawyers.

The dean at Howard Law had told me that if I came to Baltimore City I had to look up Charlie Howard, another graduate of Howard Law. When I met Charlie, Mike and I were in our late twenties, and I think he was in his late forties. Charlie was the president of the National Bar Association, and he became like a godfather to me. Baltimore City also had

George Russell and another up-and-comer by the name of Billy Murphy. But Attorney George Russell was the man, and Charlie Howard was not too far removed. In terms of the young folks, Mike, Billy, and I were it. I came to Baltimore City driving a "white-on-white in white" Tornado with "gangster whitewalls" and a car telephone connected to an antenna on the back (a car phone was a big deal in those days). Of course, I wore a big-brimmed hat cocked to the side and a black, leather coat—and wondered why I was always being pulled over by the police.

One of my first big clients was Ed Hooks, who was president of the Organization of Baltimore Cab Drivers, as well as a businessman and owner of several stores. He retained my services on behalf of the union in a case to be taken before the federal district court. The case revolved around cab fares in Baltimore City and the cost of gasoline. The Yellow Cab Company had raised the price of gasoline contrary to a contractual agreement with the union, so the cab drivers went on strike. The court issued an injunction causing the price of gasoline to be rolled back. As a result, the strike ended and the cab fees charged to the patrons of Baltimore City were reduced. I not only continued representing the union as one of my high-profile clients, I also added Ed Hooks and his business ventures to my roster of prominent clientele. However, the Ed hooks relationship would later result in political disaster in my first Maryland congressional campaign.

Another big case during those first two years of Mitchell & Pettit involved the estate of Maryland State Senator "Turk" Scott. He had been assassinated in the Sutton Place Apartments, gunned down in the garage. There was a lot of speculation because of the two people who were charged, plus the fact that Turk was allegedly under investigation. There were actually two cases stemming from Turk's death, one criminal and one civil. We handled the civil case, the wrongful death case against the apartment complex. Gerald Smith and Ken Johnson, who was my lawyer in the Maryland bar case, represented the people charged in the criminal case. Turk Scott was married to Cecilia Scott, who had a club next to the Howard Theater in Washington, DC, known as Cecilia's. Turk and Cecilia had a gorgeous daughter, Tina Scott, who would be our client in *Scott v.*

Sutton Place, a wrongful death action on behalf of Turk's daughter and estate. Turk's notoriety preceded my entry on the scene, so I was very naïve regarding several things.

We were excited when Mike got the call to handle the Turk Scott civil case. It was a tremendous professional breakthrough for us. When Mike and I got to Sutton Place to investigate, we were the first persons allowed to enter Turk's apartment behind the police. They had pretty much torn up the place looking for evidence. We found numerous photo albums filled with pictures of lovely women and most of Baltimore City's black high society. In today's context, finding these photo albums was like finding e-mails. Mike knew all of these people, and he stood there showing me certain prominent Baltimoreans. Turk Scott was quite the man, but that was not what gave me my first encounter with the underworld. We found some keys. We could not readily determine what they opened, so we left them in the apartment before returning to our office to prepare the civil case we would later argue before the United States District Court and the Maryland Court of Appeals. Our case was based on the proposition that apartment complexes that advertised their security measures, such as security guards and video cameras, have a responsibility to assure security when they knew of prior criminal activity on the premises. When Turk was killed in the basement of Sutton Place, the video camera had been turned off and the security guards just happened to not be there.

Several days later, someone called our office wanting to know about the keys, and some questionable people actually came to see Michael. They were convinced we had taken the keys to a safe deposit box. Allegedly, the safe deposit box held a substantial amount of money and some type of narcotics; I'm not sure if it was alleged to be cocaine or heroin. This began one of the first stressful times in my young legal life, because while I was preparing the case, I got death threats in phone calls received at four and five o'clock in the morning. "You know where the shit is, and if the keys are not turned over in a certain time, you are a dead man." This was so unnerving that I resorted to keeping my short magnum rifle by the bed.

One night, I came home after a couple of drinks—a situation, along with my whole social life at the time, about which my wife was seriously aggrieved. I fell blindly into bed, not really knowing if she was there or sleeping in another room. Early in the morning, I heard the shattering of glass, and I was convinced, without any doubt, that the persons who had been making the phone calls were coming into the house. Still feeling the effect of several Scotch and waters, I immediately went into combat mode and rolled out of my bed, yelling to Barbara to get down on the floor. She began hollering and screaming, but in the waning fog of drink, I could not make out what she was saying, or more to the point, whether the yelling was coming from her or the people outside trying to get in.

Half focused, I heard Barbara screaming, "I'm sorry. I'll never do it again." I had no idea what she was talking about, so I opened the front door military style and rolled out onto the ground, looking both ways, holding the rifle before coming to my feet. I worked my way to the other side of the house and then ran to the next corner.

Barbara was still screaming, and I kept hollering, "Barbara, baby, shut up!" I didn't see anybody and finally came back inside to calm her down.

She kept babbling, "I didn't do … I won't do it again."

I still didn't know what the hell she was talking about until I realized that the bad guys hadn't broken the windows to get in. It was my wife working out a temper tantrum because of my late hours. She had thrown a bottle through the window while I slept. When she told me this, I was so damned mad that that I must have squeezed or jerked the trigger of the rifle, which was pointed at the ground, and the gun accidentally went off. The bullet blew through the floor, and she took off out the door. I left the gun and ran out behind her. She was running around in her nightclothes, and for that matter, so was I. That being a nice little Jewish neighborhood, nobody came out of their house, but I am sure the neighbors wondered what in the hell the Pettits were doing running around the house in their nightclothes, especially after hearing the gunshot. It must have been quite a sight.

Eventually Mike and I met with certain authorities, and we were able to convince others that we did not have any key or keys as alleged. This was my first major contact with the real underworld hierarchy of Baltimore City. Unlike today, where you have street gangs and corner drug dealers,

East and West Baltimore actually had well-organized crime units back then.

I first met Charlie Berman, an alleged drug dealer, when I went to a party at his home with Mike and Clarence Mitchell III. The party turned out to be a gangster's jamboree. The party flowed both inside and outside, and food and drink were aplenty everywhere. Charlie's swimming pool was shaped in the formation of a *B*, and it was surrounded by beautiful women. Someone had pulled out a video camera and casually taped the evening's events, a tape that would later be seen in federal court. When the camera came my way, the videographer asked me to introduce myself. I obliged and lifted my glass of soda as a gesture of hello. Mike and Clarence also introduced themselves when the camera panned their way.

Later in the evening, the videographer asked Charlie Berman, "Charlie, to what do you owe your success?"

Charlie said into the camera, "I just keep on pushing." Well, that came back to haunt him in court. It would also come back to haunt me when I was under consideration to be United States attorney for Maryland. Perhaps the tape was viewed by the FBI. It was also played during Charlie's trial, which Michael and I attended. One can imagine what I felt, seeing myself flashed on a screen in the courtroom!

Going to the party had been a spur-of-the-moment business decision for me where I was looking to pick up some clients, I did not know who would be there nor did I know the people I met there. And I was certainly unaware of the peripheral circumstances of the evening; it appeared to be a friendly gathering of friends and acquaintances. Two weeks later, I picked up the *Baltimore Sun* and learned who Charlie Berman was. The story reported on a raid of his home by the state police. Among other things, the state police seized certain videos. That's when it dawned on me that yours truly had been sitting in the basement of this man—an alleged notorious drug dealer according to both federal and state prosecutors— being videotaped by someone I did not know.

Mike and I handled just about anything in Baltimore City that George Russell did not want, and after him, cases that Billy Murphy did not want. Many things were not criminal cases, but they were high profile.

For example, Paul Chester was the clerk of the court who had just been indicted, and, as rumor would have it, he was trying to make up his mind whether he was going to go to George Russell or me. He ultimately did go with George Russell, but the mere fact that I was even considered was tremendously complimentary. After all, George Russell was a true icon, and I had just arrived on the scene.

To be thought of as competitive was a boon to Mitchell & Pettit. We didn't necessarily make a lot of money, but we had a continuous schedule, working six to seven days of the week. We had beautiful offices under construction, although it was shared at night with rats scurrying around construction materials. In and around 1977 I would be elected president of Monumental City Bar Association (the Black Bar Association originally founded by Thurgood Marshall). We would become involved in all types of political activity. At that time we would lead the fight to get the first African American on the Maryland Court of Appeals, Harry Cole. It also did not take long for Barbara and me to buy our first house and move the kids out of the Bonny Ridge Apartments. At that time, Mike and I worked until seven or eight o'clock every evening then headed downstairs to Longfellow's to unwind with Baltimore City's up and coming who would stop by. It was one big whirlwind, one big adventurous fun time for Mitchell & Pettit.

Mike was representing clients who were trying to promote a fight with Muhammad Ali. On one occasion, Mike and I flew into Chicago to the National Bar Association Convention, as a guest of Charlie Howard, the president of the NBA. We occupied the presidential suite on the top floor of the Hyatt Regency while promoting our new flourishing firm. Our social life took on a flair of its own: parties, restaurants, and nightclubs like The Riviera along Baltimore City's Fulton Avenue and the Red Rooster on Baker Street. At that time, I had not yet graduated to the Sphinx Club or the 5 Mile House, both of which are Baltimore City landmarks. We worked hard, and we played hard. Life was good.

Every other Friday night, I drove back to DC, my old stomping ground. Washington, DC, was still partially home. Everything in DC was wide open to me, carte blanche. I would pull up in front of the Fox Trap (not the

Fox Trap II) and park my car right at the front door. Goodman (mentioned previously), who worked at the National Archives as a Secret Service guard, had weekend parties. At the time, Gonchos was the club in southwest DC. It had a jazz entertainment and a sunken bar. I had been in the SBA when the club was started with an SBA loan for $350,000, so whenever I walked in, we got the royal treatment. The piano bar was all blue and white and generally filled with the guys I rode with in DC during my Howard and SBA days. Of course, another major social institution was Faces on Georgia Avenue. All of the major DC VIP's held court there nightly. Two of my best friends, Harold Reddick and James McEady were icons in the DC social life, and introduced me to boating and to the Seafarers Yacht Club in Annapolis. Another favorite spot of socializing for black "folk" was the famous Club Harlem in Atlantic City, New Jersey. Our family, including my father and uncles, would go to Atlantic City at least once every summer with their wives. John Pettit and I would meet at Club Harlem to catch one of their famous shows, such as the Temptations, Redd Foxx, etc. The club was on Kentucky Avenue and that was before integration and casinos when blacks had their own businesses.

Around this time, in the middle 1970s, Barbara had to be in DC for a conference just prior to one of Howard University's homecoming games, and we had arranged that I would drive down before the game on Saturday and pick her up at the hotel where she was staying. Not only was my Tornado decked out with flashy gangster whitewalls and a car phone antenna on the back, I was also high styling in a pinstripe suit, a white high-collar shirt, a white, silk tie, a long, black, leather coat, alligator shoes, and a wide-brimmed, black hat. You could not tell me that I wasn't the cleanest thing in the world. I was dressed. I was not home that morning, so before leaving Baltimore City, I had emptied the chamber of my .357 Magnum (for which I had a permit to carry) and placed it in its shoulder holster inside the locked glove compartment of my car.

When I pulled up to the hotel where Barbara was staying, I called to let her know that I was downstairs and then waited. As usual and expected, my wife was late. I sat there waiting and waiting and waiting, until finally I noticed police cars approaching from all different directions.

I thought to myself, *Hmm, I wonder where all of these police are going? What in the hell could they be looking for?* I checked my watch and noticed it was by then almost noon, and because Howard's homecoming game was scheduled to start at one o'clock, I decided to go inside and get Barbara. Before getting out of the car, I glanced in the mirror, and that's when I noticed the police had blocked off the street, as well as the alleys on both sides of the street. The next thing I knew, a big piece of steel tapped me in the back of the head. It was a shotgun. Police were all around me with guns drawn.

"Don't move! Put your hands on the steering wheel. Don't move!" My window was down. The cop was so nervous I could feel the shotgun shaking up against my head. He yelled, "Do you have a gun?"

I answered, "Yes."

He said to me, "Get it."

I told him, "You have lost your damn mind. You get it." I didn't move, and I didn't take my hands off the steering wheel, because I really believed that if I did, I'd be a dead man. After taking my keys, one cop reached into the glove compartment, and then I got pulled out and thrown against the car with my hands held behind my back. I was ordered to get in a spread position up against the car.

After they had my gun and all of the commotion had died down, I said, "Now, gentlemen, I don't know why all this is happening, but I'm a lawyer. Go in my pocket and pull out my identification. You'll find my gun permit and a card showing that I am a lawyer."

Everybody froze, literally. This is not an exaggeration. There must have been thirty or forty police officers out there and at least ten or fifteen squad cars. No one moved until a captain, naturally a white guy, showed up a few minutes later. He came up to me, looked at everything, went back to his squad car, and then returned with a question, "Well, if you're a lawyer, why in the hell are you dressed like this?"

I asked my own question, "Well, Captain, what is it about the way that I'm dressed that offends you? Is it because I have on a black hat with a big brim? If this is going to cause all of this attention, you all can have the hat and coat. What's the problem?"

He said, "Counselor, it's just the way you're dressed—and this here car."

As it turned out, I was apparently sitting across the street from a bank that had been robbed about three weeks before. The coincidental yet interesting thing about it was that the alleged bank robber was a former classmate of mine at Howard, John Dorch. The first I knew of his involvement was years later when he wrote a book mentioning me as his lawyer and the robbery, not together of course. Until then, I had no idea I was sitting in front of the same bank where a black female police officer was killed during the robbery or that I sort of matched the description of one of the robbers. Of course, it was beyond me to wonder why in the world the cops would believe that one of the bank robbers would return to the same bank within a few weeks in broad daylight on a Saturday morning.

At any rate, that was the explanation given for all of the attention I drew sitting in a white car with gangster whitewalls, wearing a black, leather coat, a wide-brimmed hat, and a big Afro bush, across from the scene of a bank robbery and cop killing just three weeks before. The captain said to me, "Okay, Counselor, you're a lawyer. We apologize. It is not our business how you are dressed. But why would you have this gun in the District of Columbia? This license is for the state of Maryland."

I said, "Okay, Captain, if I can talk now without anybody shooting at me, let's examine this. Where do you live? I know you don't live in the District of Columbia." He told me he lived in Virginia. I continued, "So, living in Virginia, what do you do with your gun when you go home? Do you stop and bury it under the bushes? I know you carry it home with you, because Virginia respects your permit when you carry your gun home from the District of Columbia. Then you carry it back. It's the same for me living in Maryland. I think the District of Columbia has to respect my right to come into the District of Columbia even though I am not going home. If I happen to step across these lines for social, political, or business reasons, the District of Columbia should have no beef so long as I stop before getting here to take off my gun, which I did. I put it in the glove compartment, unloaded, locked with the bullets secured in the trunk.

The captain stepped back and convened a little sidewalk head-to-head conference. By this time, my wife had come down the steps, and she was screaming, hollering, and crying, wondering what happened and what had I done. It's always what did I do! Trying to control her, I pointed out that if she had not been late, I would not have been sitting there for two hours, no one would have called the police, and the police would never have mistakenly connected me with a bank robbery.

Finally, the captain came back over to me and said, "Well, Mr. Pettit, the District of Columbia will hold the gun. You can go ahead to Howard's homecoming with your wife. You can come back on Monday morning and pick up your gun with our apologies—and your bullets, which we found in the trunk."

I couldn't help but say, "Captain, if you also want my hat and leather coat, they're yours." Of course, he refused.

Shortly after this incident, I decided that as a young black male I would be wise to reduce the size of the hats—even though presently I still wear my hats and leather coats. As I was under thirty years of age, driving an expensive car, and going back and forth between Baltimore City and the District of Columbia, this was a necessary personal period of transition.

Opening of Mitchell, Pettit, Davis & Gill Law Office

Uncle Hayes, Dad, Dwight, Mom, Cousin Leon Conley

Chapter 14: Politics at Its Best

After we moved to 222 Saint Paul (and reverted from Mitchell, Pettit, Davis, and Gill back to just Mitchell & Pettit), I handled another big case, *The State of Maryland v. Smith*, which was also around the time when I first encountered Jimmy Carter, the next president of the United States.

Mitchell & Pettit was not particularly thriving, but the firm did begin to develop all around. Among other things, Mike was elected to the city council; his brother, Clarence Mitchell III was already a state senator. They were the sons of Attorney Clarence Mitchell Jr., who had been the chief NAACP lobbyist for nearly twenty years, and Juanita Mitchell, who was one of the top lawyers in Maryland. The brothers, Mike and Clarence, were the nephews of Congressman Parren J. Mitchell (now deceased). The elder Mr. Mitchell, whom I affectionately referred to as "Old Man Mitchell," also established an office at 222 Saint Paul upon his retirement from the NAACP. As architect and chief negotiator for the NAACP, his work led to the successful passage of the nation's most vital civil-rights legislation. He was also one of the nicest men a person would ever want to meet. Once at 222 Saint Paul, Mr. Mitchell maintained a close friendship with the Supreme Court Justice, Thurgood Marshall. Furthermore, Mike's mother, prominent Baltimore City Attorney Juanita Jackson Mitchell, was in and out of our firm's office on a daily basis.

Our firm had essentially become two firms: one being Mitchell, Mitchell, and Mitchell, and the other being A. Dwight Pettit, PA. I still enjoyed a very close relationship with the family, but it did become somewhat strained. I began to feel that there were certain family decisions directing the firm. In other words, as much as I loved Michael as a brother, I believed that before we could discuss anything, he more or less had to get his marching orders from his family—from his mother mostly, not so much from his father. I really believed that Mr. Mitchell was removed from our law firm. But Mrs. Mitchell and her son Clarence III were heavily involved in what was taking place in the firm of Mitchell & Pettit. This became evident when I made the decision in 1975 to involve myself in politics.

Having just come back home to Baltimore City in 1973, I did not have any name recognition, but I really wanted to get involved with the presidential campaign. While still in our offices on Charles Street, I began a one man study of who I thought would be the presidential candidates, and who would be successful in 1976. In doing this, I finally focused on two Democrats, Jimmy Carter of Georgia and Reubin Askew of Florida. Nixon was the president and was being impeached when I left the Small Business Administration, and I knew that Spiro T. Agnew would not be considered because he was going to be indicted as a result of payoffs he received while governor of Maryland. When Nixon stepped down, Ford became president. Then I read an article in either *Newsweek* or *Time* magazine about the fact that Governor Jimmy Carter of Georgia had hung a picture of Martin Luther King Jr. in the Georgia state capital. Being a spiritually led person, I said to myself, "With all this press, maybe this guy has already been tapped to be the president of the United States." After that, I focused on Jimmy Carter. I also researched Governor Reubin Askew of Florida. The reason I zeroed in on these two was because I knew that to beat the Republicans, the block known as the "Solid South" would have to be broken, or at least seriously cracked. I believed this had to be done by a Southern white man, either Carter or Askew. One of them would have to run.

In an underground newspaper, I read about the Trilateral Commission founded by David Rockefeller. Among its highly politically placed members were Henry Kissinger, Zbigniew Brzezinski, and this fellow Jimmy Carter.

Additional research revealed that Carter was an engineer and former military man who had been the commander on a nuclear sub. He had also been sent to Japan for studies in higher international economics. It was generally acknowledged that he was extremely smart. As luck or providence would have it, I was serving on the Johns Hopkins University Board for Minority Affairs and I saw a bulletin. The bulletin said that Jimmy Carter was coming to Baltimore City to speak, so I figured, "I've got to go and listen to what he has to say." I went by myself. In his speech, Carter said flat out that he was going to be the next president of the United States. Having said that, he got heckled by some of the people in the audience, but he just stopped, looked out into the auditorium, and repeated, "I am going to be the next president of the United States." He said this with such confidence that he was almost arrogant. It was as if he knew it, and we did not know it. *Oh shit*, I thought. That's when I figured it out. *This good ole boy is going to be president of the United States.* I knew I was right. Something or someone had already chosen him. He was already ordained.

I ran to the telephone and immediately called my wife. "Barbara, trust me, sweetheart, no matter what you are doing, stop. Get in your car, and come down to Johns Hopkins' campus. I have just met the next president of the United States of America! He's walking around by himself, and no one knows he's going to be president but me." I ran back, and I found out where the reception was going to take place. In the reception room, there was just one aide, perhaps twenty-five or so people who, like me, out of courtesy and curiosity, had come from the auditorium, and no security or Secret Service.

Before Barbara showed up, I approached Governor Carter and said, "Sir, I heard what you said, and I enjoyed your presentation. And, truthfully, I believe that you will be president of the United States. In fact, to show my sincerity I want to give you a campaign contribution right now." Then and there, I gave him a check for five hundred dollars. He looked at me, somewhat surprised.

When Barbara came, I introduced her to him, and he offered a compliment, "Oh, you are so pretty. Where are you from?"

Barbara said, "I'm from New York." I bumped her elbow, because she may have grown up in New York, but she was actually from Mississippi. I whispered to her that she should tell him so he could relate to her.

She turned around and said, "I mean, I grew up in New York, but I am really from Mississippi."

"I knew it," he said. "I knew you were a Southern girl." And with that, they hit it right off.

The next week I got a call from Atlanta, Georgia. The young man on the other end of the line introduced himself as Hamilton Jordan. He was the campaign manager for Jimmy Carter's presidential campaign.

He said to me, "Mr. Pettit, Jimmy told us how you warmly embraced his candidacy in Baltimore City. Let me be direct. You are actually one of the first African Americans outside of Atlanta to have done so. We are very excited by your support, in particular because we found out that you are a civil-rights lawyer and an activist in the black community. I hope you are truly on board, and, if you do not mind, we would like to fly a large part of the national staff into Baltimore City to meet you. What we would like to do is give you the direct number to our headquarters here in Atlanta. Would you arrange lunch at a hotel in Baltimore City? We would like you to invite other distinguished black Baltimore City leaders to this meeting. The governor will not be coming, but I will. We would like very much to sit down and talk to black leaders outside of Georgia. We have some very strong leaders in Atlanta working with the governor—Andy Young, Mayor Maynard Jackson, Senator Ben Brown, Martin Luther King Sr., Mrs. Coretta Scott King, and many others. You are one of the first outside of Atlanta. If this is acceptable to you, can you make those arrangements and call us back? We would be very appreciative."

I hung up the phone, and I thought to myself, *Oh my God. I am on the ground floor.*

I was so excited, and I did everything they asked. I set up the meeting at the Hilton Hotel downtown. I immediately lined up attendees, including my mentor, Samuel T. Daniels, grand master of the Prince Hall Masons; Danny Henson, a friend and political operative who would later serve as Baltimore City's city commissioner of housing under the Schmoke administration and prior to that SBA regional director in the Carter administration; and Larry Gibson, professor of law at the University of Maryland and now a member of Ron Shapiro's firm in Baltimore City. It was difficult to bring others to the table in that it was early in the campaign, and others were either committed or holding out for other presidential candidates.

Hamilton Jordan brought the Carter staff, which included a fantastic young white guy by the name of Peter Bourne. I would later also meet his lovely wife, Mary King. From the moment I met the Carter staff, we hit it off. I was a part of the team. I became Carter's operative in the state of Maryland, and I opened up the Carter headquarters, albeit with a limited budget because at that time Maryland was not a target state. I was also asked to arrange a reception at my house for Chip Carter, Governor Carter's son. This was quite a task because at the time no one knew Jimmy Carter. However, I packed my house in West Baltimore for the reception. While organizing the campaign I found a building on Charles Street, pasted posters in the windows, and suddenly found myself in the newspapers. I also made news of a different sort back at Mitchell & Pettit.

Shortly after starting the Maryland campaign, my office door suddenly flew open and Mrs. Mitchell stormed in, despite the fact that I had clients in my office. Caught off guard, I overlooked the interruption, and I simply asked, "Mrs. Mitchell, what can I do for you?"

Unexpectedly, she started in with, "Young man, I am so disappointed in you. You are such a disgrace, a disgrace to Negro Americans. Here I worked my tail off to see that you got an education, and that you were placed in that white school. We spent hours and hours working with you and your daddy. Here you come out of school and come home to work for a Southern racist farmer, a Southern farmer who has no ties to Negroes whatsoever. Who are you to come back here working for a southern redneck? I am so disappointed with you."

And with that, she slammed out of my office. I had no chance to explain anything because Mrs. Mitchell would not let me talk. I really wanted to explain to this great lady and legal giant why I felt I was doing the right thing for our community and nation. This, and two other factors, ultimately led to the dissolution of the relationship between the Mitchells and me. Unfortunately, these issues would come back to haunt me later, especially in politics.

Even before Jimmy Carter, there were other factors that contributed to my first race and my loss in the state's attorney election in Baltimore City. These factors dated back to when I won *George D. Pettit v. United States*. Mrs. Mitchell had come to me and asked, "How much money are you going to get, and how much do I get?"

I said, "Mrs. Mitchell, I came to you about the case, and you indicated that you had already done what could be done and that I could just take the case out of the office. We never discussed the case after that, and you never did anything on the case from that time on, although I recognize all that you did to get the case to that point. I took the case out of your office, all the way to the US Court of Claims by myself."

I later called my parents, and my father said, "Dwight, Mrs. Mitchell was paid, and she was paid well."

My mother also said, "Mrs. Mitchell would call your father on a Friday night and say that she needed five hundred dollars for a hearing on Monday morning. In those days, five hundred dollars was a lot of money, and your father would run all over Baltimore City borrowing fifty dollars here and one hundred dollars there from wherever he could get it. He went to his brothers, his friends, and everywhere. He made sure he had Mrs. Mitchell's money by Sunday night. She would call the house on Sunday night and say, 'If you don't have the five hundred dollars tonight, I won't be there tomorrow morning.'"

According to my parents, this was something that went on for months and years.

My mother said, "We do not owe Mrs. Mitchell any money, and neither do you. Now if you want to give her part of your money, you can. But we do not owe Mrs. Mitchell anything."

As I reflect on it, the better part of valor, I will now say, the correct thing would have been to give Mrs. Mitchell part of the recovery. She had labored for years on that case, and, in reality, my father could not have possibly paid her for what she did. I was young, arrogant, and stupid. I tried to rationalize that a large part of my portion was going into her son's and my business anyway, but that was probably just justification for my arrogance. That probably would have completely changed the political future of A. Dwight Pettit. It could have changed the entire political history of Baltimore City. I do not say this out of ego, nor in a falsely pompous fashion. As this book reveals, this bad decision on my part has haunted me repeatedly. What I did at that time I firmly believe created a major political enemy, and it was not my law partner, Michael Mitchell. My decision possibly produced one of the most formidable, intense, and dedicated political enemies conceivable, namely State Senator Clarence Mitchell III, otherwise known as The Bear. This feud between us would continue over much more petty and insignificant issues, but the fire had been ignited.

At that time, he was the political star of Maryland and, for that matter, one of the political stars of black America. Clarence, considered by any standard to be a pretty boy, drove a flashy white convertible Cadillac and was the youngest black legislator elected in US history. Although he had attended law school, he never completed the program as his brother Michael had. Yet he was becoming one of the most powerful voices in the Maryland State Senate. He was loved, hated, and adored by the citizens of Baltimore City. He had lost the race for mayor, along with George Russell, because they split the black vote, allowing William Donald Schaefer to become mayor. Moving all of that aside, he was still, at that point in time, at the height of his political career. My issue with his mother, in my opinion, gave him reason to manifest ill will against me, although that ill will might have resided there anyway for other personal reasons. Whether my disagreement with Mrs. Mitchell ignited or just fanned Clarence's hostility, I will never know. However, I do know that I had ignited a major issue with the leadership of a political dynasty in the African American community. I was deemed an individual with no political background whatsoever who was now an enemy of the leader of the Mitchell dynasty (namely, the senator), so when Mrs. Mitchell registered her disappointment and staged her tirade, her son Clarence followed up with a political battle that would rage backstage throughout my Baltimore City political career. I would later discover that the senator had possibly blocked my appointment to the Public Service Commission by former Governor Lee and also my appointment to the Circuit Court of Baltimore City by Governor Hughes. I would also find out later that he and his brother Michael Mitchell (my former law partner) almost derailed President Carter's national campaign in Maryland.

At one point in time, during the congressional race that Kweisi Mfume won, we were brought together, Clarence and I, by a mutual friend, James "Biddy" Wood. We met at my house over spareribs and beer and attempted to air our differences and bury the hatchet. The deal would be that he would drop out of the congressional race, throw his support to me, and in return I would assist in his representation and attempt to help him in the WEBTECK investigation, which ultimately led to his indictment and conviction. My argument had been that he could not win anyway due to the ongoing investigation. And, because of the firm, we shared the same political base. He almost agreed, but at the last few minutes of the meeting, he reneged. The pattern was set. I always found Clarence Mitchell III on the other side of an issue or in some way manipulating the other side of every potential issue in which I was involved. For example, as I moved forward with the Jimmy Carter campaign, Clarence became the local organizer of the campaign for Senator Henry M. "Scoop" Jackson, while Congressman Parren Mitchell endorsed Congressman Mo Udall. However, during the latter phase of the 1976 presidential campaign, Clarence flipped his political machine to support Governor Jerry Brown, who was by then a formidable challenge for the Carter campaign. The nation's history almost changed here in Maryland.

The presidential campaign was very intense. The Carter campaign billed me as a close personal friend of Jimmy Carter's. I got phone calls on a weekly basis from Atlanta, saying, "Dwight, we want you to go to Florida and tell them about your personal friendship with Jimmy Carter." Or, "Dwight, we need you to speak to two hundred union people in South Carolina tonight. You'll be introduced as a civil-rights lawyer and a friend of Jimmy Carter."

Everything was always prearranged for me. My ticket was always waiting at the airport, my hotel room already booked, and my ground transportation handled by a Carter aide. Even though I had only met Governor Carter the one time, it didn't seem to matter, because I was already touted as being a friend of Jimmy Carter's. Two or three days later, I would be off to someplace else.

During this time, on a trip to Tennessee with the Carter campaign, I, along with Dwayne Wickham (later the president of the National Black Media) and the late Norman Wilson of the *Baltimore Sun*, met a young woman in her late teens, Oprah Winfrey. This was well before she came to Baltimore City. Oprah and I would develop a close friendship that would carry throughout her years in Baltimore City. We hung out together with the crew that included Danny Henson, Maria Broom, Pam Fields, George Minor, and others. In fact, before she left Baltimore City for Chicago, she attended my wife's fortieth birthday party at our home.

As I see Oprah now in the media, I am not surprised that she would become the person she is today. In my opinion, she was always destined for greatness. I have always believed that some people are touched by the hand of God. She was and is a very bright, intelligent, and sophisticated woman. She is now a very rich, bright, intelligent, and sophisticated woman. Even though the close friendship no longer exists, I have always wished her well.

As the Carter campaign picked up speed and garnered more and more national recognition, the press began echoing, "Jimmy who?" Then as he began to win primary after primary, the question became, "Who is this Governor Carter?" and, closer to home in Maryland, "Who is this representative of Carter?" Once it became obvious that he was an unbeatable competitive force heading into the primary election, attention turned to the naming of the campaign leadership in Maryland. This was really a test for the Carter campaign. Hamilton Jordan, Peter Bourne, and Mary King flew into the state. Because I had been working hard in the city and around the country, I was named cochairman of the Carter campaign for the state of Maryland. Not only would I work directly with Jordan and Joseph "Jody" Powell but I would also meet with the deputy national campaign manager, Senator Ben Brown.

Ben's story was unique because he was an alleged bisexual black man who was very close to being openly gay and was near the top of a presidential campaign. In 1984, gay rights would later play a major role in the Jackson campaign organized under the banner of the Rainbow Coalition. Senator Clarke was named the other cochairman for the state of Maryland. He was a farmer out of Howard County, Maryland, with a distinct southern drawl, who had some reservations about me being named to such a high position in the campaign. However, I could tell he was not a racist; rather he was just concerned about the possibility of turning off white people in the Maryland race. After all, I was not only a black American; I also looked a bit militant at the time.

It was Peter Bourne who announced my appointment, making clear to all that "Atlanta [meaning Jimmy Carter, himself] has discussed it, and the decision has been made. Gentlemen, it's not an issue. The decision has been made that Dwight Pettit will be a major player in this campaign in Maryland. This may be a first in the nation, naming him cochairman along with Senator Clarke. Let me say this again: this is from Atlanta. He will be the cochairman of the campaign along with Senator Clarke. Jim Rouse will be the financial chairman for the state of Maryland and will also be on Jimmy Carter's national fundraising staff. Gentlemen, it's a done deal."

Now, the reason I repeated this is because I want to direct attention to the fact that none of the politically prominent Democrats in Maryland, including the mayor of Baltimore City, William Donald Schaefer, were consulted. Or, even if they had been, the decision had still been made in Atlanta. They may not have had input with the Carter campaign, but they were still the players within Maryland politics, including the Democratic Party candidates vying for state and federal offices. Those players included Congressman Paul Sarbanes, who was running for the United States Senate.

As goes the presidential campaign, so go local campaigns. The old truism was troubling to many. Thus, just as my appointment had a limited impact on the national election, it had a major impact in Maryland. All of the prestige and responsibility that came with my appointment also brought resentment and an extreme amount of jealousy. This was even more so after Jimmy Carter won the nomination. I remember arranging a breakfast at a downtown hotel for one of Jimmy Carter's trips to Baltimore City. All of the major players in the state were duly assembled in a large conference room while Press Secretary Jody Powell and I were in the back getting Governor Carter ready. When we entered the room, we discovered that all of Maryland's big shots—Paul Sarbanes, Mayor Schaefer, longtime Maryland State Comptroller Louis Goldstein, and others—had taken up all of the chairs at the main table except for the one reserved for Carter.

When the governor got to the table, he looked around and, before seating himself, said, "We need another chair beside me for Mr. Pettit." Everyone paused, looking surprised. Governor Carter continued, "I want Mr. Pettit seated right here beside me."

I could see the tension in those white men. Their narrowed eyes said it all. "We don't give a damn what this boy's title is, Governor. How dare you come into our state and dictate that you want this black man to be seated next to you."

Feeling this, I said, "Governor, don't worry about it. It's not a problem."

If one was to know Jimmy Carter, you would know that was not the case. It was a problem until it was solved.

He said again, "We need another chair." Whether that moment served me later in Maryland politics, or whether it served as boiling political resentment, only time would tell. However, I knew I had not only made enemies with elements of the Mitchell family, namely State Senator Clarence Mitchell III, I had now made possible enemies with Congressman Sarbanes (who would become Senator Sarbanes), Mayor Schaefer (who would later become Governor Schaefer), and several others who perceived in me an unacceptable arrogance.

I guess I should have said, "No, boss, I can't sit beside you here 'cause only white folks can sit beside you in this room." That was what I was supposed to say, but I didn't. Maybe that's one of the reasons I am not an elected official today.

James Rouse, a man I later became very fond of, was also initially antagonistic to the idea of my appointment. I think his resistance was born from the arrogance of wealth and unquestioned power, not the arrogance of racism. He was the renowned developer and builder of major buildings, shopping malls, and even cities across the country. In Maryland, his projects included the development of Columbia, Baltimore City's Village of Cross Keys, and later the Inner Harbor. Every time I said something to him or made a suggestion, he would look at me as if to say, "How dare you question me." We even had words on occasion as to the line of authority— that is, until one morning, after a tense meeting, when we actually glared at each other until we silently came to a mutual understanding. The tension never resurfaced.

The Carter campaign continued to grow in Maryland and the nation, but we came close to losing momentum when Senator Mitchell and Baltimore County executive Ted Venetoulis came together for Governor Jerry Brown of California. Venetoulis was a sort of a young pretty-boy political figure. With Clarence Mitchell III and Michael Mitchell, he went to California to counsel Governor Jerry Brown that he should come into Maryland for the purpose of stopping the Carter campaign, not only in Maryland but nationally. Thus, the war for the White House would crystallize in Maryland and in Baltimore City.

Another major player on the scene was the former vice president, Senator Hubert H. Humphrey of Minnesota. He had not formalized his run, but he was considered a popular unannounced contender. The Mitchells and Venetoulis believed that when Scoop Jackson's campaign failed and when Udall hadn't taken hold in the primaries, Jerry Brown could derail Carter in Maryland and create a draft momentum for Humphrey. What no one knew was that Hubert Humphrey had cancer and would ultimately not seek the nomination due to his health.

At any rate, Jerry Brown narrowly prevailed in Maryland, but the intended results did not come about. Further, it should be noted that Governor Brown did not win the Seventh Congressional District, the black political district in Baltimore City. Venetoulis would later come to me during my 1978 campaign for the state's attorney post and suggest that we join forces. My political naïveté as to what was taking place at that time caused me to reject the offer and subsequently lose that local campaign.

In the wake of Jerry Brown's perceived threat in Maryland, the top campaign command immediately came in from Atlanta. This dynamic brought Governor Carter and me closer, unlike the more distant relationship of "candidate" and "campaign operative." Normally the Democratic Party's presidential candidate would not come into Maryland because we are not a large or populous state nor were we at high risk of going Republican. Maryland was (and still is) generally bypassed by the national campaign. So, in this instance, what appeared to be a negative in terms of Jerry Brown's projected success in the race was really a positive for me. Candidates are only sent into those states that are considered battlegrounds. So, but for Jerry Brown, Maryland would not have become essential, and Jimmy Carter would not have been brought in. Moreover, with the growing necessity to carry Maryland, we got additional funds from Atlanta that we would never have received as a nonessential state. I had already hosted Carter's son, Chip Carter, at a reception at my house, and we hit it off quite well. Then, when Governor Carter came in, I had the opportunity to deepen our one-on-one relationship and develop a very nice friendship with Mrs. Carter, a great first-lady-to-be. When she came, it fell on me as the state's cochairman to take her through the black community. At that point, Carter's candidacy had not risen to the level where Mrs. Carter was going to be mobbed or surrounded, so a security entourage was not required. Thus, my wife and I, along with a campaign aide and driver, took Mrs. Carter to various private homes and churches, including the home of Mr. and Mrs. Roland Patterson (Mr. Patterson was the former superintendent of Baltimore City Schools). Mr. and Mrs. Patterson held a major reception for Mrs. Carter. One Sunday alone, we took her to four different black churches in Baltimore City. She was such a pleasant, wonderful woman, and I thought to myself that she would be a perfect first lady for this country. She was so dignified, so poised, and so well-spoken. It was just a very nice experience, moving throughout the city on a very peaceful Sunday with a simply wonderful person.

The trajectory of the campaign generally ran smoothly except for incidental, out-of-context comments made by Governor Carter along the way. For example, he put his foot in his mouth with his "lust in my heart" remark during an interview with *Playboy* magazine. The press jumped on that one. Even more damaging was what became known as the "ethnic purity crisis." This took on the proportions of being a national event, not just a press event. In an offhand remark, Carter said something to the effect that, "The ethnic purity of neighborhoods was a good thing." It was, of course, taken out of context, but it was said, printed, and repeated. He later explained his comment by saying he saw nothing wrong with an Italian neighborhood preserving its Italian heritage and culture, likewise a Greek or Chinese neighborhood and so forth. The press also characterized this explanation as being the bias of a Southern governor, and when it hit the national news networks, the entire campaign trembled on its foundation.

What Carter believed was an innocent misunderstanding of his view of the cherished rainbow fabric of our nation's heritage, was played out in the media as a racist remark. His use of the term "ethnic purity" generated references to Nazi Germany and Hitler's pure Aryan race.

I thought, *Oh no! What have we gotten into here?* I immediately sat down and on my own initiative prepared a five-page telegram telling Governor Carter precisely what he should do and how he should do it. I still have this telegram. I called the Carter headquarters to find out where the governor was at that time, and I was told that he was in Ohio on his way to Illinois. I then dictated my letter over the phone to be sent as a telegram directly to the highest-ranking person traveling with the governor's entourage. In my telegram, I laid out certain specific things that needed to be done: a seven-point plan. I told Governor Carter he needed to come straight back into the black community to reestablish his ties, reaffirm his commitment, and explain what happened. He also needed to contact the major national black religious leaders. He also needed to get on black radio stations. I told him he should be seen in the cornfields of Nebraska in the morning, but heard in Harlem on the radio, not TV, by night. My telegram explained, "I know your relationship with black Americans. White Americans are not going to want to see you embracing black Americans in too great of an extent. You should be in black communities and on the black media networks at night talking to black Americans and then back in Nebraska, Oklahoma, or Missouri during the day, so the national news networks carry you at six o'clock."

When Carter spoke in Harlem, he again said something "off script" that gave me pause: "You and I are going to the White House together!"

I said to myself, "Mr. Carter, I did not tell you to say all of that. Don't scare the white folks into thinking that you and black folks are going to have a big party in the White House!" It was later reported to me that when Governor Carter received and read my telegram, which was before giving a speech in Chicago, he turned to the audience and said with visible emotion, "This is from a young black civil-rights lawyer in Maryland." He was apparently very moved by the substance of the telegram. The next morning I received a call indicating Governor Carter would be in Washington, DC, the next day, and I was to meet him for breakfast at the Washington Hilton. I left Baltimore City that morning, not quite believing that I was going to have breakfast with the probable next president of the United States. I arrived at the hotel and was taken directly to his suite, where I found staff and two people of national prominence already there with the governor. Carter got up from the table, came over, and gave me a hug.

He said, "Young man, I want to thank you for what you did, and I will never forget it as long as I live." It was a very moving moment.

Whenever I was with Governor Carter, on the campaign trail in Maryland, he always insisted that I remain by his side, no matter who else was there, be it governors or senators. I had sort of become an extension of his campaign staff. I had the opportunity to observe personal conversations and negotiations during meetings with national leaders, and I also attended several of Carter's meetings with just Hamilton Jordan and Jody Powell. I had reached a status that was quite unique in the campaign. My advice and opinions had been helpful. We overcame the "ethnic purity crisis," we retained the black vote, and, of course, we maintained the white vote. By then, Maryland was a crucial battleground state. Everything was breaking for me like the hand of fate. An unimportant state was now an important state. A lawyer who just knew Carter incidentally was now a lawyer who knew him personally. I could not only get the national campaign headquarters on the phone, I believed I could also get Governor Carter himself on the phone, at any time, though I never tried.

Then the call came in to me: "Ham" was coming to Baltimore City.

Hamilton Jordan was the national campaign manager. In his wake, the campaign's bigwigs out of Atlanta descended on Maryland. The entire brain trust of the Carter campaign was now in Baltimore City, and the little campaign office that I had opened became the core of the Carter campaign, spilling over into my private law practice at 222 Saint Paul Place. I found one thing amusing about this fascinating transition. My 1973 Mercedes 450 SLC had a telephone. That was a big thing at the time, a novelty. When the good ole boys from the South arrived, they thought of it as great fun. Everyone who got in the car wanted to call back to Atlanta. It became the talk of the Carter campaign in Baltimore City. Stationed in Baltimore City were the people who would eventually staff the White House, including Ellen Metsky, Peter Bourne, Mary Ellen, Mary King, Jody Powell, and of course Hamilton Jordon. Later, after Maryland, all of us arrived in Pennsylvania together for the Pennsylvania primary, where Carter almost clinched the nomination.

Georgia state senator Ben Brown also arrived on the scene in Baltimore City. He was the deputy national campaign director. I had talked to this young man a number of times by phone, and he had told me that he had heard of the fine job I was doing, and he was looking forward to meeting me. When the day came, I was at the headquarters on Charles Street, and someone said, "Dwight, Ben Brown is at the airport, and he wants you to go pick him up." This would start my friendship with one of the sharpest personalities in backroom politics that I have ever had the opportunity to meet. Other major public black figures in the Carter campaign were Andrew (Andy) Young, Maynard Jackson, and of course, Coretta Scott King and Martin Luther King Sr., all from Atlanta.

Andy and Maynard were on a political level on par with Carter. Senator Ben Brown was like Hamilton Jordan: an operative, the brains, a political guru, and wheeler-dealer. He organized the troops, put endorsements together, and coordinated the black Atlanta base into the national web of Carter's black support. As a politician, he was brilliant. What I did not know initially was that Ben had some baggage. As soon as I picked him up at the airport, he got into my car and said, "You are a handsome little thing. You are just lovely—just as pretty as I thought you would be."

I thought to myself, *Oh hell*. I tried to change the conversation, but the next thing that I knew Ben's hand was on my knee.

Once out on the exit road from the airport, I pulled the car over to the side of the road and said, "Look, Ben, we've got a campaign to run. We have a president to elect. I've heard rumors of your sexual persuasion. I have no problem with that, none whatsoever. I have no problem with one's sexual choices or preferences, and I have no axes to grind and no prejudice against homosexuals. But, let us understand something here and now, my friend. I am straight. You and I … it is not going to happen. It is not in the cards. It is not even a consideration. It is not a discussion, and it is nonnegotiable. It is not my thing." While I was saying this, I picked his hand up by his wrist and placed it on his own knee. "Now, Ben, I hope you understand. If you do, let's get on with the business of electing a president, and we will not have to cross this bridge again."

Ben sighed, "Okay, no problem."

This was something rarely discussed in 1976. A lot of things were different then, as they say, "in the closet." Ben was well out of the closet even though he was married and had children. Eight years later, in the 1984 Jackson presidential campaign, being gay was an open and essential part of the Rainbow Coalition. Nevertheless, in 1976, it still had an undermining affect.

I realize then that Ben's raw power and personal actions as demonstrated were a potential disadvantage to him. But his power did not extend to me. I did not report to him. I reported directly to the Carter inner circle. I could do things that other people could not do because I did not come in through Ben Brown. He understood the political meaning of that and the political nuances.

I was the only one who could, and would, say, "Ben, get your act together." No matter what Ben thought of himself, I knew this man was not going to be able to go into the White House. I had to assume the campaign operatives only tolerated his conduct for political purposes and because of his political brilliance. This man who I had developed a strong political friendship with over the months of the campaign and who I had grown to admire for his political savvy, was now not being politically realistic.

So I wrestled with the question, "How is the black connection to power going to be maintained in the White House once Carter becomes president?" In other words, who was going to be the black presence in the White House with access to the president and his inner circle? Andy Young would not be there. He was sure to receive a cabinet appointment. Maynard would not be there. He would remain the mayor of Atlanta. It dawned on me that no one would be there to fight on behalf of the national black community. In any political organization, there is a hierarchy. True, I had direct access to Hamilton Jordan, Jody Powell, Ellen Metsky, and Peter Bourne—the top persons in the campaign—but they were all white.

Different color badges reflected your campaign status. I wore a blue badge that gave me unrestricted access, even to the candidate himself. The only issue was that I had to wear the badge clearly visible on the outside of my clothes for security reasons, which attracted a great amount of attention, especially from the national press.

In fact, one night while on the convention floor, a reporter actually came up and said, "Mr. Pettit, Walter Cronkite is up in the booth, and he wants to go national with you live. We have information that you know who the vice-presidential nominee will be."

I looked up, waved at Mr. Cronkite, and said to the reporter, "You must be kidding," before politely exiting the conversation.

Along with my hotel room, I was given an entertainment suite and asked by the campaign to entertain and socialize with the media. I was also asked to host parties and receptions for the delegates and prominent figures like Jesse Jackson, Maynard Jackson, and Isaac Hayes who were all at the convention. What a week! Andy Young introduced me to Reverend Jesse Jackson, but the future presidential candidate was not too friendly at the time. Little did we know that I would later chair his Baltimore City campaign during the 1984 presidential race.

My access to everyone and to the nominee during the convention was solidified and continued through the transfer of power on the way to the White House. I was more of an independent operative. However, what continued to bother me was that once this was over, who would be the strong person in the White House able to continue advocating the interests of the black community? We needed somebody who would have a direct line to Jimmy Carter. I knew Ben was not going to be there, and I could not understand why he did not know.

To compound this, his wife called my home one night. "Mr. Pettit, I have only had the opportunity to talk with you once, but Ben is such a fan of yours, and he speaks so highly of you. I am going to ask you to do something very personal for me. You know that Ben is gay?"

I said yes.

She went on, "You are one of his few straight friends. He respects you and listens to your advice. The word is coming back to Atlanta that during the campaign he has become more open than ever. I've suffered through this here in Atlanta, but now it's becoming national. I really wish someone could sit down and talk to him."

I promised I would, and shortly thereafter, I called Ben and told him I needed to talk to him. He was in Washington, DC, so we arranged to meet at a restaurant midway between there and Baltimore City.

Ben wanted to invite Attorney Bill Borders, a mutual friend of ours and a campaign operative. Bill, known in DC as "Sloppy Borders," would go on to play a very interesting and major part in both the Carter campaign and the Carter White House with the judiciary. He would also become the president of the National Bar Association. On that evening, the three of us met for dinner, and I laid it out to Ben. "I am hearing things that I do not like, plus your wife called me. I hear through the grapevine that you have an apartment in Washington, DC, equipped with a big round bed generally occupied by four to six men. The FBI is not going to let you take this act into the White House; you have a responsibility bigger than yourself. You have a responsibility to all of us. I mean, you're the man. Andy is going to be busy, and Maynard will still be in Atlanta. We need someone in the White House, but you're not going to be that person. You're not going there. I know you think you will, but with your conduct, your chances of going are quickly dissipating."

Ben looked at me and said, "Dwight, maybe you're right, and the campaign knows about me; I've been cleared by the campaign, and I've been cleared by the FBI. Jimmy said that I will go into the White House with him, and it's not a problem. I know you're my friend, and you're trying to help, and I appreciate it. But, chill out. I promise you, I'm going into the White House, and you'll have access just as you've had during the campaign. You won't have to go to the white boys; I will be there representing black interest."

As it turned out, unfortunately I was right. Ben did not go to the White House. Instead, he went to the Democratic National Committee, not as the national chairman, but as the deputy chairman.

The Carter campaign appointed me to be a delegate-at-large from Maryland and a floor whip at the convention. I was off to the 1976 Democratic National Convention in New York City.

The swirl of activity at the Democratic convention was at its greatest intensity when my wife came down with an allergy attack due to shrimp. Barbara cannot eat shrimp, but she ate some by mistake the night Carter was chosen as the Democratic Party's presidential nominee. She had to be rushed to the hospital but, given the crescendo of activity at the convention, she argued that I stay. My uncle, John Pettit, was there so he took her to the emergency room. After Carter received the Democratic nomination to be the president of the United States, the battle immediately focused on Gerald Ford and the general election. I remained the cochairman in the general election with Senator Jim Clarke and experienced close-combat politics at its most intense level until Carter finally won the presidency.

One of the nicest people controlling communications in the black community at the time was a woman by the name of Ms. Elizabeth Murphy Oliver. She was the city editor of the African American newspaper, *The Afro*. It was home-based in Baltimore City and had tremendous status in that day with a widespread readership up and down the East Coast, including Washington, DC. Ms. Oliver did a great deal for us during the party primaries and leading up to the general election. No matter what the story line, she ran it. Whatever I sent to the AFRO about Jimmy Carter, she ran on the front page. Politically, Carter was the feature of the *Afro* newspaper in 1976. All I had to do was supply the story.

After the Democratic Convention, Ms. Oliver called me and said, "Dwight, Jimmy Carter owes us a favor." She wanted an exclusive interview with Carter. My initial response to Ms. Oliver was that it was impossible to get to him at that time. He had just returned to Plains, Georgia, exhausted after receiving the Democratic presidential nomination, and he was resting in retreat before heading into the general election. No one could gain access.

Nevertheless, with Ms. Oliver's urging, I made a call and got Hamilton on the phone. He gave me Carter's phone number and told me to call the house. When I called, I got Chip on the line and finally Roslyn. I said, "Mrs. Carter, I have the *Afro* newspaper bugging the heck out of me, and I know I'm being a pest to you and the president-to-be. They really want an interview, and I think if you will consider it, it will really help. As much help as they've given us in the primary, I have no choice but to ask. I'm sure it will help us in the general election."

About an hour later, to my surprise, I got a return call from the nominee's house in Plains, Georgia. The caller said, "Dwight, the tickets will be at the airport. Reservations are for a flight into Atlanta. Transfer tickets will be in Atlanta, and you will be flown into the airport closest to Plains. You will bring Ms. Oliver, and your wife is also invited. The Democratic nominee is looking forward to seeing you."

This was on a Monday. On Wednesday, Ms. Oliver, Barbara, and I flew into Atlanta, and in the midst of a thunderstorm, we boarded a small plane to Plains. On the way down to Atlanta, I nursed a vodka and tonic because I simply could not fly without a drink.

Ms. Oliver, being a good Christian woman, kept looking at Barbara and me critically.

"Boy, you are sure enjoying that vodka."

But once that storm rattled our small plane on the way to Plains, Ms. Oliver yelled to the flight attendant over the engine noise, "Give me a couple of those little vodkas!"

Bobbie and I fell out with laughter. From there on, we flew calmly and happily into Plains.

From the airport, we were taken immediately to the Carter residence where we met with Governor Carter in his den. Governor Jerry Brown was exiting as we arrived, and we engaged in a brief debate over the Maryland primary, with Governor Carter stepping in between us and cutting off the discussion.

Before the interview got underway, Barbara sat in the kitchen talking with Mrs. Carter. She also met Amy, the president's daughter. The interview was in the den. Barbara eventually joined us in the den, and Jimmy Carter put his arms around her and took pictures. We would also meet Billy Carter and the president's mother, Ms. Lillian. Jimmy Carter would go on to defeat Gerald Ford in the general election. Then began the start of Jimmy Carter's transition to power.

The change from one administration to another begins with the transition of power, or more to the point, the orchestrated transition into and out of power. This being the president-elect's new administration, new people and résumés came out of the woodwork, followed by round-the-clock interviews. Suddenly, strangers appeared from everywhere, including Harvard, Yale, and other esteemed halls of academia. A framework was set up for the transition. The Maryland players involved with this process were Congressman Parren J. Mitchell (P. J.), who had served as an advisor during the general campaign; Danny Henson, who would later go into the Small Business Administration as a regional director; Larry Gibson, who later would become the associate deputy attorney general of the United States (Criminal Division); and Paul Vance, who became the superintendent of the Montgomery County school system and later, superintendent of the DC school system. Also in that group were George Minor, special assistant to Parren Mitchell, and yours truly. We were the core group from Maryland involved in the transition for the new Carter administration.

Interestingly, being one of the "locals," I often ferried people back and forth from the airport. I ran the most exciting car pool of my life. I remember very distinctly going to the airport to pick up Congresswoman Shirley Chisholm, the former presidential candidate, when she delivered a speech in Baltimore City.

One day, I picked up Andy Young at the airport, and he asked me, "Dwight, what do you want in the administration?"

Being as naïve as can be, I was caught off guard and said, "What do you mean, 'what do I want'? I haven't really thought about it."

"Well," he said, "the time has come. So, what do you want for yourself in the Carter administration?"

There I was, just thirty years old, in casual conversation with a national figure known to be one of the closest people to Carter, being asked, "What do you want?"

In a split second, without really thinking about it, I responded, "Actually, I don't know."

Andy said, "Well, it's time you know. What about a federal judgeship?"

To that, I readily responded, "I don't want to be a federal judge." I felt that I was too young to be saddled on the bench. After a moment of reflection, I said, "I think I would like one of two things: either to be named the United States attorney for Maryland or to be a special counsel to the president."

Now, being a counsel to the president did not mean I had to be "the counsel" to the president, rather I could have been assistant counsel to the president or a deputy counsel to the president. That might seem far-fetched to younger readers of this book, but it should be remembered that John Dean was a young man, only thirty-two years old, when Richard Nixon named him White House counsel to the president. Of course, he may not be such a good example, given what ultimately happened to that relationship. As for an appointment as United States attorney, I think facts will support me that I would have been the first black United States attorney representing a state. Although Carter appointed Billy Hunter (a classmate of mine and now the executive director of the National Basketball Players Association) as the United States attorney for the Northern District of California, to the best of my knowledge, no black person had yet been named United States attorney for an entire state.

At any rate, those were my off-the-top choices. Andy basically nodded his understanding and indicated he would relay my choices to the correct channels. If Ben Brown had been in the White House where he should have been, not only could these things have been more aggressively pushed, it might have happened. As stated, Ben was moved to the DNC, and his hopes to be an actual power in the White House faded.

The fighting and struggle for power by the new people coming onboard intensified, and, of course, none of these new people had anything to do whatsoever with Carter's election. In fact, what can happen in presidential politics is that political enemies are allowed in, sometimes intentionally. In Carter's case, the people who had laughed at him, calling him a hillbilly and a southern farmer, were the same people wanting to share in power. In his effort to heal the party, Carter thought it necessary to put some of the people who were formally his opposition into positions of power. The problem with that approach, trying to be everything to everybody, is that you cannot give major power to your political opposition, although in present day politics one can see that repeated with Obama and Hilary Clinton.

President-elect Carter did not seem to appreciate that political fact. As I watched the parade of characters during the transition, I witnessed the infiltration of the political opposition. The absence of Ben Brown on the White House staff was monumental. Instead, he was sitting over at the DNC. Maynard stayed in Atlanta, refocusing 110 percent of his attention as mayor, and Andy was very busy in New York after being named ambassador to the United Nations. I witnessed firsthand the very fears I had warned Ben about come into reality. Nevertheless, in my early thirties, my access to the president-elect continued, unabated.

My parents and I were invited to the inauguration, and, in fact, I was tapped to be on the National Inaugural Host Committee. Barbara and I danced the first dance in the presidential circle roped off at the first presidential ball with President and Mrs. Carter, Senator and Mrs. Chuck Robb of Virginia, and Mr. and Mrs. Jim Rouse. I was so nervous when we danced; I told my wife to just move her arms up and down, without really moving her feet because I was afraid we might trip and fall in front of worldwide television.

The next morning I was part of the breakfast entourage. After that, I had total access to the White House; it was just a matter of picking up the phone. I attended many White House functions and Barbara and I received regular invitations to state dinners. The first state dinner we attended was for the prime minister of Canada. Our table was just one table removed from the head table, and I was seated next to Mrs. Jackson, the wife of Senator "Scoop" Jackson, while Barbara was seated next to Harry Belafonte. I also attended the signing of the Egyptian-Israeli peace treaty by Anwar Sadat and Menachem Begin. My access was complete, and the relationships I had developed were maintained.

As it turned out, or should have been anticipated, my new unimaginable access to power alienated the top levels of the Maryland political network. It had not endeared me to Senator Paul Sarbanes or Mayor William Donald Schaefer when President Carter had said, "Excuse me, please let Mr. Pettit sit down."

Once, when meeting President Carter with others at the airport, I was standing beside him. Senator Sarbanes (now retired) literally elbowed me out of the way and rolled his eyes at me as if to say, "How dare this young man stand between me and the president of the United States." Of course, he was right. I should have given him his due and arranged for him to stand next to the president, but I was too arrogant at the time. Small things become so major in politics. I had definitely fanned Senator Sarbanes' wrath, which probably caused him to become the major impediment to my becoming the United States attorney for Maryland.

My access to the White House became so complete that I was able to take on a very different type of clientele professionally. For the first time I was no longer handling just robberies, rapes, murders, and narcotic-distribution cases. For example, I took on cases for Fallston Hospital in Maryland and a hospital out of Memphis, Tennessee, as well as the case of a Republican out of New Mexico by the name of Nathan Twining (*Department of Housing and Urban Development v. Nathan Twining*). I picked up criminal cases before federal courts because of my perceived access, or because it was believed I would be the next United States attorney.

One evening, I attended a Sugar Ray Leonard fight in Baltimore City, actually his first professional fight, and found myself sitting next to two white men, Chester Price and Richard Protee. I did not know who they were, but Richard Protee turned to me and asked, "Aren't you Dwight Pettit?"

I responded, "Yes," and we shook hands, traded some brief small talk.

We watched the fight until he turned to me again and said, "We've got a couple of big problems we want to talk to you about, Counselor. Can we get an appointment?"

I said, "Sure."

He asked, "Can we see you on Monday?"

That was not a problem for me, so come Monday they showed up at my office. By then, my own research indicated they were both Republican businessmen.

They began, "We have a problem, Mr. Pettit. We inadvertently underpaid our Medicare premiums to the government, and the extra funds ended up in our hospital's reserves. The government is now taking it back on a monthly basis. Of course, one of the biggest law firms in Maryland represents us, but they haven't been able to stop the flow of money back to the government. What this reverse flow of money is doing is destroying the hospital, because they're taking it back at a rate of $1.5 million per month, and we're a small private hospital, one of the few private hospitals in the state of Maryland. If we could possibly retain you to conduct an investigation to see whether you can help us, we'd really appreciate it. We don't have any connections with the White House, and we understand that you might."

I decided to play big shot. I picked up the phone, and I told my secretary to call the White House and get Peter Bourne on the phone for me. Among other things, Peter Bourne was a doctor and was now President Carter's White House special assistant for health issues.

Peter's voice came through the loud speaker on my phone, "Hey, Dwight, how are you doing? Jimmy was asking about you. When are you going to come over and see us? We're having a cookout next week. And how's Barbara?" I glanced over at my visitors. Their eyes were as big as saucers. Peter went on, "In fact, you want to say hello to Jimmy? Mr. President, Dwight Pettit is on the phone."

I quickly said, "No, no, no, just tell the president I said hi, and I'll be over there shortly."

Peter asked. "When can you come over?"

I said, "How is Friday? What time is good?"

Mr. Price and Mr. Protee now sat openmouthed.

Peter said, "You don't have to have a time; we haven't seen you in a couple of months, and we'll be happy to see you as soon as you can get here." I asked about Peter's wife, Mary, exchanged some more small talk and then ended the call. The gentlemen sitting in front of me had a look of utter fascination. Richard Protee never said another word; he just wrote out a check and pushed it across the desk. It was a blank check.

Carter eventually appointed me to the National Democratic Compliance Committee of the DNC, a very potent spot. The responsibility would involve implementation and enforcement of the party delegate seating rules for the 1980 national democratic convention. Not only did access to presidential power result in a new and completely different clientele for my private practice, it also resulted in a different class of money. For the first time, from a dollar percentage, I had more white clients than black. More to the point, I had white Republican clients with money who needed access to the Carter administration for differing reasons. I always maintained appropriate records, because I remembered the difficulties encountered by former Attorney General Richard Kleindienst when he left the Nixon administration. He apparently received a $250,000 fee for making a phone call that was investigated by the Department of Justice. Being a black man, I knew that I had to be particularly careful about what kind of money I received—from whom and for what.

Such prudence bore fruit, especially when I took on the Fallston Hospital case. I hired a very dynamic young woman by the name of Alee Pinderhughes to help in handling this matter. (Alee's mother Alice would later become the superintendent of the Baltimore City schools.) During the Maryland attorney general's later investigation of Fallston, a review was conducted of my relationship to the hospital—specifically to determine whether I had been retained to do work for Fallston or merely to exert influence. Fortunately, I had documentation indicating that I had assigned Alee to directly handle the Fallston case. We had done substantial work for Fallston, including advising the board of directors and commencing extensive federal litigation. (Interestingly, Alee later went on to serve as an assistant attorney general in Maryland; she is now the senior partner in her own firm.)

My Baltimore City practice experienced several major internal changes. My secretary Ingrid, who had been with me for years, decided to go back to DC, and she was interviewed by the Carter administration for a secretarial position to the president. This particular opportunity did not happen; however, she accepted a position with a large Washington, DC, law firm. Betty Brown and then Aggie Valdez became my secretaries. Betty was a dear person who was also a ground soldier in the Carter campaign. Aggie had joined the office at age nineteen as a receptionist during her early college years. She later went on to law school and became my law clerk before passing the bar exam, after which she became an associate of mine.

We had a nice little team at 222 Saint Paul. However, Michael and I finally reconciled to the fact that his practice was more on course with his family. We decided to go our separate ways. So, we had the carpenters come up and partition our 222 office. They cut in two doors, one leading to "A. Dwight Pettit, P.A." and the other to "Mitchell, Mitchell, and Mitchell," meaning Michael, his mother, and his father. Although his brother State Senator Clarence Mitchell III was not a lawyer, he spent a considerable amount of time in the Mitchells' office.

Still bathing in the glory of having run a successful state presidential campaign, I found myself pushing buttons as to where people would go in their careers and what these careers would be. Attorney Larry Gibson, who had orchestrated the general operation for the Carter campaign in Baltimore on election day, was pretty much on his own because he had a former professional relationship with Attorney General Griffin Bell and later Attorney General Ben Civiletti. Larry and I had worked together on behalf of others. Larry called me one day about sending Danny Henson to the Small Business Administration, so I met with Senator Clarke and Carter officials, and Danny's position was secured. I was also contacted by some people from Montgomery County's board of education inquiring about Paul Vance as a potential superintendent of the Montgomery County school system. I gave glowing praises about his work as a main point man and operative in the city on the Carter campaign, and he got the appointment.

All of these people moved into certain positions of power, and I began getting vibrations and hearsay feedback that I was being put down from inside of the Carter administration. Allegedly, certain people that I had moved into certain positions were bad-mouthing me, saying I was a ladies' man and a player. Negative vibrations made their way inside the Carter White House. No one was there to watch my back except white folks. Ben Brown was not there. Once Ben and I passed the bullshit, we could really sit down and talk politics. Even though Peter and Hamilton were there, I couldn't talk to them in the same way I could talk with Ben or Andy Young. I didn't have anybody of color within the inner circle of the White House staff. Although a young man of color by the name of Kurt Schmoke, who would later become mayor of Baltimore City, was appointed to the President's domestic policy staff, headed by Lou Eisenstat, he came by way of his Harvard and Yale connections, not the political trenches.

Out of the blue, I got a phone call one day from a man with a raspy voice. "Mr. Pettit, we need to talk to you."

I asked, "Who is 'we'?"

His name was Marty Rosen, and he said he was across the street in his law office. He gave me a time when he wanted to see me, but he didn't explain why. This was intriguing, so later in the week I moseyed across the street to keep the appointment. A young politician, State Delegate Ben Cardin (now US Senator Ben Cardin), occupied one of the offices in the firm. His brother Howard Cardin, a well-known young criminal attorney was also in the office. Mr. Rosen occupied an office in the rear. The receptionist ushered me into this back office; just like in the movies, the room was dim with low-level lamp lighting.

Mr. Rosen formally introduced himself and took a long, penetrating look at me before saying, "Young man, take a seat. I've got something to tell you." Uneasily, I sat down as he began to explain, "The word has come out of New York that you are going to be made."

I said, somewhat sarcastically, "Made what? Who's making me, and what am I going to be made into?"

Rosen replied, "The deal is done, you are going to be made the United States attorney for the state of Maryland."

All of a sudden, it hit me. The word was coming down from the White House through the Jewish connection in New York that I was going to receive one of the three things I had discussed with Andy. I did not get this from the White House; instead, I heard it from a Jewish lawyer right across the street from my office.

So I asked, "Well, who told you this, Mr. Rosen? I haven't heard anything from the White House."

He said, "Trust me, young man. The deal has already been cut. Congratulations. Now, there are some people I want you to meet."

So we went to a restaurant in Baltimore City's Little Italy. There we were met by a Jewish and Italian contingent of people. There were no other patrons in the restaurant, and again, just like in the movies, the shades had been pulled down. Although I knew Jewish people in the Carter campaign, I did not understand how the Jewish connection related to Maryland. But as they were telling me that I was going to be the next United States attorney for Maryland, the connection was made clear. Governor Marvin Mandel, Maryland's first and to-date only Jewish governor, had been tried for racketeering and mail fraud. A mistrial had been declared. A decision about a second trial was going to be made by the White House and the Justice Department. I had met Governor Mandel at the Democratic Convention. He was part of the "anybody-but-Carter movement" in Maryland, a force I had battled at the convention while serving as a floor whip.

Mr. Rosen said, "The deal is cut, but there is a question. The next United States attorney will have a big say in whether or not to try Mandel a second time. There are certain people who are aware of your connections with Washington, DC, and with Mr. Carter. Certain of these people—and Jewish people in general—will support you even though the deal has already been made. The quid pro quo is that although we do not want any promises, we are asking you to consider the fact that you, if appointed, will be asked whether there should be a second prosecution of Mandel. How do you feel about that?"

I said, "Well, Mr. Rosen, all of this is happening so fast. Mr. Mandel said some very negative things about President Carter during the campaign.

I don't think Carter took it to heart. In fact, I don't think that he was personally aware of Governor Mandel one way or another. I have no problems with Mr. Mandel. To be quite honest, even before all of this came up, I thought that the first prosecution of Mr. Mandel was biased and without substance. I've had that personal conviction regardless of what's being said in this room. So even though I could never sit here and say or formulate a political position, I do have personal views on the matter."

When I got back to my office, I immediately called Peter Bourne and asked if it was true that the president was going to seek my appointment as the United States attorney for Maryland. True enough, Jewish political power was quite strong in Maryland. Nevertheless, raw power was still in the gentile community.

Little did I know that newly elected Senator Paul Sarbanes would oppose me with a vengeance. It became such a struggle that the *Washington Post* ran a story entitled, "Pettit Blowing in the Wind. Who appoints US Attorneys—Presidents or Junior Senators?" Although federal judges and US attorneys are nominated by the president, "senatorial courtesy" actually calls for the senator representing the state in which there is a vacancy to recommend the candidate for nomination by the president, who almost always acts accordingly. The White House would not formally make a nomination without Senator Sarbanes' recommendation, and Sarbanes refused to make the recommendation.

Hamilton and Peter both told me not to worry. "It's going to happen. It's just a matter of time."

Nevertheless, the next day I would still read in the newspaper, "Dwight Pettit under Consideration" in the *Baltimore Sun* and "Pettit Blows in the Wind" in the *Washington Post*. The trigger had not been pulled. In fact, it had become such a stalemate that the *Afro* and other black media began to attack Senator Sarbanes. As it turned out, some good came out of all this for the citizens of Maryland, fortunately. The appointment of the first black federal judge in Maryland, Joseph Howard was a result of this stalemate.

I got another strange telephone call one morning, this time from Pete Marrudis, assistant to Senator Sarbanes. Pete would later become the special assistant to the mayor of Baltimore City, Kurt Schmoke. Pete called to arrange a meeting at which he told me, flat out, "Senator Sarbanes wants you to back off."

"What do you mean back off?"

"He does not want this to continue; he wants you to withdraw your name from consideration for United States attorney. And you should understand that you could get hurt if you continue."

I said, "Pete, am I being threatened?" In those days, I was arrogant and brash, so to me this was like a threat. "Is this a threat from a United States senator? What do you mean by 'I might get hurt'—economically, physically, or politically?"

Pete just said, "Dwight, you can take it any way you want. I'm just delivering the message."

That was when I began to realize how serious this issue had become. The blue-blood law firms had always controlled the office. I realized later that it was not about me, it was first and foremost about the power remaining in the hands of those who had always held it, and second, it was about a determination to separate Mandel and his Jewish connections from their power. In my opinion, they could not take the chance of having me become the first black person named the United States attorney for the state of Maryland. They could not take the chance that the larger law firms would not control the most powerful office in the state of Maryland. It was not about me. It was much bigger than that.

Sarbanes' next move was a stroke of political genius. He reached out and nominated Joseph Howard Sr. to be the first black United States district court judge in the state of Maryland. This confused the black support in place for my bid for United States attorney. This political trade-off for the black community scuttled my chances. Everybody loved Joe Howard, including me, which took the spotlight off me. In fact, people used to joke, "Dwight, you made Joe Howard, Sarbanes didn't." Although the White House continued to buck the idea of making anyone else United States attorney, Sarbanes then nominated a man by the name of Russell T. Baker who was already in the justice department's criminal division. Thus, instead of appointing a United States attorney from outside of the justice department, which meant that the White House would have been able to block it, Baker was a lateral transfer into the position. Sarbanes had thus accomplished two things: the black community got the first black federal judge and the White House got outmaneuvered. These things made clear to me that my opposition was neither in Washington nor in the White House. Rather, my opposition was in Maryland and more particularly among those in Maryland who had political axes to grind.

My understanding of the Maryland culture up until this time was developed through a number of enlightening relationships and conversations. Parren Mitchell (affectionately known as PJ) was a great human being. Although he might have had pressure from his relatives, particularly the senator, I enjoyed what I thought was a very amicable relationship with him until his death in 2007. I always felt that I could consult with Parren, and I did in later campaigns. As previously stated, I also enjoyed a very good relationship with the senator's father, Mr. Clarence Mitchell Jr. His name is on my certificate as the nominating attorney recommending my admission to appear before the United States Supreme Court. Even in his senior years, after the dissolution of Mitchell and Pettit, I could always go across the hall to sit with him and discuss politics and world events This man was the major author and lobbyist for the nation's major civil-rights legislation. Although Martin Luther King Jr., Whitney Young, and others received credit for most of the achievements of the civil-rights movements, it was Mr. Mitchell who in fact was the architect of the legislation enacted by President Lyndon Baines Johnson and the United States Congress (which at the time included a Republican-led Senate). A contemporary and friend of Mr. Mitchell's was Thurgood Marshall, who had been appointed by President Johnson, first as the solicitor general of the United States and later to the United States Supreme Court. I immensely enjoyed the chance to talk to history about history—especially about local history still in the making.

During this time, I also maintained ongoing conversations with William (Bill) Borders, the president of the National Bar Association—who had the status of being the leader of the nation's African American attorneys. Bill was the individual who met with Ben and me in an attempt to correct some of Ben's behavioral difficulties. After Bill was appointed by President

Carter to the Appellate Judicial Nominating Commission, I handled a lot of his federal practice in Maryland. Bill shared a fantastic office with Jimmy Cobb, a former president of the National Bar Association. I always used to say these two were the real superstars of the legal profession. They had offices in a beautifully converted embassy building on Embassy Row in Washington. Jimmy's office was on the second floor, where he discreetly kept a little scotch in his desk drawer. On the third floor were big lounge chairs and a pool table, and many of the guys I would later meet, including O. T. Wells, a former president of the national bar out of New York, would sit around there and talk law. I hung out with Borders in Jimmy's office on Friday afternoons when in Washington for the Carter campaign or on a court appearance or some other business. Being around these giants, listening to them talk law, was an educational process in and of itself. I was like a kid on the block, listening in on the big boys' conversations. I did not talk; I listened and absorbed.

Once Carter became president, I served on occasion as his advance man, for example, when he attended the Congressional Black Caucus. Mostly they were political events, which for me were a lot of fun. I would party a little, and at the same time introduce myself, network, and make people aware of the new president's agenda and his hopes for the African American communities. Basically, it was my responsibility at or during these events to "keep him moving" in the right direction, or at least that was what the Secret Service kept whispering in my ear, with a nudge on my back, as we moved into and through crowds, just as we had done during the campaign. I had become use to the drill because President Carter made several trips to African American events.

My first assignment was at the Congressional Black Caucus event after the presidential election. Waiting for him outside of the Washington Hilton, I watched the crowd, all excited and anticipating. Being a black event, most in the crowd were black, some with their own agenda chanting, "Jimmy, go home!" Then I saw something quite extraordinary, the effect of raw political power. The president was not a commodity seen up close by many people, particularly not by black people because we seldom interacted with raw power, except maybe to some extent with the Kennedys. All of a sudden, I heard sirens and saw motorcycles with flashing lights round the corner. There were at least ten or twelve motorcycles with US flags mounted on the back leading the president's limousine, with Secret Service agents running alongside and behind. When they pulled up in front of the hotel, the police bike motorcade officers looked sharp in their shiny helmets and tall black boots, and then almost in unison, they braced their bikes with one booted foot. It was an awesome sight. Aided by the Secret Service, the president of the United States stepped out of the limousine smiling. He waved his hands, and the black folks—even those who only moments before had been shouting, "Jimmy, go home!"—started screaming instead, "Oh God, its Jimmy! Oh, Lord, it's Jimmy! It's him!" It was amazing. People were waving, and women were trying to touch him.

I said to myself, *This is power, raw awesome presidential power.* Any hostility that had existed moments earlier just dissipated.

I stepped from the curb and took President Carter by the arm, "Mr. President, follow me, sir." When we got inside the ballroom, I led him to the stage, and as directed by the Secret Service, I also continued onto the stage with him. As a footnote, I vowed not to go to another Congressional Black Caucus event because being there as just an observer, not a participant, would never feel the same after being there with President Carter. I promised myself that I would not go back unless I did so as a congressman. Many years later, I think in 1997, Congressman Elijah Cummings invited me to a Congressional Black Caucus event, and I finally relented, attending just as a regular citizen. However, going to the Congressional Black Caucus in 1977 and advancing the president was one of the more exciting moments that I can remember in politics.

At another time, Attorney General Griffin Bell attended the National Bar Association Convention in New Orleans, and I was asked to facilitate his meeting with the organization and to participate in a compilation state by state, district by district, and circuit by circuit of those African Americans who should be considered for President Carter's judicial appointments to the federal bench. In those days, federal judges were rarely African Americans. However, the National Bar Association was proactively prepared to change this dynamic. Thus, when Senator Sarbanes looked for a federal judge from the ranks of black lawyers and judges in Maryland, the list had already been developed. Joe Howard was on that list. His brother was Charlie Howard, now deceased, who was also former president of the National Bar Association. He was one of my best friends and mentors.

When Mike and I arrived in Chicago for the swearing-in ceremony, there were about 2,500 people at the luncheon.

Being the new young lawyers out of Baltimore City, we were introduced as the "New Turks" of the bar. Charlie Howard had an employee from Baltimore City at the time by the name of Georgia Gosley, who was a lawyer in his office and was scheduled to be on the podium with him. When Charlie's wife arrived from Baltimore City, Charlie could not be sworn in until later, in private. One issue was deciding who was going to hold the Bible for the swearing, Ms. Gosley or Mrs. Howard. Nevertheless, Charlie, Michael, and I had a great time.

President Carter's appointment of Bill Border's to the Appellate Judicial Nominating Commission was for a six-year term. As we know, Carter lost the 1980 election to Ronald Reagan, which meant Bill's appointment overlapped two presidential administrations. This complicated President Reagan's plans regarding the appointment of judges to the United States Court of Appeals because Borders had the temerity to tell President Reagan where to go and what to kiss when Reagan asked him to resign. In my opinion, this put into motion the setup of Borders by the Reagan administration for a sting operation leading to Bill's arrest for soliciting bribes and the impeachment of Judge Alcee Hastings. I ended up representing the infamous William Dredge, the client referred to me by Borders, and thus I was the lawyer unknowingly representing the FBI plant who was part of the sting that brought down a US federal district judge as well as Borders himself.

Even though I had great relationships with the white staff within the White House, this was still not comparable to having a relationship that one black person would have with another in terms of pushing the black agenda. Yes, the White House inquired as to any interest I might have had in being the deputy director of the Peace Corps, and yes, I did interview for that position, but I think my lack of enthusiasm showed through. Even though I went for the interview, I never really pushed any buttons to follow through, so I just politically (as the *Washington Post* stated) floated in the wind.

My father was firmly convinced that my problems becoming United States attorney stemmed from other things, not just the politics of my Maryland enemies. My father was not pessimistic, but he said, "Dwight, if you become the first black US attorney for Maryland, I would be the first to applaud it, but I don't believe it's going to happen. It's just like when you thought you were going to become quarterback. Son, just don't get your hopes up too high. I know Carter is a good man, but you have many other people, black and white, who have to make a decision and support you. So don't be naïve."

That brought to mind what I had been told as a kid, "Just don't get too far up on cloud nine." Dad said, "With this president you are politically involved; you know him personally, and he knows you. We all went to his inauguration, and we've all been to the White House. But don't get too far up on cloud nine when dealing with this structure known as America, because you're a black man, and no matter how much you feel they like you, it will still be a major-transition type of appointment by the White House." I was forewarned. Dad added, "There are certain things that they could use against you that they won't use against other people." Again, my father would say, in Yogi Berra fashion, "Son, the world is yours but not really yours."

Mary Ellen and Ellen Metsky, Peter's administrative Assistants were both close friends of mine from the Carter campaign days. They were now powerful operatives in the White House, having moved into the West Wing. Ellen and Mary approached me about being appointed to the Democratic National Committee's Compliance Review Commission, which was an arm of the DNC. My appointment would assure that there would be proper representation by minorities going into the 1980 convention. However, what was intriguing about this appointment was the major power struggle being waged with the Ted Kennedy forces that wanted to seize the 1980 nomination from President Carter. Because my appointment to the Democratic National Committee's Compliance Review Commission was made, I became directly involved.

This commission, comprised of twenty-five members, including former governors, congressmen, and others who had held high political positions in the party, met on a monthly basis to take and act on testimony in conjunction with DNC rules to ensure that minorities would be seated fairly in proportion to the population of the respective congressional districts. At the time, Jesse Jackson was an actual mover and shaker on the national stage on this important issue. Four years later, I became Jesse's campaign chairman in Baltimore City for his first presidential bid, and I was also active in his second. The issue of minority representation in the seating of delegates would continue to be a major issue in the Democratic Party.

The flash point began when Kennedy moved to seize power within the compliance commission. These preliminary steps, taken early on, were totally unknown to the public. However, I saw signs of weakness within the Carter organization. The commission formulated the rules and regulations governing the seating of delegates at the upcoming convention, in essence naming those who would decide the next Democratic presidential nominee. The White House determined that Kennedy was going to attempt to take the nomination from the sitting president. He was going to overthrow Carter from within his own party. This became openly apparent as the 1980 campaign season progressed. Not only was the struggle for power taking place within the Democratic Party in general, but also within the DNC. However, President Carter never seemed to take an interest in things such as this during his administration. For example, in a reconciliation move after his election, he had appointed Joseph A. Califano as secretary of Health, Education, and Welfare. That made no sense to me. Califano was one of those individuals who had put Carter down as a country hick. The Carter administration brought on some of the same people who still considered him a joke, people who had no loyalty to him at all. Why appoint your political enemies to such powerful positions? I know there is a saying that you should keep your enemies close where you can watch them, but it is never a good idea to put your enemies right within your decision-making team.

Before I went into commission meetings, Ellen Metsky and other

Carter insiders would brief me on the upcoming agenda. They would tell me who the Kennedy people were going to be, and who was going to testify. They would also tell me where the cross-examination was expected to lead. My duty was to derail, if possible, the Kennedy witnesses on cross-examination. I was to block the Kennedy forces from achieving their agendas. I was to be the pit bull, the legal infighter of the compliance commission. For example, when the Attorney General from Massachusetts testified, I was the one who cross-examined him. Through this overall aggressive strategy, the Carter forces were able to hold the Kennedy forces in check. I like to believe that I was one of the soldiers from the inside that the public never saw who helped President Carter defeat a takeover, an attempted coup, from within his own party. This was not a Republican effort. It was internal. It was an immensely fascinating and challenging experience being deputized by the White House to spearhead the defense of the sitting president as we prepared for the Democratic nomination for the 1980 convention.

Eventually I became disenchanted with what I saw. I saw Ben Brown, the catalyst for many minorities, gradually removed from the center of power. I saw the descent of his power beginning in the early part of 1978. By this time, I had influenced the placement of several people. I had also converted nonbelievers in the black community and, despite campaign battles, brought many of the same "Jimmy who?" people into the White House to meetings with Carter's insiders.

In fact, President Carter awarded Clarence Mitchell Jr. the Presidential Medal of Freedom, the highest civilian award in the nation. This was without question a well-deserved honor. Unfortunately, the tide began to turn, and I began to see all of us, the loyalists, being transferred outside, while all of the newer intellectuals were being taken inside. It was almost as if they were sitting on the inside, smugly laughing at those of us now on the outside. At any rate, the Carter political staff had to get ready for the upcoming 1980 campaign. Late in 1978 or early 1979, the White House invited back the black leaders who had been the guts of the original Carter movement to work on the next political battle strategy. The meeting, which included some new black participants, brought those who had been instrumental in the 1976 Carter election back into the fold, under one roof as a black political network. This group included Roland Burris, then state comptroller of Illinois and later United States senator; Wellington E. Webb, the mayor of Denver, Colorado; and of course the aforementioned regular Atlanta crew. I exited in the middle of the meeting to catch a train to New York. This was my private personal protest. I would not be invited back to the White House again under Carter's administration. The next time that I would see the inside of the White House would be under George Walker Bush when he and Secretary Condoleezza Rice returned from Africa. And the last time I was invited was when President George W. Bush signed the extension of the voting rights act in 2006 on the lawn of the White House. Most of the national civil-rights leaders were in attendance.

Pettit opens Maryland / Carter Headquarters 1976

Pettit and Parents with Ben Brown and Chip Carter

Bobbie, Dwight and President Carter

Dwight, Ora Reid and Ben Brown

Dwight and (Grady) Whitman Mayo 1976 Presidential Election

Mr. & Mrs. James Rouse and Dwight

Chip Carter at Pettit's House

Danny Henson and Dwight

Barbara, Dwight and Maynard Jackson

President Carter and Wife, Dwight and Barbara
share their first dance at Inaugural Ball

First State Dinner with Prime Minister Pierre Trudeau

Dwight introducing Carter to the Baltimore Community

Dwight and Hubert Humphrey at
1976 Democratic National Convention

Barbara and Mrs. Carter

Carter and Dwight

Carter and Dwight in Downtown Baltimore

Chip Carter Meets the Pettit Men

Chip & Bill and Anne Bouche

Dwight and Gov. Jerry Brown debate Maryland Election in Plains, Georgia

Dwight at the White House

Dwight brings Carter into Baltimore

Dwight, Mrs. Carter, Ken Wilson and Parren J. Mitchell

Jesse, Dwight and Barbara

Larry Gibson and Mrs. Carter

MD Delegation 1976 Democratic Convention

MD. Democratic Convention with State Senator Steny Hoyer,
Congressman Paul Sarbanes, State Senator Verda
Welcome, Louise Keelty and Dwight

Roland & Mrs. Patterson, Mrs. Carter and Dwight & Barbara

Barbara, Mrs. Elizabeth Oliver, Carter Press Secretary Jody Powell
and Dwight in Carter home in Plains, Georgia

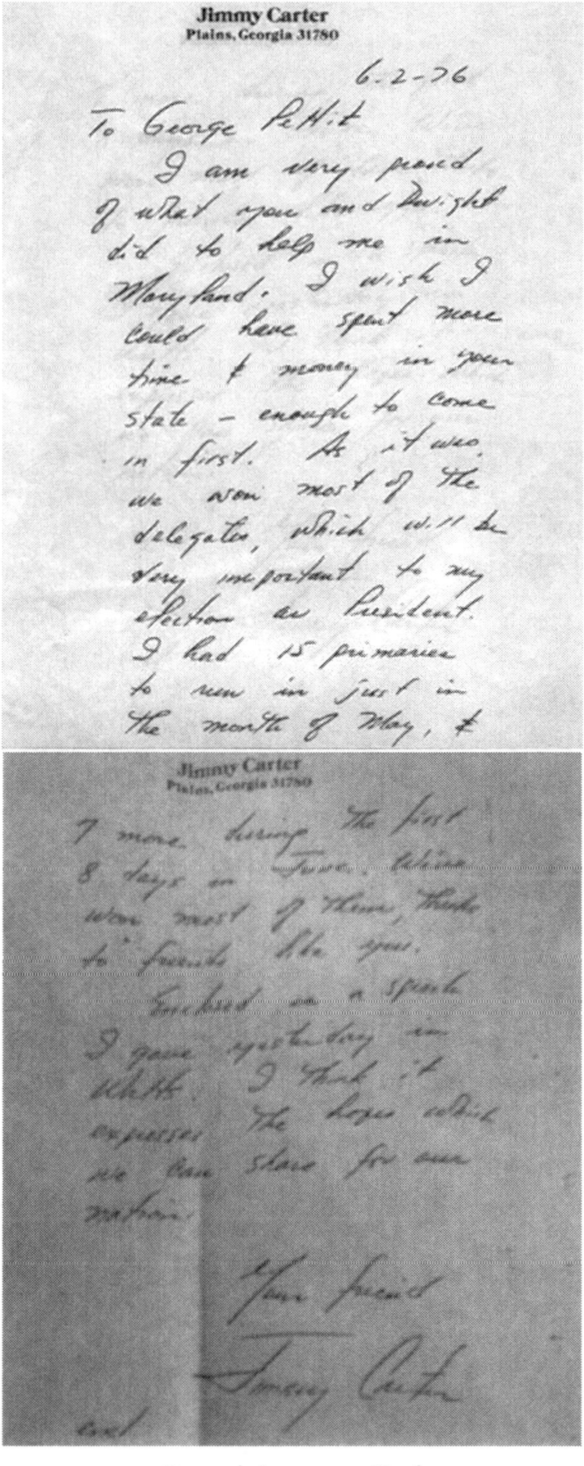

Jimmy Carter
Plains, Georgia 31780

6-2-76

To George Pettit

I am very proud of what you and Dwight did to help me in Maryland. I wish I could have spent more time & money in your state - enough to come in first. As it was, we won most of the delegates, which will be very important to my election as President. I had 15 primaries to run in just in the month of May, &

Jimmy Carter
Plains, Georgia 31780

7 more during the first 8 days in June. We won most of them, thanks to friends like you.

Enclosed is a speech I gave yesterday in Ohio. I think it expresses the hopes which we have shared for our nation.

Your friend,

Jimmy Carter

Carter's Letter to Dad

Jimmy Carter and the Pettits at the White House

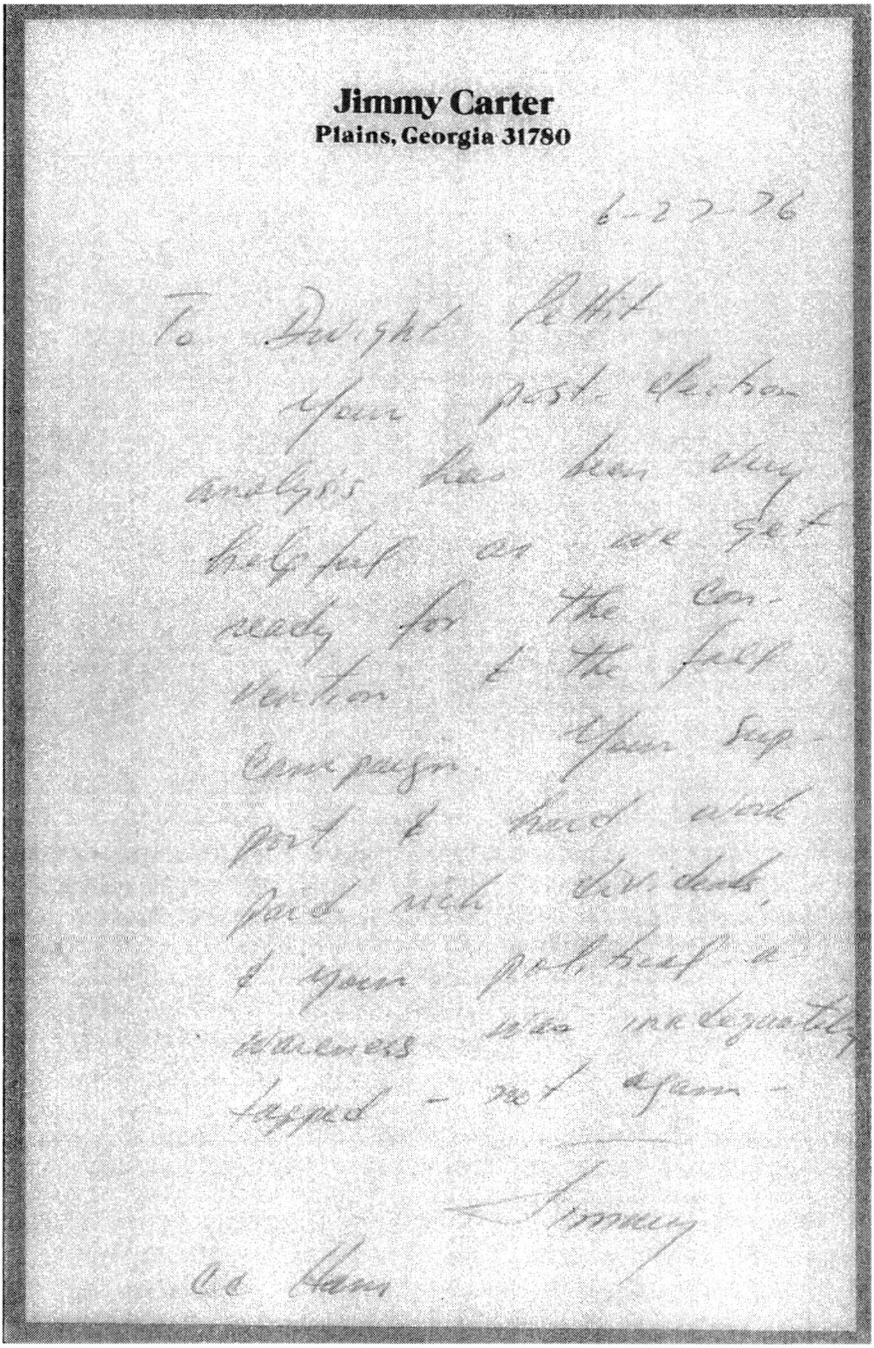

Jimmy Carter
Plains, Georgia 31780

6-2?-76

To Dwight Pettit

Your post-election analysis has been very helpful as we get ready for the Convention & the fall campaign. Your support & hard work paid rich dividends, & your political awareness was inadequately tapped — not again —

Jimmy

Cc Ham

Carter's Letter to Dwight

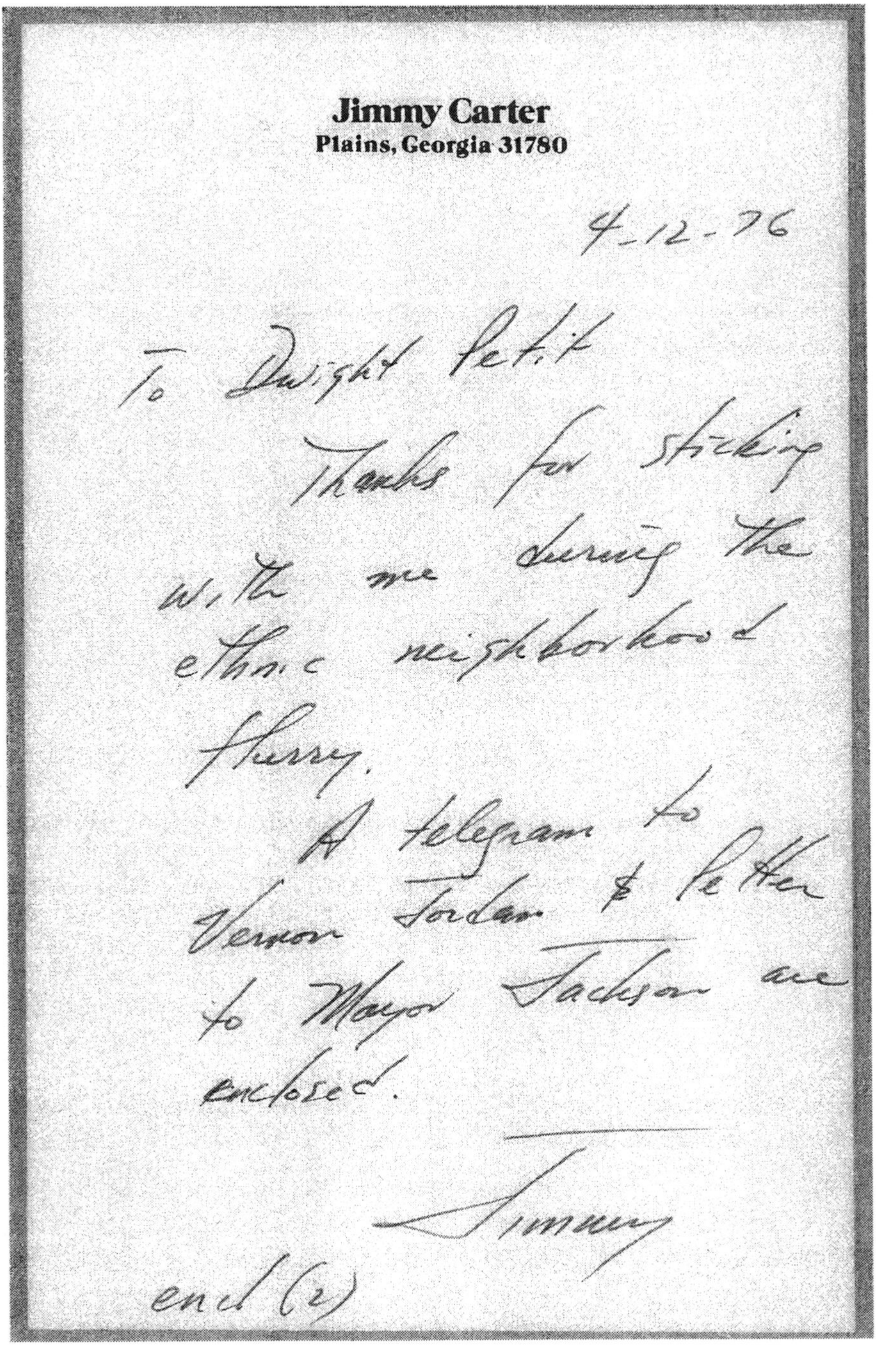

Jimmy Carter
Plains, Georgia 31780

4-12-76

To Dwight Petit

Thanks for sticking with me during the ethnic neighborhood flurry.

A telegram to Vernon Jordan & letter to Mayor Jackson are enclosed.

Jimmy

encl (2)

Carter's Preconvention Letter to Dwight

Clarence, Dwight, Chip Carter and wife,
Barbara and Michael at Pettit home

Dwight, Carter's mom (Ms. Lillian) and Barbara

Bobbie and President Carter in Plains, GA

Chapter 15: After All That

Having come out of the Carter campaign and the United States attorney battle around the summer of 1978, I returned to a quiet and somber office. The staff was a little depressed but somewhat inspired about the things we had done and what we had accomplished. On staff were Betty Brown, Aggie Valdez, Alice Pinderhughes, Benny Frazier (who later worked in Federal Pretrial Release Services), and Florella (Happy) Dabbs. I changed gears, and my agenda was to once again focus solely on my private practice. However, I would seek public office on several occasions in the coming years. I would run for state's attorney, for Congress twice, and for city council. Although, I was always high in the polls, it would seem that my campaigns would fizzle in the end, mainly due to my inability to beg for and raise money. For example, I specifically remember being at a political fundraiser and being introduced to a financial "heavy hitter" in Maryland politics, who congratulated me for my standing in the polls with so little financial support. He said to me, "Dwight, I would give you some money, but I am afraid that the next day when I turned on the television I would see you screaming 'black power.'"

During this time, I would have the occasion to befriend such people as David Brice, who worked in all of my campaigns; Danise Dorsey, who would manage my second congressional campaign; George Collins, my media consultant and the first black news personality in Maryland; Attorney Arthur Frank, who would be my major fundraiser and who later introduced me to Congressman Robert Ehrlich, who would become governor of Maryland; Congressman Elijah Cummings, who would run my first campaign as well as be one of my adversaries in my last campaign. Clarence Mitchell III and others would be my various opponents. I would also have the opportunity to meet such national figures as Al Green and Demond Wilson of *Sanford and Son*, who would in fact come in and campaign for me in the various campaigns. I would also have the opportunity to campaign with another powerful local politician by the name of Larry Young, who at the time was running for president of the Baltimore City council. He would later go on to be a very powerful state senator and is currently a very popular radio talk-show personality in Baltimore along with (Coach) Butch McAdams. I would also have the good fortune to meet and become close friends with Bernie McCain, another renowned radio talk-show host.

The social climate was still receptive to civil-rights litigation. This was an era when you could still win in court just on being right. It was socially, politically, and legally acceptable to take Title VII cases. One of our successful cases was *Billingsly v. the United States Department of Health, Education, and Welfare*. Mr. Billingsly had been an HEW administrator who was denied a promotional opportunity. I took his case before the administrative board with negative results. So I took his case to the United States District Court for the District of Maryland and pulled Judge Edward Northrop who was at that time chief judge of the US district court in Maryland. He was known to be quite conservative and not a champion of civil rights.

When I first appeared in his courtroom, he gave me a dignified good-ole-boy speech about what he expected. "Well, I don't know too many of you folks here, but here is what I expect in my courtroom." Apparently, he felt the need to give some type of up-front warning emanating from what he had heard about black lawyers or blacks in general. Nevertheless, Judge Northrop and I ended up establishing what became an excellent relationship in both the Billingsly case and later the Twining case.

What made the Billingsly case interesting was that no one in the Baltimore City legal circles had ever known Judge Northrop to find for the plaintiff in a discrimination case. It was just unheard of. When I told people that I would be appearing before Judge Northrop, all I got was "Good luck," a smile, and then silence. As it turned out, Judge Northrop had a fantastic secretary by the name of Ms. Smith. She was a very nice middle-aged white woman, and we had a very cordial relationship. I really believed she was one of those secretaries who helped decide certain matters for the judge. In the Billingsly case, Judge Northrop could not bring himself to find discrimination; instead, he found that there had been retaliation against my client. My client received the same relief as a finding of discrimination. What I found amusing about this victory was the evidence of Judge Northrop's stalwart conservative ways. He could clearly discern and rule against discrimination, but simply could not find his way to actually say the word "discrimination." The word retaliation was more acceptable to him.

I successfully tried another major civil-rights case, this time against Amtrak in front of Judge Shirley Jones, a former Baltimore City circuit court judge who was then at the United States district court level. I mention this because I noticed during the development of my private practice that a change of the political climate was in the wind; a change regarding what was winnable and what was unwinnable. Justice in America, both in terms of criminal law and civil law, is dictated by what is politically acceptable and what is unacceptable. At that time, it was popular to use the civil rights statutes 42 U.S.C. 1981, 1983–1985. These civil rights were developed post-civil war. It was also popular to use Title VII. We were dealing with judges, even those appointed by Eisenhower and Nixon, who found that even if civil rights weren't acceptable, the law would at least be enforceable. Despite these judges' conservative ideology, they were not hostile to the political movement of blacks or other minorities. Affirmative action was accepted at that time, having been approved by the federal courts in conjunction with the support of a Republican administration. So these cases were still popular and could still be won. In addition, the civil-rights legislation enacted by Congress provided for the financial compensation of attorneys, thereby providing an economic incentive to take and win these cases. However, this "acceptable" period was coming to an end as Ronald Reagan came to power.

My caseload still included criminal law, some domestic relations, and increasingly more business-law matters. The latter evolved from my background with the Small Business Administration. Added were more high-profile state and federal cases.

One of my former law professors, Jerome Shuman, called and told me that he had the daughter of a Mrs. Smith in his class, and she had told him a very tragic story. Her mother, a Jewish lady, was losing her family's business. The business and property were being taken away by the courts for allegedly violating the Consumer Protection Act of the state of Maryland. This legislation, enacted in Maryland to codify consumer laws with criminal sanctions, was new, and Mrs. Smith's case would be its first legal test. The events in question took place in Hagerstown, Maryland, a small town located in the mountains of western Maryland in Washington County.

This would be my first case in this region. Generally, Maryland's geography and population represent a good sampling of America, good and bad. Baltimore County is conservative but not as conservative as other areas. (Baltimore County and Baltimore City are two separate political entities.) I had tried cases all over the state, including Ann Arundel County, where the slaves were brought into port. The Eastern Shore, on the other side of the Chesapeake Bay from Baltimore City, was like being in the heartland of Mississippi in the '50s and '60s. To refresh memories, the Eastern Shore is where H. Rap Brown was put into a dog cage during the civil-rights movement before they attempted to blow him up in Bel Air, Maryland. Like the Eastern Shore, racial prejudice and hatred existed heavily in the mountains of western Maryland.

Washington County, which lies about seventy miles west of Baltimore City, was the jurisdiction of the infamous Judge John P. Corderman. In Washington County, Judge Corderman was the power to be—the next thing to God. He was more powerful than the mayor or county executive. I knew him from the Carter campaign, when he was a state senator before becoming a judge. I thought of him as a collegial associate of mine because when I served as the cochairman of the Carter campaign, then State Senator Corderman had been a Carter delegate. I did not anticipate receiving any benefits or any preferential treatment appearing before him as the sitting judge, but I did anticipate that I would be meeting once again a political colleague and associate. The reason for Judge Corderman's notoriety was that, in my opinion, he was the epitome of judicial arrogance in the highest form. He eventually reached such a level of infamy in Maryland that he actually received a bomb in the mail. When he opened the package in his lap, it blew up. He survived and just recently passed last year; he had so many critics that the FBI could never trace where the bomb might have originated.

To further set the stage, my client, Mrs. Smith, was a nice woman, a little older looking than her years. She was a white Jewish woman in her mid-to-late forties, married to a sickly husband who had heart problems. They operated a mom-and-pop furniture store that sat in the heart of Hagerstown. She came to me in Baltimore City upon the recommendation of Professor Shuman. She indicated that she had hired several lawyers without success, and her finances had been exhausted. She told me she was going to go through great efforts to pay me and said she was going to borrow the funds. Little did I know that I was about to embark upon a case that was going to consume over a year of my life. I actually traveled from Baltimore City to Hagerstown so often that I almost lived in Hagerstown rather than just trying a case in Hagerstown.

As related by Mrs. Smith, several lawyers had handled this case, but during the discovery proceedings they had bowed out, one by one, giving varying reasons, before the case even got to trial. It appeared that all of this tension was because of Judge Corderman. It was my first belief that Jews, like blacks, were not popular in Hagerstown, or the powers that be simply wanted the Smiths' property for whatever reasons. (I expect that if I went there today, I could find out what those reasons were by tracing back from whatever is sitting in that space now.) By the time I got the case, Mrs. Smith's store had been seized by the sheriff pursuant to provisions of the Consumer Protection Act. Mrs. Smith and her husband had been evicted from their own business, and, for all practical purposes, I guess they were expected to fold. But, this was a tenacious little Jewish lady. She was a pure warrior, right out of the books in terms of what is believed about the nature of Jewish moms. She had confidence in herself and confidence in me. Thus, she retained my services.

My first visit to Hagerstown was with Professor Shuman. Now I am a large man, about six foot two and about 215 pounds at the time. Professor Shuman was a big burly man about six foot three, weighing in at about 230 pounds. He arrived in his big black Rolls Royce. Although Shuman taught corporate law, finance, and legal accounting at Howard and Georgetown, and although he was considered a corporate law genius, he had never practiced law a day in his life. In fact, I do not think that Professor Shuman had ever stepped foot in a courtroom. He had no concept where he was going, none whatsoever. On the morning we were scheduled to meet for the proceedings, we picked up Mrs. Smith at her house. When we got to the court in the center of Hagerstown, the cameras were everywhere, both from local TV stations and the *Washington Post*. However, the press completely ignored me. They were more inclined to catch the image of Mrs. Smith, a short slightly stout white woman about five foot one, getting out of a big black Rolls Royce and standing next to Jerome Shuman, a large dark-skinned black man. I did not make "good press" because of my light skin. The next day the headlines rolled out pictures of Mrs. Smith with this big burly black lawyer from Washington, DC, coming up the courthouse steps.

This was a classic scene almost like vintage 1960 Mississippi, except in reverse. Once we got into the courtroom, I expected nothing from Judge Corderman other than fairness. Instead, he dashed onto the bench in all of his grandeur, leaping up the steps. He sat down, reared back in his chair, and then looked down at me with this evil, hostile glare. I gave a nod and a little smile as if to silently say, "Hi, Judge, good to see again. Remember me?" There was no return look of recognition, certainly no friendliness. I said to myself, *what have I gotten myself into?*

Once the case of *Maryland v. Marilyn Smith* began, I was very aggressive during cross-examination, so much so that within the first few hours it became obvious to the judge that the trial was now real, and Mrs. Smith was prepared to seriously confront her accusers. The fabrication that the State put together was systematically being taken apart. The prosecutor, a man by the name of Jonathan Atkins, was an assistant attorney general who also came from Baltimore City to try the case. Under my cross-examination, his first three witnesses practically recanted the statements they had given the State, one by one. Everything these people had stipulated to in sworn testimony during the administrative proceedings was destroyed in a matter of only hours.

Judge Corderman very quickly picked up on the fact that I was getting ready to totally embarrass the State, so he intervened and asked very distinctively, "Is there anything that we can agree on?"

I said no sir, so the prosecutor was obliged to continue.

I could tell Corderman was going to embark on a strategy to save the State's case, however, before he could intervene, Shuman reached over to me and whispered, "Can I take a witness?" He had gotten excited at my initial success of dissecting the State's case so quickly, and he assumed it must have been easy.

I said to him, "Jerome, I don't know if you really want to do that right now. Have you done any trial work?"

He answered, "No, but I've watched you." I wanted to point out the obvious that he had only watched me for a few hours, but instead I gave Professor Shuman the next witness.

Professor Shuman had barely opened his mouth, in fact, I don't think he got twenty words out of his mouth, when Corderman screamed from his bench, "What the heck is this? What the heck are you doing?"

The courtroom, packed with press and observers, went totally silent. I did not think it was funny then, but I recall it with amusement now. Judge Corderman gave us the courtesy of approaching the bench.

He asked Shuman, "Are you a member of the Maryland bar? Do you practice law? How many cases have you tried?" He just tore into Professor Shuman.

Well, needless to say, the next day the Rolls Royce did not show up, and Professor Shuman did not show up. The case went on for another year, and I never saw Professor Shuman in Hagerstown again. He disappeared from the case and left that monstrosity in my hands.

Corderman and I went tit for tat, back and forth, for over a year. In time, he became so arrogant in his disregard for the law that I actually took him to the Court of Special Appeals, where he was reversed during the trial. In fact, in one appeal, the appellate court said that if the court had just listened to counsel (referring to me), it would have saved the State and the Court of Appeals a lot of expense and a lot of trouble. Instead, this lady was put through a horrible experience. This shows that when the system is moving against fairness, fairness is nonexistent.

Near the end of the trial, the sheriff broke into her house under the pretext of serving a summons. After doing so, the sheriff charged her with assault and battery. This would cause her husband to have a heart attack, and I would also have to defend her against these new charges. Later in the trial, Judge Corderman charged her with perjury and ordered her locked up. She was lead out of the courtroom in handcuffs in a quasi-criminal/ civil proceeding. That led to a second criminal trial on top of the assault charge before a different judge who would not put her in jail although Corderman wanted her there. We actually got to a point in the trial when Corderman threatened me from the bench, asking me if I wanted to take the stand next.

I said, "Judge Corderman, I'm counsel, not a witness."

At that, he glared back and said, "Mr. Pettit, if you want to take the witness stand, you are invited to do so."

"No, Judge," I replied, "I'm the lawyer."

Aggravating everything was the fact that Judge Corderman repeatedly postponed the case in the middle of the day, knowing that I had to drive back and forth, to and fro, from Baltimore City to Hagerstown. So I actually got a room in town to stay two or three days each week as the trial proceeded. But the day he threatened me with the hint that he would put me in jail, I came back to Baltimore City that very afternoon and went straight to my office. I drew up a federal complaint against Judge Corderman for violation of my civil rights and asked for an emergency restraining order and a temporary injunction. I rushed it to Judge Miller, a United States federal district court judge, who was chambers judge that very night.

He looked at it and asked, "Mr. Pettit, are you serious about these allegations?" I said, I certainly was, and not only that, upon arriving back in Baltimore City, I called the Civil Rights Division of the Department of

Justice. With Corderman being as threatening as he was, I actually worried about his agents, the sheriff and state police.

Judge Miller immediately called Judge Corderman, and he said, "John, I have Mr. Pettit in my chambers, and I'm reading some allegations concerning things you've said as well as some of the things you've done. I don't want to believe these things. However, if Attorney Pettit is correct, you have a serious problem. I told him you were a friend of mine, so he consented to my calling you. So now I'm calling you as a friend to tell you that I know these things didn't happen. Did they, Judge?" (Apparently, on the other end of the line, Corderman said, "No, sir.") Judge Miller continued, "And if anything like this could have happened, it won't happen again. Will it, Judge? I mean, I can rest assured that if I don't sign this order, Attorney Pettit will be treated with all due respect as a member of the bar and in accordance with the law when he comes back to Hagerstown. Isn't that right, Judge?"

That telephone call, from a United States federal district judge to a local state judge, telling him that the signing of an order was eminent, was a test of local enforcement of the Constitution of the United Sates. It was also the testing of a rogue judge who had threatened a black attorney representing a white woman. It stopped Judge Corderman's outlandish abuse of power even though one judge was reluctant to sign an order against another judge.

When I got back to Hagerstown the next day, I walked into the courtroom expecting to see the sheriff and state troopers. Everybody was on pins and needles.

The law clerk came out and said, "Mr. Pettit, Judge Corderman wants to see you."

When I entered his chambers he said to me, "Dwight, my buddy, my friend ... Dwight, why would you do that? Why would you make those allegations against me?" He looked at me as if he had no recollection of how he had treated me over the past months, no conscious memory of how he had threatened my being as an attorney, notwithstanding what he was doing to my client. Nevertheless, he apologized for any misunderstandings, saying it would not happen again. He also suggested that we should be able to work out the Smith case. It was then that we sat down.

Of course, Mrs. Smith lost her store, more so for financial reasons than for legal, but she never went to jail. Talk about injustice, her family's property had been taken, she was put through two criminal trials, her husband had a heart attack, the sheriff had broken into her house, and she had been arrested three times. Her bank account had been seized, her daughter had dropped out of law school due to lack of funds, and her family had been abused. And all of this was done in the name of justice.

I said to myself, "My God, this was a white woman, a hardworking white family, all-American white people in a white community." They just happened to be Jewish. If they could visit this type of tragedy upon this family, one of their own, a family of means, a family that owns property, a family that owns a business in Maryland, USA—a state that had a Jewish governor and elected progressive leaders—what more could they do in the name of justice to black people? Just throw out the Constitution? Throw out equal protection? Throw out due process? What in the world would happen to black Americans, particularly in the counties and rural areas? Well, the answer is easy. A black family would have never been able to open the business in the first place. But then again, maybe the people in power weren't doing this to themselves. After all, the Smiths were a Jewish family. Obviously, religion was a distinguishing element. Gentiles distinguish between themselves and Jews just as they distinguish between themselves and blacks.

On reflection, I remember the Jim Parker ("Big Jim" of the Baltimore Colts) divorce case where the lawyer said to me, "You don't want to try this case in Howard County, Dwight, because they don't like Negros and Jews out there." It did not matter that the Smiths were a white family; they had been destroyed. I came to a clarified realization about the nature of justice in America, not that I had been so naïve as to misunderstand that the protections it provided were only afforded to certain classes of people so long as those protections were political and popular, or in present terms, politically correct. I had seen the viciousness of the so-called arm of the law when political protections were no longer provided to certain litigants standing before the bar of justice. In my opinion, Mrs. Smith had her liberty because she was not incarcerated, but even this was only because of the intervention of a federal judge near the end of the process when it became so obvious what was taking place. The situation became an embarrassment to that jurisdiction, that county, and the state of Maryland. It was a rude awakening for me, returning from high-profile presidential politics back to good ole Southern white-folk justice. And it all took place under the color of law.

Sam Daniels, Arthur Frank and Mike Mitchell

Mitchell the 4th and Dwight

Dwight ushers Jessie Jackson into Baltimore

Barbara, Bernie McCain, Michael Mitchell and Dwight

Demond Wilson, Dwight, Barbara and Son

Dwight and Alice (Alee) Pinderhughes

Dwight Campaigning

Marie Davis and David Brice

The Pettit Family

Barbara, Dwight, John and Ruby Pettit
At the famous "Club Harlem" in Atlantic City, NJ

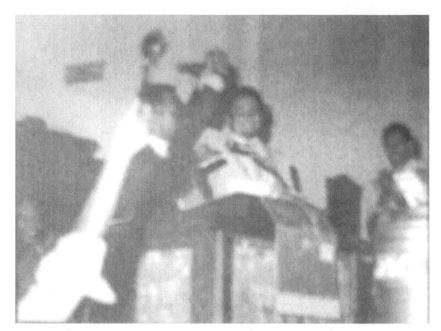

Parren J. Mitchell and Dwight

Rev. St. George Cross, George Collins and Michael Mitchell
introducing Dwight at a campaign rally

Chapter 16: Cases after Smith

After the Smith case, I moved into more generalized cases in my private practice. In 1978, I also allowed myself to be encouraged by the community into the race for city state's attorney. One of the other candidates, challenger Antone Keaton, pulled a brilliant campaign maneuver. He went on TV and offered one hundred dollars to anyone who could verify that I had tried a criminal case before a jury in Baltimore City. The irony was that he specified "Baltimore City." Although I had handled many civil cases in front of a jury, and although I had tried criminal cases in front of Baltimore City judges, I had never actually tried a criminal case in front of a jury in Baltimore City. I had been a part of a trial team facing a Baltimore City federal jury, but I had never tried a criminal jury case in Baltimore City by myself. Of course, given that the state's attorney was a strictly administrative position, this was irrelevant.

Nevertheless, I became very, very eager to fill that gap in my occupational growth and put that lack of experience behind me. I was determined to focus on being the best jury trial lawyer that I could be. Not only did I represent Fallston Hospital and Nathan Twinning, I also expanded my client portfolio to include a broader variety of matters. During the Carter years, I had corporate clients on retainer, which had rather removed me from the regular legal work. So my caseload became more of a mixture moving into the late '70s and early '80s.

People do not realize that an association with the president of the

United States brings on much more than the reward of a job. There may not have been publicity or power, but there was money to be made. An example was John Rolli. This gentleman allegedly had connections with organized crime. He retained my office through the recommendation of Al, the main man in Little Italy at the time. (Everybody in Baltimore City knew Al as the maître d' of Sabatinos Restaurant, a political meeting place in Baltimore City.) Rolli had left a knife in a man in a Baltimore City restaurant and then strolled into the back of his limo. The restaurant had been packed with patrons including police officials.

When he came into my office, he pulled up in a limousine, with a briefcase full of money, accompanied by a beautiful blonde woman. This was strictly Italian, straight out of a movie. John Rolli took my staff and me out to a restaurant for a dinner meeting. Once the patrons left, the doors were locked. The women in our party had to be quiet during our meeting. This was typical, classical. I agreed to represent John Rolli on this attempted-murder charge.

Right after this, two FBI agents came to my office and with a smirk, one asked, "Mr. Pettit, do you know who you are representing?"

"Yes, of course, my client Mr. Rolli."

In a strangely humorous manner, the agent said, "No, sir. The question was do you really understand the nature of your involvement? If things don't work out between you and Mr. Rolli, you might need protection. Give us a call." With that, he gave me his card, and they left laughing. That was a pretty chilling encounter, especially the laughter.

Working with Mr. Rolli was a fascinating experience. His case was to be heard in the circuit court before a female judge, Judge Boothy. This was the first (and last) time that I ever had a client stand up and tell the judge, "Bitch, do you know who I am, who you're talking to?"

I was not sure she actually understood his standing in the organization to which he allegedly belonged, whatever organization that might be. But I will say this, every other week I got a call at three o'clock in the morning, and, just like in *The Godfather*, a raspy voice would say, "Mr. Pettit, do you need anything, anything at all? We want you to take care of John. John is very important to us."

I would always reply, "Thank you very much. I've been paid, and I don't need anything else in terms of assistance," and I would assure the caller that I was doing everything I could within the capacity of the law.

Then, just prior to the trial, I got a call from a federal prosecutor (now a federal judge). I remember that he said very clearly and very distinctly, "Dwight, the Rolli case is over."

I asked, "What do you mean it's over?"

He just said. "Tell the circuit court judge in Baltimore City that the federal government will resolve it. The State's action is over."

I contacted Judge Boothy, but she told me, "No, Mr. Pettit, we are going to trial. This man is going to trial."

All I could say to her was, "Judge, you can say anything you want to say, but I'm telling you now that there will be no trial. I'm telling you now there is no case, and the man doesn't exist anymore."

The last time I would see John Rolli, he was being held in federal protective custody when I visited him at his request at Rahway Prison where they made the movie *Scared Straight*. As I walked through the prison, the guards passed the word, "He's here to see Mr. Rolli. He's here to visit Mr. Rolli." When I walked into the prison yard, I saw Rolli sitting at a picnic table with his friends and a nice looking young woman. They were drinking sodas and having hot dogs and hamburgers.

He saw me and said, "Everybody, come over here, I want you to meet my lawyer, Mr. Pettit from Baltimore City." All of the prisoners came over to meet me. I met Hurricane Carter, an inmate at the time.

John said, "Dwight, do you want a soda, a sandwich, or a hot dog?" This man was in prison, and we were exchanging pleasantries. I recognized true power. The Carter campaign had given me the opportunity to experience that kind of clientele up close and personal.

I was later brought into another trial where all I was supposed to do was sit at the trial table. I was never allowed to open my mouth. The presiding judge, Judge Hargrove, was black and there were two black people on the jury, and the firm wanted everyone to see a black lawyer at the table. I sat in front of the jury for two weeks and made a substantial fee.

There were other things going on at that time that were also quite unsettling. One of those things was the sting that went down on William Borders, the DC lawyer and then-president of the National Bar Association, whose office I had visited many times early on in my career. Borders was arrested and charged with attempting to bribe a federal judge, Judge Hastings of Florida, now Congressman Hastings. I was subpoenaed into Atlanta and kept on the stand an entire day. They never brought me in before the United States Congress during the impeachment proceedings against Judge Hastings of Florida, but they did bring me to Atlanta where I was cross-examined by three judges and a federal prosecutor. They could not understand or appreciate the fact that I had nothing to do with the Borders-Hastings situation. I was not in the loop. Judge Hastings had called and asked me if I would be testifying at the Border trial. Because my name was in Borders telephone records and in the records and memos in Bill Border's office, the interrogators in Atlanta contacted me. On the stand they asked me why I was calling Borders so many times if I was not involved.

I replied, "Well, gentlemen, it's very simple. I was representing two clients of Mr. Borders. I was representing Rebecca Montgomery and Sweet Willy from Philly."

One judge asked, "Sweet ... who?"

Sweet Willy from Philly was a player and a hustler. He and I had played ball against each other in college, and we had met up again when I walked into court one day where he was appearing on another matter. His lawyer was wearing a pink suit. When he saw me, he came over and said, "You really look like a lawyer. I like the way you're dressed." After that, he and I had become very good friends. We hung out and partied together in Washington, DC. I constantly kept him out of trouble and also represented him in a case in Prince George's County. Willy was a professional hustler, and he victimized women big time: I mean houses, cars, bank accounts. I could run into Sweet Willy in the streets of Washington, probably still can now, and Willy would just go into his pocket and give me five hundred or a thousand dollars.

I would ask, "Willy, what's this for?"

And he would say, "This is for the trouble I'm going to get into."

At one point, we opened a beauty shop in Virginia that I think lasted for six months. Other than hanging out together, anytime I ran into him in DC he would say, "Counselor, take some money."

People would always walk up to him and ask, "Willy, how's your case coming?"

He would say, "Case? Man, I ain't got no case. I paid Dwight Pettit. He got a case; I ain't got a case."

Willy and I were tight. So when Willy was being represented by Borders in DC, and just before Borders went down in the Hastings-Dredge sting operation, Willy had contacted me to find out how he could reach Borders. As a favor to Willy, I rang Borders's phone off the hook. That was one of the reasons for all of the calls. I explained this to the judges in Atlanta.

In addition, Rebecca Montgomery and her boyfriend had major federal charges in federal court in Baltimore City that I was handling on behalf of Bill Borders. Rebecca had not paid me, so I had been calling Bill in an effort to get my money. Again, I explained this to the judges in Atlanta, adding that this was all well documented. All they had to do was verify two things, that Willy was in jail at the Loudon Detention Center in Washington and that I was on record as representing Rebecca Montgomery as cocounsel with Bill Borders before the federal court in Baltimore City. My telephone calls had nothing to do with the Hastings-Borders situation or the FBI sting. In fact, my only connection to the sting was that I represented Dredge, the informant—although I did not know he was the informant.

So, after a rather extensive interrogation, I was interviewed by Attorney Byron who headed up the investigation for the United States Senate into the Hastings matter, and that was the end of it. Today Bill Borders does not speak to me, or he does so only grudgingly. I do not know what the FBI or anyone else told him or what he believes I said or didn't say. However, there was nothing for me to say because I did not know anything. That was one time when I was perfectly happy being outside of the loop. I was not even invited to the party the night the sting went down. For the first time, it was beneficial being left off the guest list.

I began to get very interesting cases that highlighted my naïveté. For example, I handled a matter in Annapolis, Maryland, that was a straightforward case of wrongful death. I had never before brought a civil action in Annapolis. It should be remembered that Maryland's location along the mid-Atlantic separated the old south from the north making it the so-called "free state". Thus, Annapolis, located in Anne Arundel County, was a major slave port for the eastern part of the United States. It was the place where the slaves were first brought onto shore and then sold. This was a place with history. In fact, it was memorialized by Alex Haley in the book *Roots*. My case involved two black contractors working on a trench by the side of the road. They were working near their truck when a white kid, doing about ninety-five miles per hour, literally scraped the two men off the side of their truck where they had taken refuge upon seeing the speeding car heading in their direction. One was knocked sixty-five feet in the air and the other forty feet. Both men were killed instantly.

When I went down to Annapolis to try the case, I encountered a judge who was hostile and very arrogant. What I did not know was that the trial lawyer on the other side had gone to school with the judge. In fact, they had been school buddies. More disconcerting was that the trial lawyer was very famous in Maryland at the time, not because of his legal ability but because he had written a book. It was a joke book about African Americans and Jews. Although this material was clearly demeaning, he was nevertheless respected and accepted for his humor throughout the state.

As the trial got underway, he got up in front of the jury, pointed toward the defendant, and said, "Y'all know this boy, that's Mr. [so-and-sos] boy, lives down the street." Then he pointed at me, "Mr. Pettit is this big slick lawyer out of Baltimore City, and he doesn't understand that we stick together down here and that we're like family."

And so it began. Although I had subpoenaed the police department to bring in the pictures of the scene, the photos were, of course, lost. When I called the police to the stand and asked about the results of their accident investigation, their notes were lost as well.

Here were two dead black men, killed while they were working, by an intoxicated, speeding white kid, at five o'clock in the morning. The police had no recollection, no pictures, no notes, and no reconstruction. As for the defense attorney, he did not challenge the doctor's testimony or the medical reports. In fact, in his closing argument, he stipulated to all of the medicals and the autopsies. Then he ended by saying, "Folks, as I said when I opened this case, this is a good ole boy, and we take care of each other down here. This is Billy's boy. Y'all know him. Billy owns the grocery store down at the junction. This is Billy's boy." With that, he rested his case. The jury stayed out for four hours. That alone scared the hell out of the defense. What was keeping them out for four hours? Obviously, it was a defendant's verdict. This case was another notch in my legal education and the lessening of my naïveté: Justice could not only *not* be served—justice could be damned with impunity and arrogance. Lady Justice is not blind. That blindfold around her eyes is bullshit; her eyes are wide open as to your color, your national heritage, your religion, and your economic status. This and the Smith case were the types of civil cases I became very much involved with, as well as very interesting criminal cases.

Also around 1978, I took on one case knowing I would lose. On the Eastern Shore, an alleged black dope dealer sold dope to his white girlfriend, who turned out to be an undercover state trooper. This was a no-win case. For the jury, it was not going to be about the sale of narcotics. On the contrary, I knew they would convict him simply for going with a white woman. So, being sarcastic, I said to the all-white jury, "This man is on trial for selling dope, not for going with a white woman." The jury laughed and then found him guilty.

My next big criminal case happened around 1980 and was much more high profile. It was also my first murder case that actually went to trial. Robert Perry was a bus driver in Baltimore City who had been terminated for alleged personnel reasons. He was charged with going back to the Union Hall on Maryland Avenue, where he supposedly shot and killed a man by the name of Keys, the board chairman of the bus-drivers' union. Perry also supposedly shot and wounded another man in the office by the name of Pettis, a so-called pretty boy who had worked his way up from being a bus driver to becoming president of the local union. According to newspaper accounts, this was an unbeatable case. Perry was arrested while sitting in his van about an hour after the shooting. Reportedly, there was gunshot residue on his hand.

Pettis, who was still alive, identified Perry as the assailant. "I saw him shoot and kill Keys, and then he shot me." When Perry was arrested, they recovered a .357 Magnum from his van, which they alleged was the murder weapon. It was apparently an airtight case.

I went to see Perry, and he told me, "Mr. Pettit, I didn't do it."

Of course, I had heard "I didn't do it" and "I was never there" before, but this time there was a lot of questionable evidence.

I asked Perry, "Well, how did you get the gun residue?"

As expected, he replied, "I don't know anything about that. I wasn't there."

I pressed on, "What were you doing when you were arrested?"

"Working on my van," he said. Sure enough, when I examined the photos taken when he was arrested—supposedly while inside his van—the cover of his engine was removed. I took the case.

I brought in Attorney Kenneth L. Johnson, a distinguished criminal and civil-rights lawyer who was known for being very meticulous. In fact, he would later become a judge, now retired, in Baltimore City. Kenneth Johnson was the same person who had been my lawyer during the process of correcting the inequities of the Maryland bar. I wanted someone with experience. If I made any mistakes, I wanted his experience backing me up to ensure I would not sacrifice the client.

It was an interesting trial, which lasted ten days in Baltimore City. I had retained experts, including ballistics experts from the Aberdeen Proving Ground, and was advised that the chemical compound you get on your hands when you fire a gun is carbon-based residue. Carbon components can also be picked up from working on a car engine. What about the motive? What about the alibi? Was he or wasn't he there? I began digging into the facts. I went back to the murder scene and realized there was a door in the back of the office. A car had been parked in the back that had blocked the exit door. I went through the office looking for a second bullet. One bullet was in Mr. Keys, but I looked for the second bullet, which had passed through Mr. Pettis's arm. I never located it anywhere in the room, and finally, it dawned on me what could have happened.

I knew that the union was under investigation by the FBI for some type of alleged fraud or embezzlement. My theory was that Pettis might have been at the core of this investigation, and Keys may have had knowledge of information that would have incriminated Pettis. My theory was that Pettis set up Keys, knowing that the police would conclude that Perry had a motive. He had blocked the doorway in back with his car, so that Keys could not exit. He then shot and killed Keys. Then Pettis went downstairs where he inflicted a flesh wound in his arm. That was the reason why I could not find the second bullet. It was not in the room. After Keys was killed, everybody went to the hospital while Perry was arrested. But, where did Pettis go? Pettis did not go to the hospital to comfort the deceased wife and family. Instead, after being treated for his wound at another hospital, Pettis went back to the scene of the crime that night before he did anything else. Why did he do that? My theory was that he went back to remove the bullet that had lodged somewhere in the wall in the basement where he had inflicted the wound in his own arm.

Pettis had motive and opportunity. It was a perfect crime. The bullet was supposed to have been fired by a .357 Magnum. The State never connected the bullet to the gun. They just said that Perry had a .357 Magnum. The bullet that was recovered was a .38. The state ballistic listing stated that .38-caliber ammunition could be fired from a .357 Magnum or a .38 revolver. They never could prove that that bullet came from Perry's .357 Magnum. The wound on Pettis's arm, a clean wound, was half the size of a penny. Obviously, a smaller gun had been used. Also, the angle of the wound did not match where he was allegedly sitting or standing in the office. I observed another strange thing when I went to the police headquarters to see the clothes Mr. Keys had worn when he was shot. Perry was supposed to have been sitting directly in front of Keys. He was supposed to have shot him directly and then turned to shoot the fleeing Pettis, hitting him in the arm. However, Mr. Keys's shirt had a bullet trace indicating the bullet had come directly from Mr. Pettis's direction, not Perry's. This agreed with the path of the bullet in the autopsy. It was not a direct forward wound. Either the bullet came from the side, or Mr. Keys had turned at the last second. You could actually see the graze pattern on the shirt; it was diagonal.

I had never done a "Perry Mason" before, but it is every lawyer's dream to have a trial with a Perry Mason-type discovery. When I cross-examined Pettis, I remarked right off, "Mr. Pettis, this is a very small wound to the upper inside of your right arm. If, in fact, it came from a .357 Magnum, from where you said you were, and according to where Perry was, a .357 Magnum at three and a half feet should have torn a good part of your arm off."

Pettis, being a good witness, looked to the jury and said, "Ladies and gentlemen, I don't care what Mr. Pettit said. I don't care how eloquent he is, I saw Perry kill Keys, and I know that Perry shot me."

I came back on cross-examination, "Mr. Pettis, I've heard your elegant testimony to the jury. I'm not going to take you through this again about where you were sitting or standing and how the bullet hit you, clearly going through your arm. I have just two questions for you on another subject. You went to college. Is that correct?"

"That's correct."

"Please tell the ladies and gentlemen of the jury what you studied."

"Criminal law and criminal justice."

"No further questions."

In closing I said, "Ladies and gentlemen of the jury, a murder has been committed, I concede that. And I concede that the murderer is in this courtroom. But, ladies and gentlemen of the jury, the murderer is not sitting beside me; the murderer is sitting in the audience." I turned, looked at Pettis in the rear of the gallery, and went on to explain. After ten and a half hours of deliberation, the result was a hung jury.

Judge Ward declared a mistrial. He would later say to me, "Mr. Pettit, you really didn't believe what you told the jury, did you?"

I told him, "I really believe it, and the facts support it."

I had taken the Perry case because it was high profile, realizing that Mr. Perry didn't have any money. As it turned out he only had about $3,500, and I spent well over $10,000 of my own funds, including the expenses of cocounsel and experts.

When the State later retried the case, I was called to the courtroom by the new attorney, a young woman by the name of Joann Suder, a public defender. She was very concerned and told me, "Mr. Pettit, I don't know what to do. Mr. Perry will not come out of the lockup, and I don't want him brought in front of the jury chained and gagged. He says he won't talk to anybody but you."

I went to him and said, "Robert, I hung in there for the first trial. I did it spending my own money. I can't do it a second time." This was the negative side of justice, which I always look back on with regret. I don't know whether it was a lack of principle in terms of dollars or principle in terms of necessity, but it still hurts me today that I did not handle the second case. They tried the case in Mr. Perry's absence because he refused to go into the courtroom. They convicted him in the second trial on the charge of second-degree murder. That was in 1982. I never heard from Mr. Perry again. It was very unfortunate that the first trial did not acquit him. The Perry case was the perfect crime with a perfect setup that unraveled in the first trial.

Years later, I took on the Eric Stennett case, which I will discuss later. It was also labeled "airtight" yet came apart, which only goes to prove the proposition that no case is airtight in front of a jury. Trial is all-out war; it is not just combat. I think that a trial is one of the most intense, mentally competitive things you can do as a lawyer. Doctors have a very compelling and exacting profession, but they bury their mistakes. Even in police work, there is the advantage of numbers against an adversary and the force of society. But for a trial lawyer, it is a one-on-one battle with an advocate who is just as trained, as learned, as competitive, and as determined. I think it was Chief Justice Burger who said (and I may be paraphrasing), "Out of all the lawyers in the nation, trial lawyers are but 1 percent, and only 1 percent of them are competent trial lawyers."

Another high-profile case that I handled around this time was the case of Mr. William Johnson. William Johnson could not hear nor speak, a condition often referred to as being a deaf-mute. He had been a tremendous athlete in high school, and as I tried his case, I developed a special respect for him because we had played against Gallaudet University, a school for the hearing and speech impaired, during my first two years at Howard University.

When I met Mr. Johnson, I learned that he had married the love of his life, a woman who was also a deaf-mute. They had an intense love affair. I saw this woman's picture, and it was evident that she had been a beautiful woman, with a beautiful face and great body. She already had one daughter, and they had more children together. Unfortunately, after they had been married for some time, she left William, and William went off the deep end. Although William and family members persuaded the wife to come back home, William did not feel good about where she spent her time and what she was doing.

One day at church, while his wife sat up in the choir loft, one of their little boys pointed and said, "Daddy, that's mommy's friend. He's the one sitting next to her. He comes over to the house all the time when you're not home."

During their separation, William's wife had gotten deeply in debt, upward of $10,000, and in an effort to get her to come back home, William had paid off all her bills. When William got home that night after church, which happened to be Valentine's Day, he went upstairs and found her in her lingerie, wearing a ring he had given her. In sign language, he asked, "Why aren't you happy?"

She turned to him and said in sign language, "I am just so sick of you. I am sick of your face. I am back, but I can't stand to look at you." She took off the ring and threw it in William's face, signing, "Yes, I have someone else, and I despise you."

With that, William went back downstairs and got one of three kitchen knives. He went back upstairs, where he stabbed her eighteen times. In the process of stabbing her, his stepdaughter jumped on his back, and William cut her up as well. After William killed his wife, he walked past his stepdaughter, who was begging him not to kill her. However, he was not even thinking about her. He went outside, sat down on the steps, and waited for the police. The police arrived, and William confessed on video with the assistance of an interpreter. It was one of the most moving confessions I had ever seen, all in sign language.

We went to trial on charges of first-degree murder and attempt to murder in the first degree. I raised the "hot-blooded passion" defense.

Under Maryland common law, the law can excuse or at least mitigate certain conduct, even a murder charge, when it is motivated by hot blood. We tried this case in front of the distinguished Baltimore City circuit court judge John J. Prevas (now deceased). I still believe today that if William had listened to me, he would probably have beaten all of the charges, in spite of the way he killed his wife and all of the gruesome aspects of this case. Nevertheless, he was found guilty of manslaughter and attempted murder. However, we still won to a certain extent, because he was not found guilty of murder. What got me was that William was determined to testify. He went against my advice, determined to tell that jury how much he loved this woman.

There was no need for William to testify, he had already confessed, and they had his videotaped confession, and when it was played by the State, it was very moving. The lights were turned off in the courtroom, and over the course of forty-five compelling minutes, the jury watched this man confess not only his crime but also his love for his woman and the fact that she was his life. It was heartbreaking. The interpreter, Ms. Stevens, got on the stand and testified, along with a doctor, that the dependency felt by the handicapped, and particularly the dependency on another handicapped person, has a different defining effect than that which is felt by nonhandicapped people. Moreover, his dependency on his wife was more than just a male-female relationship, it was more than just a sexual relationship; they had grown up together. She was his life, someone he could communicate with when he could not talk to the rest of the world. He could laugh with her and cry with her when the rest of the world did not understand him, knowing that she would understand. This was their relationship from adolescence, all the way through high school, and all the way through life. Their bond was something so heavy that nonhandicapped individuals could not understand it. It could be such a bond that it could create the motive to not only kill her but also to kill himself. In fact, William was on suicide watch for weeks and months thereafter. The jury was so touched that you could hear them sobbing during his confession.

I begged William not to take the stand. I pleaded, "William, you have already said everything, so you don't have to take the stand." But, William overruled me and decided that he wanted to tell the jury his story. As it turned out, William effectively cleared up exactly how the murder took place, revealing even to me some additional details. He actually broke off the first knife, went downstairs, got a second butcher knife, and stabbed her again until that one also broke. He then went back downstairs, got the third butcher knife, and stabbed her and her daughter until that one broke as well. He then methodically picked up all of the pieces of the knives, took them downstairs, and put them into the wash pan. Nobody had put together the puzzle about those knives until William got on the stand and explained to the jury how he broke off all of them in his wife. It was a fascinating case, not just because it was a fascinating murder, but because of the passion and love and the compounding effect of the disabilities these people had. The cases opened a window for me to a whole new understanding of how the disabled cope, live, and survive in their world. Their world is completely different. Their friends and associates are different. In their world, William was a hero, someone who was an athlete, the star, the kid who made good despite all of his limitations. Nevertheless, in his mind, his whole life was only possible because of one woman, his wife. Without her, there was no life.

It was a classic murder trial that could have been a made-for-TV drama. The jury came back with not guilty in first degree and not guilty in the second degree, and considering his testimony, I think we beat all that we could, except the final verdict of manslaughter. Hot-blooded passion did not exonerate William, but it was a mitigating factor. As for his stepdaughter, William was convicted of second-degree attempted murder.

The next case I worked on, *Shirley Goodwin v. the Washington Metropolitan Area Transportation Authority* (1982), was, at that time, the highest verdict in history rendered against the Washington, DC, transportation system. That was one million dollars. We tried the case in front of the same judge who oversaw the Watergate proceedings. In this case, Shirley Goodwin lost her husband, who was working on the other side of the road when he was hit and killed by a DC bus. This was a case of wrongful death. This matter was brought to me by Robert Clay, a fascinating person in Baltimore City and a very good friend of mine at that time. He was probably one of the youngest black millionaires in Baltimore City. Sadly, in 2005, he was found shot to death in his office. The State ruled it a suicide, but his family, with good cause, believes it was murder.

Shirley Goodwin's case was very interesting. We did not have to prove liability, but we had to prove damages. The difficulty was that life had taken its toll on Shirley. She was a black woman left with five kids who lived in a small cramped abode. What's more, she had a drinking problem. Her common-law husband had been a good provider, but Shirley was really quite a character.

I shared the case with Mike Miller's law firm, which represented the deceased's mother. Mike is now best known as State Senator Thomas "Mike" Miller, president of the Maryland State Senate. When I met with Mike and his associate John Webster on the Goodwin case, he said to me, "Well, Dwight, if you work with us, that Mercedes you drove up here could become just one of three or four. We can win this case and win big." They worked the case up, given that John Webster was an expert in terms of wrongful death.

For two years, my responsibility was primarily to babysit Shirley. I ended up being a surrogate father to her kids, while trying to limit her drinking. I also had to curse out the men (Shirley's friends) waiting around for the big money to come in and keep them from taking what little money she did have. I made trips from Baltimore City to Shirley's house at least five out of seven days a week and sometimes two to three times a day. I even helped Shirley pick out another house and move from her place to the new house with insurance monies paid prior to trial. I basically cared for that family for two years as we prepared for trial, and on the eve of the trial I put them in a motel. With some preliminary insurance money, Shirley supplied the five kids with new clothes. She dressed them up, and I told them how we were going to go to court, and how they should look and act. We went over all of their testimony, and I kept Shirley completely away from alcohol. I literally sat guard on her family and her for twenty-four hours in a motel room before the trial. When we marched into the United

States district court for the District of Columbia on Monday morning to try the case before Judge Gazell, Shirley was well-dressed and sober, and the kids were like little soldiers.

I wanted one million dollars per child, but the judge would not let me mention any monetary amount. He warned that if I said a specific dollar amount, he was going to hold me in contempt and declare a mistrial. Judge Gazell had been very rough on me, because he said I was leading the kids during their testimony.

The defense had espoused the position that even if the bus company were deemed liable, the family had been so impoverished beforehand that the loss of their father was not measurable in terms of the loss of financial resources, past or future. Meaning that, even if their father had lived, he would have only made another forty or fifty thousand dollars total before he retired or died.

The defense attorney actually got up and told the jury, "Ladies and gentlemen, if you give this family more than a hundred thousand dollars, you will destroy these people. These people are poor. Any award above that will destroy this family. They are not use to it. You don't make a family rich just because they lose somebody; you compensate them, and in this instance, one hundred thousand dollars would be more than adequate compensation for these poor folks."

I had never heard anything like this in my life. This white man said this to a predominately black jury that victims should stay poor. I was sure that if Judge Gazell had let me say to the jury what I wanted to say, they would have awarded five million, one million per child. At any rate, John in his rebuttal closing mentioned that a million dollars was only the value of a racehorse, and I think the jury surmised that was what we wanted, and, that's what we ultimately got.

Before closing, however, I remembered something that Shirley's youngest girl had told me during an initial interview, so I called her as my last witness. She was five years old, the cutest little thing. She looked like a little chocolate doll baby, all dressed up and pretty. She had on a beautiful, little, ruffled dress. On the stand, I took her through the whole family thing as much as you can take a five-year-old without leading, and she said, "I know my daddy, and I remember my daddy." I really got her talking.

Then I got everybody hushed and quiet, before asking her, "Sweetheart, do you miss your daddy?" By that time she had her thumb in her mouth, and she was about to cry.

The jury started sniffling. I said, "Take your time, sweetheart. What do you remember most about your daddy?"

With a slight lisp, she said, "My daddy ... my daddy ... my daddy used to take me to Toys R Us."

On that, I rested my case.

The jury was in tears. I remember this case in terms of the audacity of the defense lawyer to actually argue that giving poor people too much money would be a travesty and the destruction of a family—that a large amount awarded in damages would be too much a shock and a radical departure from the poverty they were used to. I couldn't believe this argument, but I heard it. I had heard this argument in Ann Arundel County, Maryland, but I could not believe the arrogance of this lawyer making this argument in front of a black jury in Washington, DC. He didn't dispute the fact that the man had died a very tragic and brutal death under the wheels of a transit bus, and he didn't argue the issue of liability. His whole argument was that if the jury awarded this family too much money, they would be responsible for the destruction of this family.

Later I would see these kids grow up. The money was placed in a trust fund for them, and every one of those kids, every time I saw them in the malls or shopping centers, was still in school. They still had money and were taking care of their mother, and in spite of that defense lawyer's argument, they were living a good life. The money did not hurt.

Chapter 17: Reasonable Doubt

One of the biggest criminal cases in my career was the trial of Eric Stennett in Baltimore City. Like the Perry case, the Stennett matter was the classic unwinnable case but for the power of reasonable doubt. The case was tried in early 2000. One night, years after the trial, I ran into a law professor at an affair, and he told me he no longer referenced the O. J. Simpson case during lectures on reasonable doubt. He now used the Stennett case because, in his opinion, it helped his students better understand the concept. His premise was that good criminal lawyers have to recognize that the State has all of the power, including the power of money, police resources, expert witnesses, investigation tools, and the grand jury. The State has everything. No matter how strong a defense lawyer's case is, it is potentially difficult to win. Thus, what a good defense lawyer has to do is look for that one crack in the armor through which to insert reasonable doubt. Then, just like building a pyramid, that sliver of doubt must be molded and constructed into a minor doubt that becomes a major doubt that overshadows and erodes the state or federal government's case.

He said that before the Stennett case he used the O. J. Simpson case in his lectures as a classic example. He believed the unraveling of that case began when they trapped Detective Furman with his inconsistent response to the question, "Did you in fact use a racial slur in the past referring to blacks and African Americans?"

Furman's refutable answer was, "No."

The professor I was talking with was white. He said that at some point in time, most, if not all, white people in America—no matter how holy or religious they think they are, no matter how straight and narrow they appear to be, and no matter how many liberal or black friends they lay claim to—have told a joke or said something in the presence of other white people that was derogative of black people. Furman denied he had ever done it, but everyone knew that wasn't true. He felt that no white American had gotten to adulthood without having made some kind of negative reference at some point in time. For example, in traffic, someone might use the "N" word. Or, when there's a theft nearby, someone might say, "There are too many of 'those people' in the neighborhood." It has happened. What Furman didn't consider was that they had hard evidence and knew he had made derogatory statements. And, from that small piece of information—which, by the way, was totally irrelevant to anything at issue except credibility—the defense laid the foundation, built a bridge, raised a flag, and then achieved sufficient reasonable doubt. Of course, it did not hurt the defense that the glove did not fit.

In the Stennett case, as in the O. J. Simpson case, the State perceived they had a perfect case. In the Stennett case, the police actually witnessed the crime. They were there. They saw it all, start to finish. It was like the assassination of Bobby Kennedy, seen live on television and by everyone in the room. The police saw Eric Stennett ram his vehicle into the decedent's car, and the decedent was a cop. This was the absolute slam-dunk case. To create reasonable doubt and win the unwinnable case when everybody said, "I saw it happen," is the criminal lawyer's ultimate success. The professor said that he was so happy to meet me after the affair. He also wanted to tell me that in his course outline he lays out the context for establishing reasonable-doubt arguments. He said that if one could establish reasonable doubt in the Stennett case, one could establish reasonable doubt in any case.

The Stennett case was about a seventeen-year-old African American male who was allegedly involved in some low-level street drug operation. Along with his associates, he allegedly sold narcotics and was generally heavily armed. Stennett, whose street name was "Slice," had evidently gone into a neighborhood earlier that week and somebody had shot at him. In fact, the evidence showed that he had been there on several nights when gunfire broke out, but he was a victim, not the perpetrator. He allegedly came back several nights later in full body armor, carrying a 9mm handgun and driving a Ford Bronco. When he pulled up on the street in question and saw the person who had assaulted him sitting on some steps, he pulled out his handgun and opened fire.

The guy, whose name was Dorsey, took off running, and Stennett allegedly chased him on foot. As Dorsey rounded the corner, he unknowingly ran into undercover police who just happened to be coming up the street. Their statement is that Stennett was shooting at Dorsey. That led to the charge of assault with the attempt to murder. Stennett retreated back to his Bronco. Coincidentally, coming up behind the Bronco were four more undercover police officers in an unmarked car. They had heard the shooting and allegedly saw Stennett running back to the truck, holding a gun. As they pulled up behind the truck, Stennett saw them and entered the Bronco, taking off at a high rate of speed. The police gave chase for several blocks through Baltimore City until they ended up in the area of Lombard Street. Allegedly, at some point in time, the speeds were as high as 104 miles per hour.

Alerted by police dispatch, Officer Kevon Gavin approached from the opposite direction, positioning himself to act as a roadblock in front of the oncoming Bronco. The police alleged that Stennett intentionally gunned his engine and accelerated his speed before ramming his Bronco into Officer Gavin's vehicle. The Bronco ran on top of the police vehicle, crushing it and thereby killing Officer Gavin. Because a police officer was down, police emptied into the streets of Baltimore City in full force. That became part of the problem, because when they converged on the street, there was chaos, mass confusion, and unbridled emotion. As a result, the investigation left a lot to be desired. The State's attorney indicted Stennett, in fact she over-indicted him because of the emotional aspect of the events. He was charged with first-degree and second-degree murder and manslaughter. They also indicted him with assault and attempt to murder. There were no offers made for plea negotiations.

I hired an expert out of Prince George's County, a former police officer who was an accident-reconstruction expert. Our first contact with the authorities was when we went to the police yard to look at the Ford Bronco. My expert found an interesting fact that would later come back to haunt the State. He drew my attention to the tire marks. The tire marks specifications matching those in the street referred to in the reconstruction report did not match the specs of the tires on the Bronco. This was important, because these marks were the justification for the first-degree murder charge. The tire marks were supposed to have been made due to the sudden acceleration of the Bronco, and that acceleration was presented as evidence of Stennett's intent to kill Officer Gavin. The marks did not match the Bronco. They were not the same size. Instead, the tire marks appeared to be from an unknown vehicle. They had measured old tire marks left there before the alleged crime in question.

My expert took his equipment and electronic instruments to inspect the Bronco. The police stood around looking very curious during the inspection. Nevertheless, they still exuded confidence that they had an unbeatable case. My expert did not have much to say to me at first, so I worked at establishing a rapport with him. I found out that being a former police officer who still played golf with comrades in Prince George's County, he was not too happy about the assignment he had accepted. In fact, at one point he told me that he did not see how he could help me in terms of testimony. However, he had already earned his fee and helped me by revealing the tire-mark discrepancy.

Next, we went to look at the police vehicle, which was located elsewhere. Unbelievably, the police vehicle was missing. It had been towed and destroyed, even though I had written a letter asking for the preservation of all evidence. Despite this, someone had authorized and allowed the police vehicle to be destroyed. Finally, we went to look at the pictures of both vehicles taken at the crime scene. What the tire error did was cause a return trip to the crime scene by the police expert to try to reconstruct his reconstruction. This was the same expert who had measured the tires and tire marks for the original report. We did not find this out until later when we got a late discovery report showing a new report dated after our inspection. It was my expert who brought this new inspection date to my attention after receiving the second report.

There were other police mistakes. The police expert's first report indicated that the Ford Bronco's engine block had accelerated at the point of impact and left the chassis of the Bronco. This was corrected in the second report because this finding could not be sustained by the State police expert reviewing the Baltimore City expert's first report. Then we received information that Stennett did not have any gunshot residue (GSR) on his hands, and there was no indication that he had been wearing gloves. They had wrapped his hands, taken him to the hospital, tested his hands for residue, locked him down in cuffs, and sealed off his room. So, where was the residue?

The next thing we discovered was that two of the four undercover officers in the vehicle that had chased Stennett were Lieutenant Ellerman (a female) and Sergeant Wiemer. They both wrote reports indicating that Stennett appeared to lose control of his car and veer to the right. Lieutenant Ellerman did not change her report, but she testified differently at trial. However, Sergeant Wiemer went back and wrote another report. Yes, once again, another report. The Sergeant's second report indicated there was no loss of control and that the impact was caused intentionally.

All of a sudden, we had conflicting statements by Lieutenant Ellerman and conflicting reports by Sergeant Wiemer, with all of the changes being made within a few days after submitting their first reports. We also had another inconsistent accident report by another officer on the scene. That police report indicated that Stennett allegedly shot the young man he was chasing, leaving a graze wound on his ankle. This was the basis of the attempted murder charge. However, there were no holes in Dorsey's socks and pants leg where the bullet supposedly went through. And, as it turned out, there were no pants or socks entered into evidence. They were released back to Dorsey that night. The police had released evidence needed in an attempted murder case. That left it somewhat questionable whether there was ever a bullet or if Dorsey's wound was simply a scratch that he could have received while fleeing Stennett.

Although we had several openings in the State's airtight case, they were nevertheless very cocky. No offers were made.

We drew Judge Carol Smith, an astute jurist intolerant of bullshit in her courtroom, who also allegedly happened to be a former nun. Then we picked a jury of ten blacks, one Hispanic, and one white male. After about seven to ten days of motions and testimony from one witness after another, the State's case began to come apart. It happened during my cross-examination of the State's reconstruction expert, Sergeant Howard. Referring to his resume, I questioned him about his qualifications. I remember when my father had wanted me to study engineering, I had rejected the idea. Now, as an adult, I finally understood. Mathematics stays in the back of your mind, and its application is essential at certain times. Over Dad's objections, I had not taken trigonometry. However, I did take physical science in college. I remember very vividly asking the State's expert witness whether he had an engineering background, and when he answered, "No," I knew the door was open.

I asked him if he had taken calculus.

"No."

I asked if he had taken physics.

"No."

I asked if he had taken any higher-level mathematics.

"No."

I asked him if, outside of the police department and as a consultant, whether he had taken any courses in physics, speed, math, movement, inertia, or anything like that.

"No."

Then I got more specific, asking him about human factoring.

Human factoring is the study of human reaction intertwined with certain scientific data—in other words, a human being's ability to react, a human being's ability to assimilate information, his reaction time, and the consumption and digestion of information within a certain time period. Years before, I had done an excellent cross-examination of a forensic doctor in a murder trial. I remember spending several nights digesting information regarding the determination of rigor mortis and the time of death. I learned enough within seventy-two hours, despite not being a doctor, to know the intricacies of the medical testimony. I don't say this in a braggadocio way, I just say this to point out to young lawyers that sometimes cross-examination provides the basics you need for establishing reasonable doubt.

Then, as I stood in front of the jury and in front of the press, thoughts of my father kicked in. I always believed that my father's spirit and other spirits are like guardian angels. God sends certain people to watch over us. In this trial, I felt that my father's spirit had entered me, and I felt totally invincible questioning the State's expert witness. I checked his qualifications, and I found out how deficient he was. Then I took him step-by-step through the inconsistencies in his report. That was not a big thing, because his report was open. Reports speak for themselves. If he measured the wrong tire (and he did), if he developed the wrong conclusion as to speed (and he did), if he made the wrong determination about the engine separating from the chassis (and he did), these things were on paper.

When I continued my cross-examination, I stood directly in front of the jury.

"Officer Howard, we are going to do a demonstration for the jury, you and I. We are going to compute speed. You are aware of what I am talking about, Officer, are you not?"

He answered, "Yes."

"Let's do some mathematics together. I am going to give you the data, and you are going to give me your conclusion. I want you to explain for the jury how you calculated speed and mass. Without going into Einstein's $e=mc^2$ or anything as complex as that, I want you to tell the jury the closure rate per foot if a car is moving at a certain speed. For example, if a car is moving at one hundred miles per hour and the car is fifty feet from a nonmoving target, how do you calculate the closure rate, in terms of feet per second? We'll give the jury the mathematical equation and then compute it. But, before we start, let's review the situation. The facts say that Officer Gavin pulled onto the street at a certain angle in front of Stennett who was, according to your report, a distance of 50 feet away. What was the closure rate in feet per second and the time to impact?"

He pulled out his calculator, performed a few calculations, and then looked up again, "Well," he said, "it would be six seconds to impact." He was wrong.

I said, "Officer, that's not right," and the jury looked at me. It was one of those great moments during a trial. It was similar to the glove situation in the O. J. Simpson trial. He had gotten so nervous because I had cross-examined him so efficiently that he made a minor mistake. But in a trial, minor mistakes are major.

He said, "No, no ... my calculations, Mr. Pettit ... I'm looking at them ... six seconds."

I said, "No, no, officer, don't you mean six tenths of a second?"

He shook his head, "Damn it, you're right."

"So, we are not talking about a full six seconds—one thousand one, one thousand two, one thousand three, one thousand four, one thousand five, one thousand six. No, we're talking about a closure time of a vehicle doing one hundred miles per hour. We're talking about a fraction of a second closure time—a *fraction* of *one* second when this young man had to make a decision to go left, right, or try an evasive movement. In other words, Officer, he didn't even get a full second. Am I right?"

Reluctantly he replied, "Yes," and I closed my cross-examination. At that point, even though I still did not know whether the case was won, I thought that was one of my most successful cross-examinations. I had implemented engineering concepts that I had heard my father talk about for years. A lot of people may not have known such things. Even my expert may not have been aware.

If you really think about it, the police department should have been ashamed of itself. They were in big trouble because they should not have made this type of mistake. They had top experts in ballistics, pathology, and forensics. I could not believe that they put forth all these shining-star experts with the exception of the most crucial expert, the reconstruction expert. He was the one who was going to tell the jury how it happened within a reasonable degree of scientific certainty, yet he was simply not qualified to counter the specter of reasonable doubt.

We began to list for the jury the difficulties in the State's case. No one other than police had positively identified Stennett as the shooter or the person getting into the Ford Bronco. Dorsey, the young man allegedly chased by Stennett, reportedly made a photo identification of Stennett but recanted that identification in court. We knew from his statement that he was going to say that he never identified him. I reiterated for the jury that no civilian witnesses had taken the stand and identified Eric Stennett as either the shooter or the driver.

Once we began to break the credibility of the police, we began to break the whole chain of testimony. If the jury believed the police lied about their reports, if they believed the police lied about changing their statements, if they believed the reconstruction expert was mistaken about the tire, got sloppy on other details, and then perhaps lied about it, then why wouldn't the rest of them be less than truthful about the conclusions, testimony, or other facts given on the stand?

There was no bullet or bullet hole consistent with Stennett's firing a gun because the alleged victim's pants and socks had not been retained as evidence. Hypothetically, I could have asked the testifying officer, an eighteen-year veteran, if the young man running from Stennett had suffered a bullet wound. Instead of affirming a wound, he could have said, "Mr. Pettit, here are his pants, and there is a bullet hole." One does not have to have a wound to have a bullet hole; however, one does have to have the hole in his pants to have a wound.

So I asked a series of questions. "Why, Sergeant, would you release his pants rather than hold them for material evidence? Is that reasonable?" "Did you take pictures of the hole or did you release the pants without pictures?" "Was Mr. Dorsey taken to a hospital? Is there medical verification by a doctor showing that a wound existed?"

At the crime scene, a police officer made the mistake of actually using his bare hands to pick up the gun. Therefore, there were no valid fingerprints on the gun, certainly none belonging to Eric Stennett, who was barehanded when arrested. In addition, the shells were not carefully handled. There were ten spots "circled," but only nine shells retained as evidence. Apparently, after picking up the shells, an officer was told to put them back down for the crime lab pictures. The officer put them back down where he thought he had picked them up. The fingerprints later found on the shells did not match Stennett, although he supposedly loaded the gun. The boxes for the cartridges found in the Bronco were covered with fingerprints, but again, none of them belonged to Stennett. Although there was residue on Dorsey, the person being chased, there was no gun residue on Stennett. There was testimony that Stennett supposedly had a scarf that might have protected him from the residue. (During this testimony, the scarf changed from red to blue and then black in color.) The problem with this theory was the listing presented by the State of the items seized as evidence included everything on Stennett down to his underwear and socks, but there was no mention of any scarf. Even more interesting, were the changing statements by Sergeant Wiemer, Lieutenant Ellerman, and Sergeant Howard, the reconstructionist. There were no dates indicating which reports were written by Sergeant Howard or when. He also indicated that he never talked to any witnesses in the area who may have observed anything.

When I went down to police headquarters to look at the evidence, I was shown a black rag, although it was not tagged and listed. The testimony at trial was that Stennett was searched three times before he was put into the paddy wagon. If he had in his possession or on his person this big black scarf or rag that the police said he had around his face, neck, or hands it would have been seized and listed. This was not the case. All of a sudden, at the time of trial, they said, "Oh, yeah, here is the rag." Judge Smith wisely sustained my objection due to inadmissibility.

Another compelling misstep by the police was brought to the jury's attention. After Mr. Stennett was arrested, and before the entire incident even hit the news, I received an urgent call from his mother asking me to represent her teenaged son. I immediately called the Baltimore City police department and advised them that I had been retained by the family, and I asked when I could see my client. I was told he was in the hospital. I called the next day and through the weekend, but they refused to let me see him.

When I finally went down to Central Booking and Detention on Sunday, they told me that he had been moved, and I still could not see him. When I went back to the Baltimore City detention center on Monday, they told me that it was against the rules for lawyers to see clients on Mondays. They held this young man from Thursday until Tuesday, when I finally got to see him. Well, that may be acceptable police conduct to show that kind of arrogance. But, it's not acceptable when one gets on the witness stand and tells this to a jury.

My questions were simple: "Sergeant, didn't I call you?"

His response, "Yes."

"Sergeant, didn't I talk to you personally?"

"Yes."

"Sergeant, didn't I tell you I was retained by his mother, and didn't I ask to see my client?"

"Yes, Mr. Pettit, you did those things. But, Eric didn't ask to see you, and he's the client, and he has a right to a lawyer, but the lawyer does not have the right to a client."

When he said that, I could see the hairs stand up on the necks of the mothers on the jury. What audacity! There was actual testimony on the stand that this young man, still a minor under the law, was injured, taken to the hospital with a concussion, subjected to police interrogation, and placed under complete surveillance for five days. What's more, although a lawyer had been retained by the family on "day one" to represent their minor son, and although requests were made repeatedly by the lawyer to see his client, the police refused because of their belief that a lawyer does not have a right to speak with his client. Remember, Eric had no way of knowing that his family had retained counsel.

I think that was the straw that broke the camel's back. The jurors were shaking their heads.

Then came one other piece of testimony, which I didn't want to touch with a ten-foot pole. However, the jurors picked up on it all by themselves. It was in the autopsy report on Officer Gavin. His alcohol blood level was 0.04. The jurors felt it was relatively high, even though the pathologist testified that this was the result of the decomposition of the body. According to this testimony, the chemical that the body secretes during decomposition could create the 0.04 blood alcohol level. Now, in the state of Maryland, a 0.04 level is a violation for commercial drivers.

However, I later checked this with several top pathologists, and they all said that the decomposition process could produce a blood alcohol level no higher than 0.01. The body would never create a 0.04 level. So technically, under Maryland law, Officer Kevon Gavin was impaired. I did not touch this because in no way did I want to incur the wrath of the jury. I did not want to do or say something negative to discredit Officer Gavin's character. The only way that I came close, without going there, was in closing. I reminded the jury that this is the real world. He was not Batman or Robin. He was not Wyatt Earp. He was not the "Duke" John Wayne or Clint Eastwood. You just don't run your car into somebody, get up, and walk away.

"What in the world, ladies and gentlemen, had compelled Officer Gavin, when he heard on his radio that a Bronco was coming at him at a speed in access of 104 miles per hour? He was on another street, a street of safety. What compelled him to turn his vehicle into the path of a much bigger vehicle that was moving over 104 miles per hour or higher? I couldn't answer the question. I'm asking you, as a jury, to ask yourself that question. What would make a rational, reasonable person do that?"

I believe that the jury answered that question in their verdict. Some believed that Officer Gavin might have been impaired. What remains to be seen was whether they believed he had stopped somewhere and got a beer when he had lunch that night, or whether he might have been using a medication, because the autopsy revealed he was suffering from mild pneumonia. In either event, he should not have been working that night, and it was the jurors themselves who raised the issue that there might have been something affecting or impairing Officer Gavin's judgment in those last few seconds.

The judge took a phone call at the bench and interrupted the trial. Upon her finishing her call, she said, "Mr. Pettit, do you want to close now, or do you want to close after lunch?"

I said, "Judge, I would rather not close now with people hungry and thinking about lunch. I'd rather close after lunch." When I came back after lunch, the courtroom was closed to the public. But, when they opened the door, the room was immediately packed with police officers, the media, and public observers. In no time, it became standing room only. Sitting next to me was one of my associates, a young man by the name of Matthew Bennett, who had been my cocounsel during the trial, an excellent sidekick or, as they say in the business, "second chair."

He leaned over to me and said, "Boss, are you nervous? Can you handle this with all these people?"

I looked around and then said to him, "Matthew, let me tell you something. Look at these people. Look at these cameras. Look at this crowd. Feel the tension in the air. Look at the officers' faces. Look at the jurors. We're on live, living stage, television, media—everything is live. This is locally what the O. J. Simpson trial was nationally. If you are not ready for this, if I am not ready for this, then we're not ready to be trial lawyers. Five minutes from now, I will be standing on center stage in front of the world, and the only reason that you wouldn't want this, would be if the case represented a deficiency in your preparation or if your skills were lacking. But if you are confident that you are prepared, this is every trial lawyer's dream. I have nothing else to say. I'm in the zone. I will be on stage in five minutes."

The papers said that the defense counsel had to be shocked at the verdict—Stennett was found not guilty on everything. At the very least, we all expected a verdict of at least negligent homicide or manslaughter. I won't say that I was shocked, but I would say that I was pleasantly surprised. I had told the jury, at one point, that even though I didn't expect them to let my client walk out of there, he was not guilty of murder.

What they did not put in the paper was that I had concluded my final closing argument by saying to the jury, "Ladies and gentlemen of the jury, if you look at all of these mistakes, if you look at all of the inconsistencies, look at all of the misstatements of fact, and look at all of the arrogance of the State, including the release and destruction of evidence … if you can put all of these things together one by one, they create reasonable doubt. If reasonable doubt is created over and over on any of these things, and if that generates reasonable doubt overall, then under our great system of laws you are compelled, you are compelled by law, to come back 'not guilty.'" And that's what they did.

The press immediately went to jury nullification. The underlying assumption was that this was a verdict rendered by undereducated black people. People called in on talk radio from all over the state. They called the jury everything under the sun. A police officer from Baltimore County actually went on the radio and said that the problem with Baltimore City jurors was that "they were the same people sleeping with and using dope with the people who were on trial."

I ran into several of the jurors after the trial and talked to a couple of them on the phone. One in particular told me, "Mr. Pettit, it was a tough thing we did, but in this particular instance, the Baltimore City police department didn't present its case. They didn't bring the evidence. In fact, they mutilated and destroyed the evidence, and we, as a jury, had no recourse but to acquit your client regardless of emotions and the tragedy of the loss of Officer Gavin. In this situation, the police department just didn't bring a clear and convincing case beyond a reasonable doubt. You were right. If there was reasonable doubt after these mistakes, and there were mistakes all over the place, we felt we had to acquit." They weren't uneducated ignorant black folks. They were black, white, and Hispanic folks who listened to a case that was destroyed by the police in its investigation and preparation.

As a defense team, we had the ability, and the mother had some finances. We had the resources to hire experts. We had the resources to do what a good criminal lawyer is supposed to do and what a lot of people can't afford to have done. It takes time and that means money. This is not to say that Mrs. Stennett was wealthy or could cover everything. In fact, we invested the fee into victory. In other words, I paid the experts myself.

For several years thereafter, clients would call the office and specifically tell me they wanted the Stennett defense—meaning, in their minds, they wanted the magic of guilt being turned into innocence.

$60 MILLION WRONGFUL DEATH SUIT: Deborah C. Carr, mother of Larry Hubbard, speaks during a news conference near the spot where her son was shot to death in the back of the head by a White Baltimore police officer. At left is attorney Johnnie Cochran, who filed a $60 million lawsuit on behalf of the family over the shooting. Also shown are attorneys A. Dwight Pettit (2nd, l) and William H. Murphy Jr. (r). Police said Hubbard, a suspect in a car theft, was struggling with Officer Robert Quick for his gun when a second officer, Wayne Hamilton, shot him in the head. Several witnesses said the two White officers beat and then killed Hubbard while he was on his knees pleading for his life. Named as defendants in the suit are the two officers, the acting police commissioner at the time of the shooting, the city of Baltimore and the state of Maryland.

Johnny Cochran, Dwight, (Clients) Deborah Carr,
Mr. Hubbard and Billy Murphy

Chapter 18: Onward

When one is dealing with murder cases, the question becomes, to what extent is a lawyer immune to an emotional involvement in the case? No matter how gross the facts, can one remove oneself from the emotional aspect? I have had difficulty with child-abuse cases and heinous crimes. Most murder and rape crimes are heinous, and some are more heinous than others. During the mid-1990s, I had two cases involving the murder of babies and two cases of incest. One of the incest cases allegedly involved both the mother and father of a retarded girl, and the father was a minister.

A particularly disturbing murder occurred in the late 1980s. Billy Jones was a young man who had everything. He had gone to college, his mother had a very nice home, he had a beautiful girlfriend, and he was an X-ray technician at one of our prominent hospitals in Baltimore City. Everything positive that one could imagine was in his favor, until he was charged with murder and attempted murder. Allegedly, Billy killed a woman and attempted to kill another. One of the victims survived, and that was what got him convicted. It was alleged that one Saturday night Billy was cruising an area, high on cocaine, until he picked up two young black women. He allegedly took these women to a park in west Baltimore City where he shot one in the back of the head. He then allegedly raped and shot the other one, also in the back of the head. Little did Billy know, the first girl played possum the whole night and never died. In fact, she never lost consciousness. The bullet had gone into her skull, but instead of going into her brain, it was deflected down into the neck, in the shoulder area. Her survival was by the grace of God. In this particular case, everything that they could have against Billy, they had. They had the girl who lived. She identified him. They had the car found at his house. They found fibers from the girls' clothing in the car. They did a search and seizure and found the gun above his headboard, right where he slept with his beautiful girlfriend. They found everything necessary to establish that Billy Jones committed the crime. Yet, Billy denied committing the crime.

On reflection, if he did commit these crimes, I think Billy simply could not face his mother and admit what he had done. There was no reason for the crime, no motive. We worked out an Alford plea where he pled to first-degree murder so that he would be eligible for parole. An Alford plea (*Alford v. North Carolina*) is where the defendant does not admit guilt. If he had gone to trial, he would have been convicted, and he would have received life without the possibility of parole. The State did not seek the death penalty. This case was emotionally draining for me. Still today, his mother would not believe that her little boy Billy committed these heinous crimes. In fact, after all of the money that she paid me, she hired another lawyer after the plea to recheck everything I had done. The only mistake that the killer made was not making sure that the first girl was dead. If the first girl had died, reports would have read just two dead black girls. No one would have ever suspected him. No one would have pointed to him. No one ever came forth as another witness. No one ever saw the girls get into the car. Nobody saw the murders. There was initially no evidence except that which was generated by the wounded girl. By an act of God, one girl lived, she was conscious, and she identified him and described the car.

This was one of those experiences that test the emotional side of being a lawyer. However, don't get me wrong, I gave him the best defense possible and looked at every potential avenue for acquittal. This was one of those cases that even I had to concede there was no viable, triable option. I did not advise him to plead guilty because of the heinous nature of the crime. Even though the charges were deplorable and stomach turning, I advised him to plead guilty because he had no viable defense and would have to face life without parole if convicted.

Prior to the 1996 congressional election, I handled several other high-profile cases, including *State of Maryland v. Tony M. Murphy*. This civil case received national coverage because it occurred just as "profile" stops were beginning to be widely discussed. Profile stops, which came to be commonly known as DWB or *driving while black*, expanded the frontier of litigation in the context of state and federal seizures of property. The concept of "profile stops" originated during the Iranian hostage crisis, as a mechanism to check for foreign terrorist who might be entering the country. This concept was expanded by the DEA and law enforcement as a result of the so-called war on crime and drugs.

Tony Murphy was a Washington, DC, businessman traveling on I-95 through the town of Elkton in Maryland's Cecil County. He had $71,000 in his car. He was stopped by the state police without probable cause, and dogs were brought in to search his car while he and his companions were detained alongside the road. As it turned out, the dogs did not find any narcotics or other contraband; however, they allegedly brought the money to the attention of the police. Although Mr. Murphy and his companions were not further detained, the police seized the money. When Mr. Murphy demanded the return of his money, the police not only refused, they also refused to provide a receipt. Because of this, Mr. Murphy went immediately to the state police barracks to complain. The not-so-funny thing about Mr. Murphy's demand for the return of his money was that the state police took an additional $750 that he had in his pocket. After that, Mr. Murphy did not even have toll money to get across the Delaware Memorial Bridge.

We brought the civil case in the Circuit Court for Cecil County alleging the civil-rights violation under 42 U.S.C. (1983) before Judge Donaldson Cole, considered one of the more academic judges in the state. This was one of the few times I can recall where a judge never spoke to me or addressed me by name. Although he evidentially determined that he had no recourse but to entertain my position, he did not feel that he had to be cordial during the litigation of the case. Actually, I really did not care as long as the court was fair and objective. What was fascinating about this case was that Judge Cole, despite his conservatism, decided that the tenet of probable cause had been violated, and Mr. Murphy should not have been stopped nor should his car have been searched. The court ruled in our favor but did not directly order the money returned. The judge apologized to the police but ruled correctly as to the facts. Mr. Murphy in his exuberance wanted to take me to dinner in Elkton that night. I said, *Mr. Murphy do you know where you are—this is Elkton, Maryland. There is a KKK headquarters right here. I think the better part of valor is that we be out of town before dark, but thanks anyway.* Unfortunately, the money was never returned to Mr. Murphy, even after the matter went to the Maryland Court of Appeals. Later, Mr. Murphy was brought up on federal charges unrelated to the $71,000, and the money was forfeited by advice of another attorney as part of this plea negotiation.

Later, thanks to the American Civil Liberties Union (ACLU), the state was required to keep statistics on the frequency of blacks being stopped versus whites. The New York to Washington, DC, corridor was infamous. The ACLU would later become involved and make a determination that blacks were being stopped at a tremendously higher rate than whites, despite the fact that there was no numerical basis showing that blacks were committing more crimes than whites. They were just being stopped because they were black.

After the second loss for a seat in Congress, I became invigorated. I concentrated with full focus on my law practice. I tried a case in the District of Columbia involving a shooting at Howard University, and I also took on the case of *Angela Featherstone et al. v. Marriott International, Inc.* A number of cases were significant, not because of the facts of the cases, but because they changed the nature of my practice. These included the case of *Margaret Quarles et al. v. Mayor and City Council of Baltimore,* which involved a police shooting that was caught on videotape by a bystander and then shown repeatedly on news broadcasts nationwide. This would be one of the first times that viewers across the nation would see someone killed on television in living color.

James Quarles III was holding a knife outside of the Lexington Market in downtown Baltimore City when the police approached and ordered him to put the knife down. He was shot by Officer Charles Smothers II because, according to the officer, Mr. Quarles did not act in a timely fashion. However, the videotape clearly showed that Mr. Quarles was in the process of placing the knife on the ground when he was shot and killed. This matter was not pursued with an indictment by the state's attorney, so the family brought this case to me. I brought in Attorney Allan Rabineau to assist with the preparation of this case for trial.

We took the position that this shooting was done with malice and, in fact, was unprovoked. This event stirred the state's collective conscience, as had the Rodney King videotape nationally, reigniting the controversy surrounding the use of deadly force. Officer Smothers, the shooter of Mr. Quarles, was a person of particular interest because he was already being investigated by the police department for assaulting his girlfriend (later his wife) and her then boyfriend with a gun. (He shot her car.) In fact, he was still on probation at the time of the Quarles shooting, yet his commander allowed him to return to active duty. If, according to proper procedures, he had been suspended, he would not have been on the streets of Baltimore City with authorization to use his weapon, and, more specifically, he would not have been able to shoot and kill Mr. Quarles.

It was a very tragic situation and a very tragic death. Mr. Quarles had the knife because it was a gift given to him by his father on his father's deathbed. He had only recently lost both his mother and his father. He had been in the hospital for depression, and that knife was a very dear possession to him. He was a vendor who sold socks in front of the Lexington Market, and he always used the knife to cut open the bags that held the socks. He had stopped working to watch a group of black Hebrews conducting a service nearby. In fact, that was why the videotape was running. A woman observed him standing there holding the knife, and misunderstanding the situation, she went into the market and called 911. Police Officer Smothers, who was inside the market eating lunch, received the radio call. He and other officers rushed to the scene in front of the market and, with guns drawn, ordered Mr. Quarles to put down the knife. The young man was totally startled and didn't recognize or understand the verbal orders of the police. He did not understand why guns were drawn and pointed. He was the proverbial deer caught in the headlights.

As he lowered the knife to the ground, he tried to explain why he had the knife and its sentimental value. But, after saying something to another officer, Officer Smothers just pulled his trigger.

I believe to this day that in the split second before Officer Smothers fired his gun, he said to the other officer, "I'm gonna shoot this motherfucker." The videotape of this entire event was enhanced so that it could be shown to the jury on a big screen TV, but unfortunately, the enhancement was not clear enough to be able to hear Officer Smother's exacts words. However, it might have been possible for a jury to read his lips. Then again, it is quite possible that I became so emotionally involved in the case that I perceived that Officer Smothers made this statement even if, in fact, he didn't. Nevertheless, I think when we rolled the big screen into the courtroom it was instrumental in the $500,000 settlement reached before the jury was even selected. This was a small amount considering a death was involved. But in Maryland, police are protected by what is called caps (limits on verdicts).

The Marriott case was very fascinating because it was being tried after the release of the movie *A Civil Action*. While working on another trial involving heavyweight champion Mike Tyson, I had gone to California to take depositions. Before leaving Baltimore City, I saw the movie starring John Travolta and read the book *A Civil Action* on the plane. The movie and the book impressed me so much because the story was about a lawyer suing two major corporations and what he went through preparing the case. I felt as though I was transported into the pages of the book, literally living in the pages, because we were having the same difficulties with the Marriott Corporation.

In addition to being a hotel chain, Marriott also distributes food to fast-food entities as well as schools and businesses. The case involved a young man, although underage, who helped his father load and unload one of the Marriott trucks. These trucks have carts. Food is put into a cart, and the carts are then loaded onto the truck. The carts are placed against the sides of the truck on racks called e-racks. At one point, the father was on a delivery to a fast-food chain in Glen Bernie, Maryland, and had gotten off the truck to go to the bathroom. The young man went up into the truck and somehow a cart came loose from the e-rack and crushed him to death against the truck's walls. We sued the Marriott Corporation in Baltimore City. Baltimore judge, David Mitchell, ruled over the defendant's objection that Baltimore City was the proper venue, even though the death occurred in Anne Arundal County. This ruling was based on the legal premise of "forum convenience," meaning that in this case everything else involved was in Baltimore City. The case was tried in front of Judge Murdock in Baltimore City.

The company argued that the young man should not have been on the truck in the first place because he was a juvenile. However, they knew that he was working on the truck and in fact never objected to him being on the truck because he was a "big kid," a big teenager. He was free labor. The father's testimony was that his son was constantly in the driver's lounge on the Marriott property, and everybody knew him. Even the supervisor praised him as being a big, strong, young man. One time, the yard's boss man said to him, "As big as you're getting, I know you're going to be just like your daddy. I know you're going to work here." Well, these people denied that they had ever seen him before. They just outright lied. Our trial team, a young dynamic upcoming Baltimore City lawyer Steve Silverman and I, were able to do three things in this case.

First of all, my cocounsel Steve found an expert on e-racks. (Steve found this man's name in a book on e-racks while he was in the bathroom at home.) This expert had done nothing else his whole life except study and work on e-racks. He was the world's foremost e-rack expert. He would testify that the e-rack had pulled away from the wall of the truck due to lack of maintenance. A spring in the truck was a little lower on one side of the truck and caused the e-rack to pull away from the wall. This spring defect provided the inertia that caused stress on the e-rack. Because it was improperly secured and maintained, and because it showed aging, the e-rack could have pulled away from the wall due to this stress. The young man was in the wrong place at the wrong time. It was fascinating to me that our expert could make this determination. It was also fascinating to me that although the other side had experts in structural engineering, we had the only e-rack expert in the world. This tells you that there is somebody, somewhere in the world, who does everything and anything, no matter how minute or insignificant it may seem. This man had studied e-racks all of his life. We asked him when he first got involved with e-racks, he said he use to ride on his daddy's truck as a child and looked at e-racks because they fascinated him. He went to engineering school and studied e-racks. He wrote a book about e-racks. He started teaching college courses on e-racks. These were the common everyday racks that secured cargo on a truck—something one never thinks about, but he did. To him e-racks were the foundation of interstate commerce.

The second thing was that the foreman, who was the boss man of the whole yard and who happened to be a black man, was overly loyal to the company. When he took the stand on cross-examination, we were able to cordially destroy his credibility.

I asked him, "Didn't you see this young man inside of the truck in the depot?"

"No."

"Didn't you talk to him in the driver's lounge?"

"No."

"Didn't you tell this young man that when he was big and grown-up like his daddy, he would be able to work for you?"

"No."

I pressed on, "Sir, are you going to sit here and tell us that you've never seen this young man in your life?"

"Correct."

"And you didn't know that he was on the truck?"

He broke from his one-liners, "I didn't know he was on the truck. I wouldn't have authorized him to be on the trucks. I would not have put him on the trucks, and I would not have allowed him on the trucks."

I then asked, "You are the boss man, and you run the whole yard, correct?"

"Yep."

"And you have been running this yard for twenty years?"

"Yep."

Back to the one-liners. This reminded me of *A Civil Action*. The whole company was sworn to silence. Nobody would break code. I questioned driver after driver, and all of them said they never saw this young man before.

The break in the trial came when we found two drivers who had been terminated. We found those drivers during a door-to-door canvas in Baltimore City at one o'clock in the morning in the middle of the trial. That's why I had related so much to John Travolta's character in the movie: by day we were in the courtroom, and by night we were doing old-fashioned leg work. After the foreman testified, we put our two new witnesses on for rebuttal, and they testified that they both saw the young man in the room, and they both saw the boss man talking to him on several occasions. Finding these witnesses to contradict the total denial of the foreman was the second significant element in our case.

The third useful element of our case was my father-in-law and my use of him in comparing him with the boss foreman in my closing argument. Through him, I recognized the foreman, or to be exact, I recognized the type of man he was. My wife is originally from Philadelphia, Mississippi. Her family—her father, Tommy Moore; mother, Adel Moore; sister, Sara Katherine Moore; and brother, Jessie Moore—had left Mississippi some time ago, migrating north to New York and then to Newark, New Jersey. My father-in-law not only worked as a porter out of New York Grand Central on the railroad, he also worked as an orderly at a New York hospital. He always told us how one of the surgeons that he assisted would invite him and my mother-in-law to a Christmas party at their house every year. In addition to the Christmas parties, this doctor would also invite my in-laws over for dinner and my father in-law for lunch. He always talked about this doctor who had given him his job. My in-laws were newly arrived working-class blacks, comfortable to be able to associate freely with people of high upper-income status.

I saw my father-in-law in the foreman on the witness stand. I recognized the same qualities of loyalty. Under direct questioning, I asked him how long he had been with Marriott Corporation. He said twenty-five years.

I asked him how he happened to get the job, and he said that he came to Baltimore City from Mississippi, and while in Maryland looking for a job, he met Mr. Marriott. He said that he was eighteen years old at the time, and Mr. Marriott gave him his first job. In fact, Mr. Marriott invited him over to dinner. This was a white man of means inviting an eighteen-year-old black boy from Mississippi to dinner. He said, "I will never forget that as long as I live. Mr. Marriott and I became friends. Not only did Mr. Marriott give me my first job, he also made me a supervisor, and, yes, today I am the foreman, and I run the whole truck outlet for Maryland. I run the whole thing."

I asked, "And you still go to Mr. Marriott's house, and you know his children and his wife?"

"Correct."

"And, you are like a member of the family?"

"Correct." The parallel to my father-in-law was unmistakable.

In my closing statement to the jury I said, "Ladies and gentleman of the jury, you have heard the foreman testify." One of the lawyers had referred to him as a liar. I said, "I'm not going to call him a liar. This is a good man. Let me tell you the story of my father-in-law." I then related his story. "My father-in-law is a good man, and I know the foreman is just like him. He's a God-fearing man. I know that my father-in-law raised a good family because I married his daughter, and I know that my father-in-law is just like the foreman, a hardworking man. And, I know that both men are loyal. My father-in-law loved that hospital, and this foreman loved the Marriott Corporation. So I'm not going to suggest to you that this foreman would lie for Mr. Marriott. But, I will tell you one thing," with a smile, I continued, "I know that my father-in-law would have done anything for that hospital, and I suggest to you that this foreman here would have done anything for Mr. Marriott, because Mr. Marriott gave him dignity. You're talking about twenty-five years ago, when a black kid coming up from Mississippi was just like my father-in-law. Mr. Marriott gave him a job, gave him a meal, gave him dignity, and gave him an opportunity. He brought him home to his table and made him a foreman. For a white man to do this for a black man, for a white man of power and means to do so for a black man twenty-five years ago, this black man would do anything for that man and understandably so."

The jury showed almost unanimous agreement and understanding and demonstrated it by smiling and nodding their heads

I continued, "I'm not going to call the foreman a liar. I just want to leave you with that thought when you consider whether he would lie or, let's say, bend the truth, for Mr. Marriott. You are the determiner of whether he would or wouldn't. But, I tell you one thing," this time with humor in my voice, "I believe he would do anything that Mr. Marriott asked him to do, anything, to save Mr. Marriott. And, it's logical because he's just like my father-in-law. Look at him; he's smiling now because he knows that I know him. As I look at Mr. Foreman, I look at my father-in-law. I've known my father-in-law for thirty-five years, and, trust me, I know Mr. Foreman, ladies and gentlemen of the jury. I rest my case."

The case settled before the jury came back. Later, the jurors told us that this was a plaintiff's verdict inside of thirty minutes.

That night, after speaking with the jurors, my wife and I attended a Christmas party for her office. She was the vice president at Broadway Services, a subsidiary of Johns Hopkins Hospital in charge of personnel. I picked up Barbara, and, over a few martinis, I told her the story, including that I had used her father in my closing arguments. She enjoyed my intertwining of her father's history immensely. The suspense in this case—the denials, the loyalty, and the workers sticking together—was exactly like the plot in *A Civil Action*. The only difference was that Travolta's character ultimately lost money fighting the corporations and went bankrupt. We got the money.

During the same time as the Marriott case, we were preparing to try the Mike Tyson case. Tyson had gone to a club in DC called DC Live, and while there, he was spotted by a well-known comedian, Mike Collier. Collier introduced Tyson to two lovely young women at three o'clock in the morning as the club was getting ready to close. Tyson asked the ladies if they would like to have breakfast with him and Collier. Well, the invitation to spend time with the heavyweight champion of the world and a nationally known comedian was of course accepted. Along with Tyson's personal security personnel, they all went to Au Pied De Cochon, a French restaurant in Georgetown arriving at four thirty in the morning. Getting out of the car, Tyson was immediately recognized, and they were ushered inside. On the way to the table, Tyson said to one of the ladies, "I'm going to fuck you."

She turned and asked, "What did you say?"

Tyson repeated, "I'm going to fuck you."

Being in a public place and trying to maintain her composure as a lady, she felt that the best thing for her to do was to get away from him at the earliest convenience.

Once seated at their table, she turned to her girlfriend and quietly said, "I don't think this is going to be such a good evening. We need to get back to Baltimore City." By now, everyone in the place was looking around in awe at the heavyweight champion of the world.

When the waiter arrived and asked what they would like for breakfast, Tyson said (in a loud voice), "I want some pussy for breakfast."

With that, the young lady he had been speaking with said, "Okay, I think it's time that we go."

He turned to her. "Well, bitch, how much is it going to cost? Five thousand dollars? I'll give you five thousand."

Her reply was immediate, "No, Mike, you don't have enough money; it's not about money. I'm not going to bed with you. I'm not going anywhere with you. In fact, if this conversation continues, this breakfast is going to be over, if it's not already."

The comedian Mike Collier, who was in conversation with the other young lady, was still trying to maintain an appearance of normalcy, when Tyson turned his attention to the other young lady. Tyson had heard her tell Collier that she was a correctional officer in the Maryland correctional system.

Tyson asked her, "Why in the fuck does a black woman want to work in a correction institution unless she don't have a man and gets off looking at dicks, balls, and men's assholes all fucking day."

Startled, she asked, "What did you say?"

He went on, "Well, that's the only reason I can figure why a woman would want to work in a male penal institution. To me, the shit is fucked up, 'cause if you had worked in the prison where I was a prisoner, I would have fucked you in the ass and made you suck my dick and every fucking thing else."

The comedian said, "Oh shit, the Champ is going off." By this time, the waiter returned and gave Tyson some clams Casino.

Tyson looked at the clams and said, "Motherfucker, you know I don't eat bacon. Why the fuck did you bring me some clams with fucking bacon on it? Take this shit out of here."

At that moment, someone took a picture of Tyson, and he threw a loaf of bread at the cameraman's head. People laughed.

Tyson spotted a white woman standing nearby staring at him in awe. He motioned her over, "Come here, come to the table."

As she approached, Tyson turned to the ladies at this table, "See, bitches, that's why I like white women. Look how obedient she is, how sweet she is. That's why when we choose white women you black women get upset. Y'all want to act like niggers."

The white woman could see that the two black ladies were upset. She excused herself, saying, "Champ, I just wanted to take a picture with you," and then she eased off.

Tyson turned back to the correctional officer. "Okay, bitch, I want to know why you work in a prison with all of those dicks around."

With that she said, "Let me tell you something, Mr. Tyson. I've raised my kids; I've worked as a correctional officer in a penal institution, and I'm proud of my job. I do a good job, and I make a honest living. I live comfortably, and I don't have to go around biting people's ears off to do it" (referring to the Evander Holyfield fight).

That's when all hell broke loose.

Tyson stood up, turned over the table on the women and came after her full force. He was a huge, now-ferocious heavyweight boxer, lunging at a tiny black woman who was no more than 105 pounds. As she tried to get away, she threw her coffee at him. Tyson's guards grabbed and restrained him, and they took the women into another room. The women were terrified, because there was no other exit in the room. Tyson was still turning tables over and tearing up furniture. Eventually Tyson gave the restaurant owner a wad of money, saying, "This will take care of the damages."

When the ladies finally got back to Baltimore City, they came to me. Now, the coincidental part about this was that the very next weekend the same comedian Mike Collier was working a club in downtown Baltimore City. The ladies told me I should go see him because they thought he would talk about the Mike Tyson incident during his show and verify their version. I went to the show and took my recorder. The club owner must have told Collier that the attorney for the ladies was in the audience because he spotted me in the audience during his performance and said, "See that young man over there, dressed sharp? I understand he's the lawyer for the two young ladies I had breakfast with last week with Mike Tyson. The man is sharp. Counselor, do you have a tape recorder with you?"

I told him I did.

"Will you turn it off?"

I told him I would.

As anticipated, his skit that night was in fact all about the Mike Tyson affair. He said he had never been so terrified nor had he felt such indignation at what this black man had done to these two young women. He said he was so embarrassed for these women. He led into it in such a way that after he did his moral talk he got into the humor of it. He said, "I was sitting in the middle of them, and, you know, I started to grab Mike. But … that's a big black man. Because I got a wife, a black wife, black children, and a black momma, I was going to defend the rights of these poor sisters. I was not going to let them get beat down by a black man in public. But that's a big, black man. So when Mike came over the table I started to grab him by the collar and throw him up against the wall and tell him, 'You can't do this to the sisters. You can't treat sisters like this.' But that's a big black man …" He went on and on and had the audience rolling in laughter.

When the show was over, we talked for a while in the parking lot. After that, he went back to California. The next week he did a concert in LA, repeating the same show about his night with Mike Tyson and the ladies. In the meantime, I had filed a multimillion-dollar lawsuit for damages against Mike Tyson. I told my clients not to worry about calling the police because I didn't think anything was going to happen. He would not be convicted in the District of Columbia, and I personally did not want to cause Tyson any more criminal trouble. So I brought a civil action in Maryland's Montgomery County, where Mike resided at the time, because I knew it was a conservative area, and we would have a predominately white jury who may not have been so enamored by the Champ.

At that point, Mike Tyson was probably still one of the most popular men in the world. Little did I know that before we would get to trial, Tyson would destroy his own reputation ten times over.

Mike Collier called me after the lawsuit was filed, expressing his concerns. "Mr. Pettit, I'm scared to death, man. I know you're a lawyer just doing your job, but you don't know who the hell you're dealing with, man. These people will fuck everybody up. I'm scared to even go on stage. So can you do me a favor, man? I'm changing my skit. In fact, the Muslims are going on stage with me tonight."

Collier had originally thought that the Muslims represented a threatening force acting on Mike Tyson's behalf. Instead, he said he received a call directly from Minister Farrakhan saying they were not connected with Tyson's Muslim friends, whoever they might be.

Collier said, "Farrakhan offered the Nation of Islam's protection for him." Collier told me he had been watching news of the lawsuit on national TV, and he wanted me to refrain from using his name.

Collier said, "I'm not making any further statements about it."

I asked him, "Are you going to tell the truth if I call you to testify?"

He hesitated, "I just don't know at this point in time."

As we got further into the investigation of our case, our clients, the two young women begin to feel threatened. Somebody went to their jobs, and there was a van parked in front of one of their houses. Tyson had hired a big law firm out of Los Angeles, California, to represent him, so I brought on a top civil-litigation attorney by the name of Allan Rabineau. Tyson's cocky young lawyer thought he was the only one who had a law book. It was fascinating to introduce this young man to the reality that we all have law books. Even though he might have been a prima donna with a law firm making millions a year representing people like the heavyweight champion of the world, he was in our arena in Maryland. We were also gifted and talented.

Because the Champ was in training for his first bout after losing his title, we were engaged in a legal hassle over when he could appear for trial. The judge, agreeing with the defense, did not want anything to interfere with the fight. During the discovery part of the trial, we held Tyson's deposition in the District of Columbia. I thought we would have to bring a club or a brick because of Mike's reputation for violence. In addition to Tyson's deposition, we also scheduled a deposition from his new wife, a doctor who happened to be the sister of former Maryland Lieutenant Governor Michael Steele.

Tyson walked into the room in a tight muscle shirt, and I was in awe. He was one solid, coiled mass of muscle, waiting to explode. Nevertheless, he was not that big. I had been in the presence of Muhammad Ali many times, and he was a big man. By contrast, Tyson was muscular and broad shouldered. He was a wide man but not a thick man. Flanked by his lawyers, two or three of them, Tyson came in with his entourage, including a female advisor and, of course, a crew of videographers. He sat down at the table. I had asked Allan to take the deposition because I wanted to observe Tyson. He appeared to be the nicest guy in the world, relaxed and amusing.

Before he sat down, he looked over at me and said, "Hey, Counselor, you sure are clean. Where did you get that suit? Where did you get the cuff links?"

He seemed more interested in my attire during the deposition; in fact, his lawyer had to stop the disposition to tell him, "Yes Mike, Mr. Pettit is always well-dressed and always immaculate."

Since he was so impressed, I said, "Well, Mike, if you ever need a lawyer in Baltimore City, I'm at your service."

It seemed as though Tyson was really impressed at the appearance of a high-powered African American lawyer. His sense of blackness, and his awareness of his blackness and black success were deep within him. There was a militancy deep within him too. I understood that this was real;

this was not a show. He was almost as impressed by me, a black lawyer in combat with high-powered white lawyers, as I was by him, sitting in his presence. Being a major fan of his, it was almost like being in the presence of Muhammad Ali. He was very polite to both Allan and me, maintaining his sense of humor in a tense situation.

Tyson's deposition contained very salty language, related here because of its significance in terms of the elements of the case. Our questioning and Tyson's responses were very specific, especially when we asked about his interaction with the correctional officer.

The question was, "Mike, according to the witnesses and plaintiffs, you referred to your penis, and, in fact, you told her where you would have stuck it."

Tyson responded, "I don't know; I don't think so, but I could have."

Allan said, "Mr. Tyson, you used words like *pussy* and *ass*. Mr. Tyson, you also said to her that if she was a correctional officer in your prison, you would have made her suck your dick." Allan then asked, "Mr. Tyson, did you, in fact, say that?"

Tyson responded in his high-pitched voice, "Yeah, yeah … I don't know, that sounds like me. That sounds like some shit I would say. Yeah, I guess so." With that, his lawyers rushed him, taking him out for a break.

This happened every five minutes because his lawyers never knew what was coming out of his mouth. He was so honest that it just came out. It became one of the funniest depositions that I had ever taken or been involved in. He would come back in with the biggest smile and then look at me and say, "Damn, Counselor, you sure are clean." Then, returning to the deposition, he would say, "Yeah, yeah, I think I did that shit."

I didn't know how they were possibly going to take Tyson through to trial. This was one of those cases that I looked forward to with so much anticipation that in no way did I want to just settle. I was so excited about going all the way to trial that I told my cocounsel, "Allan, we have been in a lot of cases where we have wanted to do this or that, but I'm saying to you going in, I want to take Mike in this trial. I will do the cross-examination or the direct examination of Mike Tyson. Every lawyer in the world would want to do this, but I will examine Mike."

The big moment finally arrived. We got to trial and began selecting a jury. If opposing counsel was so bright, I never understood why the LA lawyer didn't move the trial to Washington, DC, where the events actually took place. He would have had an almost all-black jury. I expected the motion for removal, but it never came. Judge Mesettie was an excellent pretrial judge, and we had an excellent trial judge, Alex Williams, a Howard University graduate who I thought would be fair. We picked a jury, striking every black man that came up and most of the black females. The defense challenged by raising what is called a Batson challenge, referring to *Batson v. United States*, which ruled one cannot strike a person solely because of their race. One has to be able to articulate an independent reason as the purpose of the strike. In other words, there are two types of strikes. There is a strike for cause and there is a preemptory strike. A strike for cause can be, for example, because the person can't make a fair decision or they are emotionally involved and can't be objective and impartial. A preemptory cause can be for any reason but not because of race. We were able to strike all of the black males and most of the black females because we were able to articulate separate reasons apart from their race. I have always been able to use preemptory reasons to strike white folks, because when it comes to considerations of black folks and justice and the criminal justice system, they have built-in prejudices and, in many cases, they cannot help themselves, especially in certain counties. So a lot of time we use the preemptory strike to get whites off of a jury and get as many blacks as possible. This was the first time in my professional career that I used the strikes to eliminate black people. I am sure that Tyson's lawyer knew what I was doing. Ultimately, we ended up with a jury of eight women, seven white females and one black female. Of interest was the fact that when we came to trial, two years after filing our lawsuit, most of the people who were in the jury pool basically disqualified themselves, because, by that time, Tyson had been charged in another assault in Montgomery County. In fact, he had been involved in a couple of other things. During jury selection, many of the perspective jurors said things like, "Hey, I believe Mike Tyson is a woman beater," and "I believe Mike raped that girl," and "I believe he beat Robin Givens, so I can't sit on the jury."

Although we ended up with an excellent jury, we encountered another very significant problem. My clients did not want to appear at trial. They had been through a lot, especially the correctional officer. She could not go back to work because she said the Muslims in the penal system were threatening her for suing their idol, Mike Tyson. The other young lady had people coming on her job, and she was scared to go to work and afraid for her child.

The night before the trial was to begin, they came to me. "Mr. Pettit, can you settle this case? There is no way in the world we can go through with what we went through before."

I tried to explain that emotions were different from before, and Tyson was no longer the sentimental favorite. He had tarnished his own reputation. People's opinions were different from what they were when my clients had been unfairly portrayed on national radio and TV as probable groupies and hustlers trying to set up Mike Tyson for money. I did not think they needed to worry about threats any longer because the hero worship surrounding Tyson had changed, thanks to the visibility of his own erratic behavior. I acknowledged the strain my clients had suffered and the horrible things they had been through. However, no matter how much I begged and pleaded for them to go to trial, they were too afraid to go. That was the only thing that saved Mike Tyson from a large verdict. I believe that if we had gone to trial with the jury that had been selected, we would have won a tremendous verdict. But, as it turned out, we settled for an undisclosed amount.

In December 1999, I took on a case involving another professional athlete, this time Ray Lewis of the Baltimore Ravens football team and three women. The women would allege that they were assaulted by Mr. Lewis. Again, as in the Tyson case the women would be characterized in the press as noncredible people who must have been lying. I was, and remain, a fan of Ray Lewis and the Ravens, holding club and season tickets. Nevertheless, out of my sense of justice and fair play, I agreed to represent the women. Before trial and during discovery the women would be subpoenaed into Atlanta concerning Ray Lewis and a homicide that had occurred January 1, 2000, following a Super Bowl XXXIV Party. I was requested by the women and the Fulton County States Attorney to accompany them to Atlanta. Upon arriving, and meeting with the county prosecutor himself, I was advised that the purpose that the state intended to use the ladies was to establish propensity for violence and "prior bad acts." However, as the court proceedings drifted on, they were never called to the stand. But in this incident in Baltimore County, Maryland, we would go to trial. The testimony by two of the women was that they had been hit and assaulted by Ray, who had knocked one of them to the floor where she was allegedly kicked and stomped by members of his entourage.

The testimony was that Mr. Lewis was coming into the Windsor Inn, a club on Windsor Mill Road in Baltimore County, surrounded by his entourage. They were allowed inside before my clients, who had been in front of them. An argument about who was in line first broke out in the lobby, and an altercation ensued between my clients and one of the smaller men in Ray's party. My clients were both pretty women of good size. They were healthy women—not fat, but full-figured. The women would testify that Ray came through the crowd full force, knocking one of them to the ground. The bouncers testified in an affidavit and trial that Ray never left the corner, that he was the peacemaker, the one calling for order. Thus, the main issue would be believability. However, on the day of the trial in Baltimore County Circuit Court, Ray was brought up in the elevator signing autographs for the sheriffs and personnel in the court, and then escorted by the sheriffs down the halls of justice. I saw this as an orchestrated strategy put on by the defense to keep their client's fame at the forefront and to appeal to the emotions of the jury. His deposition had been very different from Mike Tyson's. Ray never had a smile on his face, in fact, at one point I got the famous glare, the one he uses on the field—what I called during the trial the "Super Bowl glare."

Ray was very arrogant, but I told him, as I reached out my hand, "I'm one of your biggest fans. This isn't personal, it's just business. So let's sit down and get through your deposition." My hand stayed in midair, un-received.

Ray's was a very interesting case. Even though Ray was awarded the verdict after about four hours of deliberation, the trial had become so intense that when the jury did go out to deliberate, Ray's mother convened a prayer circle in the middle of the courtroom, referring to me as the "devil himself." I always say that the difference between the Lewis trial and the Tyson case was very simple. Tyson had lost the heavyweight championship prior to trial, and Lewis had won the Super Bowl as MVP prior to trial.

After that trial in Baltimore County, several years later Ray and I would run into each other at a downtown Baltimore Ruth Chris restaurant, where upon I extended my hand, and it was accepted without hesitation. We both agreed that as I said, "It was not personal, just business."

One day, reflecting on the high-profile trials I had been handling, my office manager, Ms. Felicia Jackson, said to me that I lived the perfect life that all men wished to live. She said that I worked and litigated hard all day and then hung out all night. However, that's not true. I know lawyers who live a much more high-level and exciting life. I think I have a reasonable lifestyle. I don't travel extensively. And, regardless of what Mike Tyson thinks of my wardrobe, I think it is modest and appropriate. I think I live a very modest life. My wife and I live in the house in Baltimore City where we raised our two children, and we have never thought about leaving the city. I appreciate the tangible things in life without being extravagant. However, I do become immersed in litigation.

After the Quarles case, just about anything that the police did in Baltimore City landed on my desk. We averaged twenty-five to thirty-five calls a week just on matters involving the police. One day, I was joking, and I told Ms. Jackson and Ms. Dabbs (then my secretary), "Don't take any more police cases unless folks are dead or half-dead."

Later in court, a judge said to me, "Mr. Pettit, I am so astonished at you. I referred a client to you, a police-brutality case. They called your office, but your secretary told them that you couldn't help them unless the client was dead or half-dead."

Oops! I could only respond, "Judge, they were not supposed to say that to anyone. I'm sorry."

At any rate, I continued receiving high-profile cases involving police misconduct. The actions of police allegedly acting under color of law appears to be the new civil-rights challenge of the twenty-first century.

One case in particular was *Eli McCoy v. the Mayor and City Council of Baltimore*. On Thanksgiving Day 1999, seventeen-year-old Eli McCoy and a friend allegedly snatched a twenty-dollar bill (never produced at trial) from a woman in a low-income area. The boys then allegedly ran away. They were eventually cornered by both Baltimore City police and officers with the Baltimore City's Housing Authority, an agency whose officers had only recently been permitted to carry guns. Officer Kenneth Dean III of the Housing Authority police reached Eli first, ordering him to raise his hands.

Eli raised his hands and, with a smirk on his face, allegedly said, "Okay, okay, you got me. What the fuck you gonna do, shoot me?"

That was exactly what the officer did. He shot Eli three times from a distance of less than ten feet. Little did he realize, or maybe he didn't care, that there were numerous eyewitnesses. Three women were up above him in a window, and three were on the street. They had clear views. Two black men on the street had partial views. They all testified that McCoy had his hands up, was partially on his knees, and had a smirk on his face.

The plaintiff's case was that the shooting was with malice. Despite the eyewitnesses, the defense alleged that Officer Dean shot Eli because he had his left hand in his pocket, going for a gun. (There was no gun.) The medical examiner ruled that a bullet through Eli's hand indicated that his hand must have been in his pocket when he was shot, notwithstanding that police are trained to shoot for center mass, not hands. We argued to the jury that the first bullet hit him directly in the chest, being center mass. Eli's hands then came down, and he fell to the ground as Officer Dean's next two shots hit him, one going through his left hand before also going through his pocket.

The authorities thought there was going to be a riot in Baltimore City. In fact, on the day of the shooting, I had gone to the scene upon receiving a call. The police asked me to speak to the crowd to restore calm. The case involving the police shooting of Mr. Quarles in front of the Lexington Market had just been settled earlier that year. There was the shooting of another young black man, Mr. Hubbard, in the back of the head, and now there was the police shooting of young unarmed Eli McCoy less than six weeks later. I had handled the Hubbard case with Johnny Cochran, Billy Murphy, and Allan Rabineau. To ward off any civil disturbances, the coroner's office issued an immediate press release that young McCoy's hands were in his pocket as alleged by Officer Dean. Very quickly, I told the public not to buy into this. Evidence would later show that eight police officers had gone into the autopsy room with the coroners as observers. They never tested for fibers in Eli's hand. If his hand was in his pocket, shouldn't there have been some fibers from the pocket in the wound? The bullet hole in the pocket had a microscopic piece of blood on the inside of the pocket against his leg. It might have been 1/32 of an inch. That little speck of blood most likely came from the impact of the bullet to the leg. They never medically concluded whether the blood and tissue on the inside of the pocket was tissue from the leg or tissue from the hand. They just summarily concluded it was from the hand. In other words, they made a speculated conclusion with no scientific basis. The public would not have been able to examine this upon the release of the autopsy, but the jury did and the jury accepted my argument, attacking the defense's conclusions as bogus and supporting mine as correct.

The trial lasted five days, and the jury came back with a judgment of seven million dollars: six million compensatory and one million punitive. However, the judge reduced this to just four hundred thousand dollars under the interpretation of the newly enacted cap on claims. Basically, the caps and their interpretation were about the devaluation of life. Two weeks before the trial started, the governor signed legislation, commonly called by us the McCoy bill, which reduced the tort cap to two hundred thousand dollars under the Maryland State Municipal Tort Claims Act as it related to judgments against the city or counties and particularly police departments and its officers.

What the system was saying was that life, and in particular that of a young African American, was not to be valued in the millions. There was no way a young black male's pain, suffering, and even his life, or his loss to his family, was worth seven million dollars. The judge, for sake of resolution, did not throw out the entire verdict; the cap just said that a life under Maryland's law cannot be worth any more than four hundred thousand dollars (or two hundred thousand per count). We would discuss an appeal with Mr. McCoy the decedent's father. Mr. McCoy would say, "Mr. Pettit, I don't know when I've had four hundred dollars at one time, never mind four hundred thousand. Take the money."

Pettit and cousin Shirley Sumpter

Dwight and Mayor Du Burns

Cousin Larry Miller and Mom

Dwight, Biddy Woods and Felicia Jackson
at Dwight's 50th Birthday Party

Gov. Glendenning, Marie Henderson, Raymond
Haysbert (President of Park Sausage), and Dwight.

Champ and Dwight at opening of Champ's restaurant

Dwight, Allan, Billy and Mitch

Dwight, Muhammed Ali and wife Veronica Ali

Gov. Glendenning "Little" Willie Adams and Dwight

Chapter 19: Equity

In the late '90s, I had decided to retest the federal courts in terms of civil rights, not so much in terms of racial discrimination, but in terms of gender discrimination. A distressed young lady, a single parent, came to my office one day. She complained not just about sexual harassment, but also that she had actually been raped while on the job as a security officer. The allegations were obviously serious. It occurred to me that this might be the perfect case to test the enforcement of Title VII of the Civil Rights Act, codified in 1972 and later amended. The original statute did not allow for jury trials. This was a big impediment to taking on civil-rights cases until Title VII was amended under the Clinton administration. The passage by Congress of the amendment did two things: it created the right to jury trials and allowed compensatory damages beyond back pay. This opened defendants to substantial exposure in a civil-rights case. Punitive damages were also newly allowed. Angel Watkins, the young lady who entered my office, would be my first test of Title VII as amended. I decided to take her case.

At first Angel seemed to be such a pitiful, little, shy, quiet girl. Her name seemed fitting. Although my first impression was that she was very insecure, deep down, she was a little warrior. She had pulled herself up by the bootstraps. She had kids out of wedlock who she was taking care of even after she was fired from her job as a security officer. She had taken a new job at the post office. She was very persuasive in her efforts to get me to take another Title VII case after almost twenty years. I think my last Title VII case was *Wrigley v. Amtrak* before Federal Judge Shirley Jones. Even though we got the verdict in *Wrigley*, by the time the judgment was whittled away, there was too little or next to nothing in monetary damages.

At any rate, I took the case of "Little Angel," the name ("my little angel") given to her by a white executive at the security company. When we met, "Little Angel" was sort of tattered, not only in demeanor, but also in terms of her plain but clean clothes. She appeared to be the type of person who would be an easy target for sexual harassment, even rape. Her attacker, a black male supervisor, probably perceived her to be so powerless that there would be nothing to fear in terms of retribution. He probably thought he had nothing to fear from this little, quiet, young, black female, especially given his seniority with the company. According to the facts of the case, Angel was in the process of being disciplined because there was something wrong with the way she wore her uniform. Mr. Kelly, the perpetrator, was her immediate supervisor, and he had called Angel during the wee hours of the morning, ordering her to return immediately from her post. When she reported to Mr. Kelly, he was the only person in the locker room where the security officers changed clothes. He immediately grabbed her and pushed her up against a locker. He then pulled up her skirt and pulled down her panties before she knew what was happening. She was pinned up against the locker, struggling, when he raped her. Suddenly, someone came through the outer door, causing Mr. Kelly to release her. When he released her to pull up his pants, she was able to pull down her skirt and get away, leaving the room. She reported this incident to her department's supervisor, who confirmed that Mr. Kelly had made advances to the other females in the work area. One in particular had filed a complaint before leaving the company.

Preparing for the trial, I learned more about Angel and all of the things she had gone through in her life, things that had gone against her. During deposition and discovery, testimony was presented that Angel Watkins was being treated for the psychological damage of rape. Mr. Kelly had been dismissed by the security company by the time of the deposition. Angel indicated that he had not used protection.

Another interesting deposition in the case was that of Mr. Fisher, who was the big boss of the company.

I asked, "Mr. Fisher," a white male, "do you have any policies concerning sexual harassment?"

Mr. Fisher looked at me quizzically, "Policies? What policies? What are you talking about? Policies?"

I spent maybe fifteen minutes with Mr. Fisher on this at deposition, not knowing that the Supreme Court of the United States would later address this as a major issue in another case.

After the depositions were taken, but before the trial began, the Supreme Court ruled that if a company had policies and procedures, and the employees were notified of same, this could be an employer's defense against sexual harassment. In other words, if a company had policies and detailed said policies as to sexual harassment, this would constitute a presumption that the company was acting in good faith. It would therefore reduce or shield them from liability. Not surprisingly, by the time we went to trial, the policies existed, and they would be invoked as a defense by the security company. Mr. Fisher took the stand and testified for almost an hour about policies—policies for this and policies for that. He testified that upon hire, employees are told about the sexual harassment policies, and they receive an employee package providing instructions about the policies. Under cross-examination, I reminded Mr. Fisher about the deposition he had given two years before. I went over the questions and his deposed responses.

"Question: 'Do you have any policies concerning sexual harassment?'"

"Mr. Fisher: 'Policies? What policies? What are you talking about? Policies?'"

I read two pages of the deposition where he went back and forth, not knowing a thing about policies. Yet, here he was on the stand, under oath, in front of a federal jury two years later, lying about these policies. I caught him dead in the middle of a lie with his own deposition. He was too arrogant to consider that I might remember his prior testimony. I actually asked him to read from his deposition where he repeatedly said he didn't know a damn thing about any policies prior to and after the event in question.

Our federal civil jury was composed of six people and originally two alternates. We had six white women and two black males on our jury. I delivered the closing argument on behalf of my cocounsel Norris Ramsey and Karen Kendricks. At the end of my closing, I told the jury, "Ladies and gentleman of the jury, I want to tell you a story. We all know O. J. Simpson."

When I mentioned O. J. Simpson, the judge looked horrified, and Norris almost fell out of his seat. (No, he would not have mentioned O. J. to these white women.)

I continued, "Let me give you an analogy. O. J. Simpson allegedly killed his wife, and he went to trial for murder in a criminal court. You remember what happened in that criminal court, don't you? He walked out not guilty. But, he didn't totally get away. Why? Because, ladies and gentlemen of the jury, he had to come back in front of a civil-court jury. Mr. Kelly was never indicted for the rape, but just like O. J. Simpson, he now sits in front of you for civil judgment. Therefore, ladies and gentlemen of the jury, you have an opportunity to do the same thing that the O. J. Simpson jury did. You have the same opportunity to vindicate the plaintiff, the victim, and render the justice that was not served on the criminal side. Therefore, I am asking you, in closing, to become the symbol of justice like the Simpson jury was in California. I ask you to rise to the occasion in Maryland. I know you will return the correct verdict, a verdict in favor of the plaintiff, Miss Angel Watkins. I thank you." The courtroom was hushed.

When opposing counsel stood, he said, "Ladies and gentleman of the jury, I don't believe what I have just heard. I am not even going to try to rise to that level of oratory. After listening to what you have just heard, I am just going to ask you to remember my summary of the facts and find for the defendant." He then sat down.

We had this old geezer for a judge, and, for the life of me, I don't understand why Congress allows federal judges to remain on the bench for life, long after they should have retired. Nevertheless, Judge Maletz was eighty-four years old when our trial began. On the day the trial started, they had actually changed judges. We had a very good judge scheduled up to that time, but for some reason they shifted this case from Judge Benson to old Judge Maletz (who I think was a visiting judge).

I asked Norris what he thought about this judge, and he simply said, "I've tried a case in front of him before, Dwight. He's not bad."

However, I could pick up from the moment I walked into the courtroom that we had a problem. As a trial lawyer, the confidence that I exude in my knowledge and competency, and the security I feel in my ability to handle the law, are often perceived by white people as arrogance. Actually, white people see different types of blacks: Negroes, arrogant Negroes, and arrogant niggers, and, as I explained about my father whites saw all three. I was perceived as arrogant on day one, and there was no doubt in my mind that this old white judge from New England perceived me to be an "arrogant nigger." It really did not matter where he came from, because racism runs rampant throughout the world and particularly in the good old USA.

Judge Maletz showed himself to be hostile from the moment I opened my mouth and said, "Good morning, Your Honor. My name is A. Dwight Pettit."

He got this strange, but familiar look on his face that read, "I got one of those arrogant so-and-sos."

From the first day of the trial, we engaged in total combat. Even in my closing argument, that SOB actually pulled a chair across from me beside the jury box. He watched me, not from the bench, but from a chair beside the jury. We even exchanged words during my closing as to what I said and what I didn't say. We went tit for tat during the entire federal trial.

I thought, *To hell with this son of a bitch.* Congress had given my client the right to a jury. *To hell with him, and everything about him, and everything he stands for.* The only problem is that one should never underestimate the depth of racism and the extent to which a racist will go to put you in a catch-22 situation. As the system would have it, this judge still had the power.

In the movie *The Verdict*, Paul Newman's character went back and forth with the judge. Paul Newman cursed him out and basically told him to kiss his ass because he was going to try his case. He was going to take the judge to the bar. Paul Newman ended up winning the verdict, after which the jury came out and said, "How much money can we give your client? Can we give your client more money than you asked for?" That was how *The Verdict* ended. The lawyer was vindicated and regardless of the judge, justice prevailed. What the movie did not tell you is that the judge still has complete power and the opportunity to intercede. Our system gives them that power, the power to interject their personal prejudices. Acting under the color of law, judges can continuously deprive black people of justice in America as long as racism exists, whether you have juries or not. Justice depends largely upon whether you are on one side of the color spectrum or the other.

Judge Maletz would not let me argue punitive damages to the jury. Nevertheless, after deliberating approximately four hours, our jury of six white women and two black men awarded this little girl, a modest sum of sixty-three thousand dollars in compensatory damages. These were good, fair-minded folks in a case against a white corporation—even though the perpetrator was black. Under Title VII of the Civil Rights Act, Congress gives counsel the right to file and argue a fee petition. I had angered Judge Maletz and pushed him over the edge during the trial, and now, probably because of the amount of the fee petition, which was reviewed under the requirements of federal law by another civil-rights attorney, he was boiling. My petition, which listed and took into consideration all of the cases I had tried and the hours of three attorneys, was in excess of one hundred thousand dollars. Instead of cutting or denying my fee, Judge Maletz threw out the jury's verdict. He threw out the verdict and ruled that with the facts as presented, a reasonable jury could have not reached the verdict that they reached. This was in spite of Mr. Fisher lying under oath regarding the existence or nonexistence of company policies. I pressed this case myself on appeal in the US Court of Appeals for the Fourth Circuit, arguing the underlying principal that Congress authorized a jury trial in civil cases and thus, the judge did not have the authority under law to nullify that verdict. By allowing him to do so, I argued that this contravened and negated the intent of Congress. Of course, I raised the issue that the Supreme Court had magnified concerning policies. After being denied by the US Court of Appeals for the Fourth Circuit, then the most conservative federal circuit in the United States, I filed a petition to the Supreme Court. Unfortunately, the high court denied the writ of certiorari (meaning they denied the review).

My argument before the Fourth Circuit court in Richmond was videotaped for teaching purposes by the Maryland Institute for Continuing Professional Education of Lawyers, Inc. Although not heard by the Supreme Court, it was used as an instructional case for lawyers throughout the state. I am not sure whether it demonstrates good or bad appellant activity, but at least it is a demonstration.

The sad part was that I don't think Judge Maletz's wrath was aimed at Angel. It was totally unfair that she had to suffer, because he was directing his anger at me. He could have just cut or easily denied the attorney's fees. To me, the message in his ruling was clear: *How dare this arrogant Negro get up here and know the law. How dare this Negro tell me I'm wrong and then cut me off after I cut him off. How dare this Negro stand in front of the white women on this jury and use O. J. Simpson as reverse psychology. How dare this Negro argue with me and then say he should get paid one hundred thousand dollars. How dare this arrogant Negro to do this in a federal courtroom in front of a predominately-white jury. I'm going to punish this Negro. If he thinks I'm going to sign a fee petition for one hundred thousand dollars, he's out of his mind. I'm just going to strike the whole thing as if it didn't even happen.*

To lose one hundred thousand dollars was painful. To lose one hundred thousand dollars after you have celebrated the victory with lobster, steak, and champagne was painful. To begin spending one hundred thousand dollars with your wife and then not get the money was painful. But the most painful thing I suffered was picking up the phone and calling this little black lady, who was actually a very strong black woman with two children, working two jobs. It was through, and because of, the trial that she had learned to celebrate her blackness and wear it with dignity. With the jury's verdict, she had cried with joy on the streets of Baltimore City. Yet, this had been taken away from her with one stroke of a pen. No hearing, no argument, no consideration, just a son of a bitch taking food out of her mouth in order to punish me. He was acting under color of law.

I had been around for a while, and I understood that the US Court of Appeals for the Fourth Circuit would not reverse on appeal. When I argued the case in front of the court, the emotion in the argument was such that three times I accidentally cut a judge off when he was asking me a question—not that I did not want to answer his question, but because I knew his question and the answer before he asked it. I should have let the question come out.

After the third time, he said, "Counsel, will you let me ask the question?"

"Yes, Your Honor, I am sorry." I listened to the question I already knew was coming and had already answered twice, but again the emotion of the case seeped out or the George Pettit arrogance raised its head. This was the same arrogance the Air Force saw when I practically won every competition placed before me. And maybe it was the same arrogance that popped up in later trials. This must have been the same arrogance perceived by Baltimore City's politicians and maybe even the electorate when I ran for political office. It was not arrogance or cockiness of superiority, but possibly the arrogance imbedded in me in terms of African blood that survived the trip to America and then slavery on these shores. Or maybe it's the mixture of my African, American Indian, and white ancestry along with the tremendous temper my father gave me. Maybe it's just the arrogance of the Zulu nation or the Cherokee nation, or the arrogance of the Mandingo or white blood running in a lot of our veins. Maybe African Americans are truly the super race. Maybe that's why we are so feared; maybe that's why racism is so rampant and why we are so hated. Maybe that's why the color of law is so different for us as opposed to white people. Maybe that's why we are not allowed to participate in the economic fulfillment of the American dream. Maybe that's why the American dream is not shared with us. Maybe that's why every time we begin to share in the American dream of economic fulfillment, the nation decides to change economic and political philosophy and proceed into a recession.

Chapter 20: State of the Nation

Regardless of what you think about President Bill Clinton, he helped usher in a time when people of color began to think of obtaining the same advantages as white people: a house, a stock portfolio, two cars in the garage, a boat, a summer house, money in the bank, and money to spend. We enjoyed the best industrial economy (supposedly the determiner of politics) that this nation had ever seen. But the manifestations compelled white America to change partners at the presidential level. There is no other explanation. So the people of America reelected a president in 2004 who said, I'm going to make the rich richer. I am going to give all of the rich people tax cuts. I am going to close down the factories and transfer them overseas. And for good measure, I'm going to declare two unnecessary wars.

In 2008, we went to the polls en masse and elected the first African American president. By the end of 2008, the nation was deep in a recession. The stock market plummeted, people lost jobs by the thousands, and foreclosures soared. The underclass, the lower class, and parts of the middle class were being destroyed, leaving only two classes—the haves and the have-nots. The wealthy remained untouched. The new president would move to stabilize the economy and energize the nation.

In the thick of this political evolution, my firm would begin to fight in the new civil-rights struggle of police brutality and would win one of the largest jury verdicts in the nation in 2004. It was the largest verdict for a case of excessive police force in Maryland's history and maybe the nation's. This was the case of *Emma Brown et al. v. Rodney Price*. I tried the case with the law firm of Dominic and Anton Iameles, a very good father and son team. Also at the trial table was a young man from my office by the name of Mitchell Treger.

Officer Price testified that he was acting as a police officer and acted in the scope of his employment in fear of bodily injury when he shot Tristin D. Little Sr., killing him. While in partial uniform, Officer Price was allegedly investigating a car outside of his wife's apartment and shot his wife's alleged paramour twenty-one times. The jury awarded $5 million per shot, for a record-breaking $105 million verdict. The State Court of Special Appeals eventually threw out the verdict, ruling that the shooting was outside of Officer Price's official scope of employment, and thus the city was not liable. We would go on to handle several high-profile cases at the time of conclusion of the writing of these memoirs. Along with co-counsel Neal Janey and Stuart Simms, we are awaiting a second decision from our highest state court the (Maryland Court of Appeals) regarding *Kevin Clark v. Martin O'Malley*. This would be a landmark ruling involving a then mayor and now second-term governor on the issue of the remedies of damages and/ or reinstatement for the illegal and unlawful termination of a Baltimore City police commissioner (who just happened to be black and was taken out of his office by a SWAT team).

Now, I have also been retained to defend the campaign manager of former Republican Governor Ehrlich's most recent campaign in reference to the robo-calls made to allegedly suppress the black votes. These allegations and charges are constitutionally suspect and nothing more than a political witch hunt designed to further crush the Maryland Republican Party and intimidate any Democrat that joins the Republican challenge on certain local political issues. In my opinion, the importance of this case is that it goes to the heart of the Constitution's First Amendment, the freedom of political speech and it's national and constitutional importance. Although I have always been a registered democrat, I believe the two party or multi-party system is necessary for our nation. This is especially so when you consider the historical injustices wrought upon minorities. History teaches that we as a people (African Americans) should never be dependent on one political party.

Prior to this legal representation, I had the experience of meeting and becoming friends with Representative Robert L. Ehrlich, who was then running for and would win the 2002 governorship of Maryland. Then candidate Ehrlich would make an unprecedented commitment to the black community by way of a memorandum of understanding of which I would be one of the signers. In his one term as governor, he would appoint more African American judges and designate more funds to the HBCU's then his democratic predecessors. But like Jimmy Carter, his forthright political honesty would cause him to lose his bid for reelection. Through that relationship, I would have the opportunity to play a major role in Maryland government and particularly in judicial appointments. During that time, I would also develop a working friendship with Lieutenant Governor Michael Steele, who would later become chairman of the Republican National Committee; former US Senator Joseph Tidings, who also sat on the board of regents; and former Governor Marvin Mandel, also on the board of regents. As previously indicated, I was appointed to two terms on the Maryland University System Board of Regents by Governor Robert L. Ehrlich. In 2006, I would be appointed to the newly created Maryland Judicial Campaign Conduct Committee by our Chief Judge of the Maryland Court of Appeals Robert M. Bell.

Lt. Gov. Steel, Dwight Pettit and Governor Bob Ehrlich

Dwight, Mrs. Ehrlich, Gov. Ehrlich and Barbara

Chapter 21: My Father's Lawyer

Working in reverse order, I must conclude with my greatest case. It was my first case. Just as in my political career, where my first political involvement was at the presidential level, my first private legal case was at the top level, later discussed by the highest court in the nation, the United States Supreme Court (see *The United States v. Testen*, 424 U.S. 392 (1976). This was the case of *George D. Pettit v. the United States* (1973).

My father had been in a fight with the Aberdeen Proving Ground and the Department of the Army, beginning in and around the late '50s and early '60s, during the time when he began the school desegregation litigation and when he was elected vice president of the Harford County branch of the NAACP. As I have already written, Mrs. Juanita Mitchell was one of my lawyers in the school case. and now my father had retained this brilliant lady to be his lawyer as well in his employment case. Through elongated hearings and proceedings, modifications, and administrative appeals, she had secured a favorable ruling from the Department of the Army finding discrimination but offering no remedy. Title VII had not yet become the law of the land, and thus no monetary remedy existed, only preferential consideration for promotion. As stated in the administrative recommendation, Dad would be promoted "providing he was among the best qualified and an opening did occur."

Thus, after twelve years of hell, after exercising his rights and the rights of his child, that was it. Case over. Thank you and have a nice life. It was ironic that he and I would go through the same judicial review of our competency, our history, our achievements, and our intellect, although his intellect was never realistically challenged by anyone during his life. Mrs. Mitchell consulted her associates on the issue of court redress and, along with others, concluded there was no legal basis for further litigation.

One Saturday morning, in the fall of 1971, while in bed reading the *Washington Post,* I came across an article reporting that a suit had been brought in the United States Court of Claims (now the United States Court of Federal Claims) by a young lawyer out of Covington and Burling, one of the world's largest and most prestigious law firms, on the issue of back pay for illegal discrimination. This was part of the firms pro-bono work. That young lawyer was Paul Tagliabue. (He would later become the commissioner of the National Football League.) This was a bolt of legal lightning. The case was *Testan v. the United States,* in its early stages.

I woke up Bobbie and read her the article, and then I jumped out of bed and called my dad. He wasn't too excited, but he listened patiently. (Parents never really believe early on that their children are really "real" professionals, lawyers, doctors, etc. You are still just their children.) I called Mr. Tagliabue on Monday and found him to be a very nice, amenable person, but one who seemed to be pleasantly amused by a young man who seemed intent on following through for his father. Mr. Tagliabue invited me down to the world's most prestigious law firm and showed me the stacks of papers and files that had brought the *Testan* case this far. Mrs. Mitchell provided my father's files. She told me that she felt that they had exhausted all legal remedies, but that I could come to the office to retrieve the files. She also indicated that her son Michael Mitchell, my future law partner, would help me gather them. I went to Baltimore City and gathered all of the existing files. Next up, being a federal employee at the Small Business Administration, I needed to obtain a waiver. This waiver consisted of making a request to the government to allow a government employee to act as an attorney against the government. My petition for waiver was granted. By, guess who, the Nixon administration.

Night after night, my secretary Ingrid Coney and I toiled over the briefs. Mr. Tagliabue reviewed them, added comments and made suggestions along the way. After months of filing motions, briefs, and memoranda, the United States Court of Claims decided to hear the case *en banc*, meaning with all seven judges. In fact, the court jumped over Mr. Tagliabue's case and decided to hear Pettit first. Dad was finally a believer. The theory behind these two cases would be that the executive orders of presidents Harry S. Truman through Richard M. Nixon called for remedial action to correct past discrimination in federal employment, and, as a remedy for unlawful discrimination, back pay was among that remedial relief. Even though Congress would pass Title VII in 1964 (the Civil Rights Act of 1964), and the Equal Employment Opportunity Act of 1972 (42 USC § 2000e) the issue of back pay for federal employees would linger. The second highest court in the land, on monetary matters brought against the United States, agreed to hear the case.

After weeks of preparation, study, and conversations with Mr. Tagliabue, I was ready. I had won my moot court cases at Howard Law School, and assisted assistant US attorneys in my SBA cases before federal courts, but never in my wildest dreams had I imagined that my real court career would start on one of the biggest and grandest stages in the nation.

The United States Court of Claims sits across the park from the White House and is almost as imposing as the United States Supreme Court. I went to look at the court from the outside, and I was even allowed by the guards to look inside the majestic courtroom. I never went to the well of the court until D-day, reasoning that that would have been too presumptuous. Finally, the morning came. As the case was called by the clerk of the court, I approached the well with just enough awe and intimidation to bring out my best. I turned my internal switch to the on position. My mother, father, and wife sat behind me, along with Ms. Coney. The associate attorney general of the United States sat across from me, with the seven learned judges in front. I believed at that moment, at twenty-six years old, that I was being touched by the hand of God. What child, what man, could ask for any more than to have the family who had given so much, seated behind him in legal battle as he attempted to rectify the wrongs and injustice that had been brought against them for asking for so little for their child. In argument, I had one of the finest hours of my career: attacking each question, pulling several judges to my cause, and enlisting them in my argument against the opposing judges.

Just as when my father had seen me fight in other outnumbered battles, he never uttered a word when we left the court and headed to a restaurant. He never opened his mouth until we had dinner, and then he only uttered a few words.

"Son, you were good, really good." It was as if, in me, he saw everything that he would have wanted in a son. I had achieved the pinnacle of his ambitions for both himself and me. He would tell me this years later, just days before his death.

The United States Supreme Court would later say in its opinion in *United States v. Herman Testan and Frances L. Zarrilli*, 424 U.S. 392 (1976):

"Respondents cite *Allison v. United States*, 196 Ct.Cl. 263, 451 F.2d 1035 (1971), and *Pettit v. United States*, 203 Ct.Cl. 207, 488 F.2d 1026 (1973) as precedent for the remand order in this case. Those cases found the employees' 'entitlement' to money damages in an Executive Order, and to that extent however might be distinguishable from the instant cases ... To the extent that *Allison* and *Pettit* rely on the concept that an admission of misclassification by an agency automatically gives rise to a cause of action for money damages against the United States, their reasoning is identical to the Court of Claims' reasoning in the instant case; and to the extent that analysis is now rejected, the analysis of *Allison* and *Pettit* is necessarily rejected. *See also Chambers v. United States, supra*."

In essence, *Testan*, the later Supreme Court decision, would have reversed *Pettit*. However, *Pettit* had settled prior to the above decision for $100,000. In 1973, that was a lot of money. I think the Justice Department settled *Pettit* and went up on *certiorari* to the high court on *Testan* because they chose not to make further national news out of a father-son team. The US Court of Claims had been very explicit, detailed, and thorough in its lengthy decision. The court would lay out what my father had suffered through all of those fourteen years adopting relevant parts of the administrative findings. The court would incorporate in its opinion the following:

George D. Pettit v. United States
Cites as 488 F.2d 1026 (1973)

b. The display of Confederate flags in Mr. Pettit's work area had the effect of saying to him and fellow employees that he was not accepted as an engineer on the same basis and with the same professional status as white engineers. The incident at the Ballistic Research Laboratory when Mr. Pettit was attempting to make a point in a panel discussion during a television program and Mr. McCain used his lighter, which played *Dixie*, and the people laughed, had the effect of including Mr. Pettit as the object of their laughter as he was the only Negro present and as he was attempting to speak at the time. This was a rude and demoralizing act, which was embarrassing to Mr. Pettit, a Negro engineer, in the presence of his white colleagues.

c. Reference to Mr. Pettit and Mr. Gentry or statements to them as "boys" did not accord them the same professional recognition as given to white professionals.

d. Failure to provide Mr. Pettit the same facilities and treatment respecting desk telephone instruments and position of name on routing slip as provided to white professionals was a denial of equal professional status and as such a denial of equal employment opportunity.

[The court further states, referring to the findings of the administrative hearing officer. The hearing officer also found instances where other black employees at HEL were denied equal employment opportunity, specifically with respect to promotions.]

Pettit v. United States

2. The evidence disclosed that there were three Negro employees at HEL who left the employment of the labs due, in part, to evidence of the *absence of further promotion opportunity at this activity.* There is further evidence that Mr. Pettit *would not take the same course of action that* the other Negro employees took to alter their situation,

i.e., take employment elsewhere. Mr. Pettit was an activist in working to integrate the schools in Harford County; he stayed and fought for equality and his constitutional rights rather than accept the status quo or move to an area where his rights would have been provided for him without conflict. Whether he should have stayed and pursued his efforts to break the patterns of exclusion is not relevant to this case, *the results of his efforts are.*

4. a. Evidence of racism runs through the testimony relating to the substance of testimony relating to the treatment of black employees under the direct or indirect supervision of Dr. John Weisz. Dr. Weisz appeared to be oblivious to the needs of his minority group employees and impervious to the acts of discrimination practices by subordinate supervisors such as Erickson, McCain, Randall, and Cruse.

[To me the additional fascination of dad's decision would be the personal analysis by the court as in my decision. *(Pettit v. Board of Education)* thirteen years earlier.]

Pettit v. United States

d. The evaluation of Mr. Pettit's performance in assigned work projects showed that of eleven assigned projects, he performed at a level above average or excellent in three, average in two, marginally satisfactory in four, and unsatisfactory in two. Consideration must be given to the environment in which this performance occurred. If we accept the conclusion that discrimination was practiced by Pettit's supervisors, then we must recognize that a harmonious, cooperative relationship could not exist between the complainant and his colleagues. His performance would have to be weighed in some manner in order to overcome the adverse conditions of his work environment.

(All above emphasis supplied by plaintiff)

Several months after my office in Baltimore City was opened, I was running out of court and saw TV trucks and reporters coming toward me.

The reporters were asking, "Mr. Pettit, have you heard? You won a four-to-three decision in the United States Court of Claims. You won *Pettit v. the United States*!" I was stunned into momentary silence. Upon composing myself, I eventually responded.

I said, "I'll be damned!" I then added, "Ladies and gentlemen, hold up. I have to call my dad. If you all can meet me in about an hour at my office, my dad will be here from Aberdeen and we will be glad to hold a press conference and answer all of your questions." I called Dad; he was very quiet, still sort of unbelieving. He said that he would meet me at my office.

My dad and I met the press together.

We would later work out an agreement with the Department of the Army whereas it was ordered that he be promoted from a GS-11 to a GS-14 "with all rights and privileges and benefits deriving thereto" (with the court designating me to monitor compliance with the courts order), including $100,000 back pay for the fourteen years of discrimination. My dad, Mom, Bobbie, and I cried tears of joy.

We had truly gone full circle from *Pettit v. Harford County Board of Education*, to *Pettit v. Gingerich and Board of Law Examiners*, to *Pettit v. the United States*.

Over the years, I would wonder about the politics of *Pettit v. the United States*. Nixon, during the Vietnam War had begun to bomb Cambodia, Laos, and Hanoi. There had been a political uprising in the nation and in Congress. Nixon had argued, as Obama does today, that for some presidential decisions he did not need authorization by Congress. Nixon, in fact, argued that presidential authority in some areas was essentially analogues and equal to executive order, thus having the effect of law without congressional action or approval. At the time of *Pettit v the United States*, the Court of Claims had several Nixon appointees. The reader hereof might consider that to be an overreaching analogy, but it is academic food for thought. The historical certainty, however, would be that *Pettit v. the United States* would stand for the legal proposition that back pay could be awarded by authority of executive order to federal employees who had been unlawfully discriminated against due to race (although the Supreme

Court, as stated, would later reject this), and *Pettit* would establish the but for test—meaning that once the plaintiff in a discrimination case met his or her burden of proof that he or she was qualified for a promotion, then the burden of proof shifted to the defense to prove that the denial of promotion was due to nonracial factors or stated another way that the person would have been promoted "but for" racial discrimination.

For years thereafter, I would walk into a federal administrative hearing or a federal court and the judge would ask if I had anything to do with, or any connection to, *Pettit v. the United States*, in that the rules of evidence would be governed by same.

I would always smile and say, with great pride, "George D. Pettit is my father, and I was my father's lawyer."

Dad in lab at Aberdeen Proving Ground

Family shot

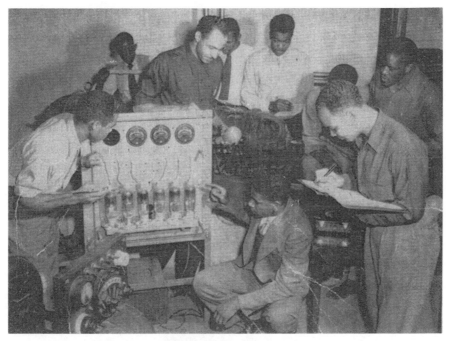

Dad at A&T lab class

Dwight and Mom

Private First Class George D. Pettit

Mom and Dad

The Pettit Family 2012

George and Dwight Celebrating Case

George David Pettit
Date of Birth : July 18, 1922 – Died: August 31, 1992
As sketched by his grandson, Alvin Dwight Pettit, Jr.

CPSIA information can be obtained at www.ICGtesting.com
Printed in the USA
BVOW08s2011030214

343828BV00002B/141/P